IMAGES
of America

AROUND GALLATIN AND SUMNER COUNTY

VOLUME II

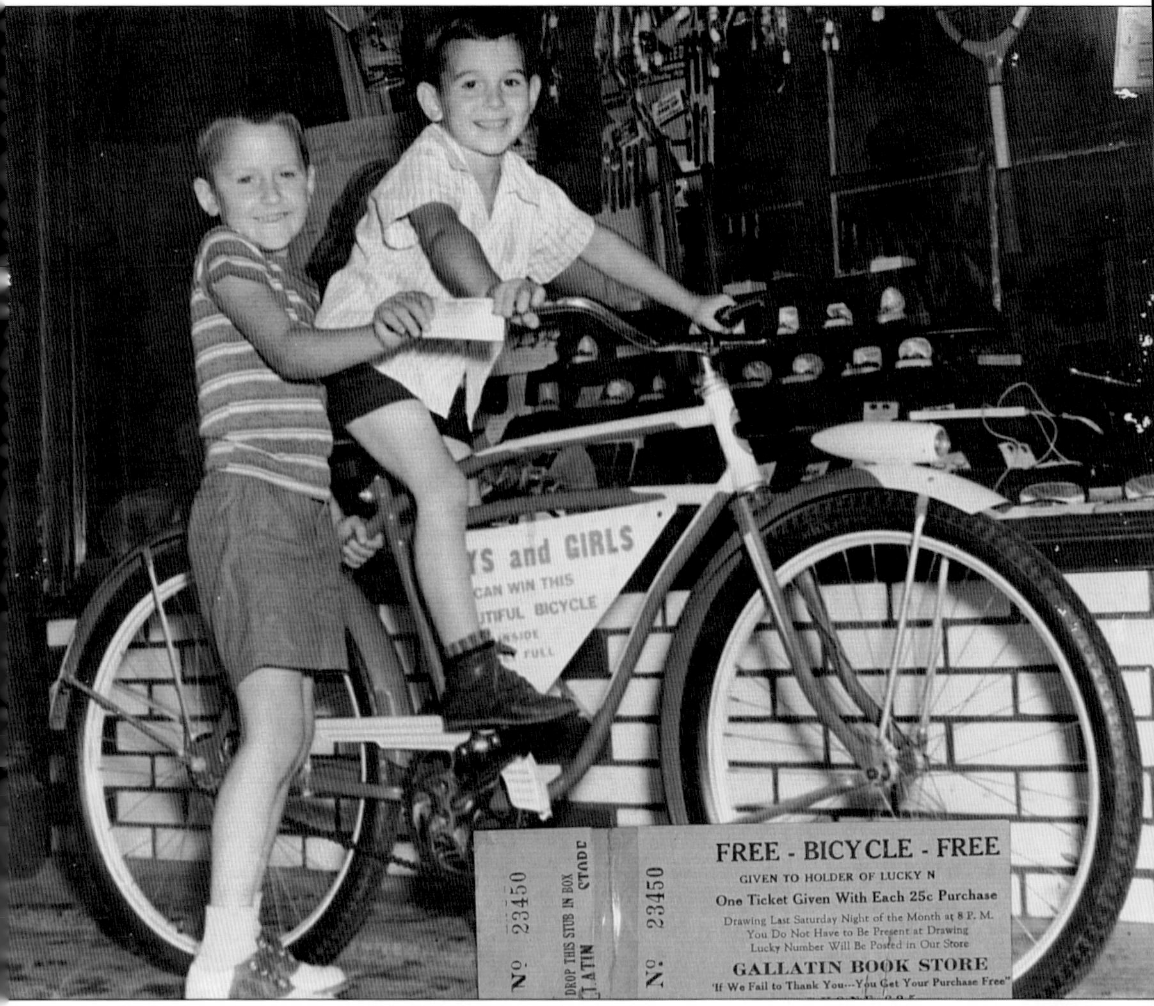

One of the happiest moments of childhood is getting a new bicycle. Lucky ticket number 23450 won this beautiful bike for Billy Wayne Anthony (age seven) and Jimmy Highers (age four), nephews of Mr. Frank Robertson of Castalian Springs. This was one of many bikes given away in a weekly drawing by the old Gallatin Book Store. (Courtesy of Sumner Franklin.)

IMAGES
of America

Around Gallatin and Sumner County

Volume II

DeeGee Lester and Kenneth Calvin Thomson Jr.

ARCADIA
PUBLISHING

ISBN 978-0-7385-6889-8

Published by Arcadia Publishing
Charleston, South Carolina

Printed in the United States of America

Library of Congress Catalog Card Number: 98-87571

For all general information contact Arcadia Publishing at:
Telephone 843-853-2070
Fax 843-853-0044
E-Mail sales@arcadiapublishing.com
For customer service and orders:
Toll-Free 1-888-313-2665

Visit us on the Internet at www.arcadiapublishing.com

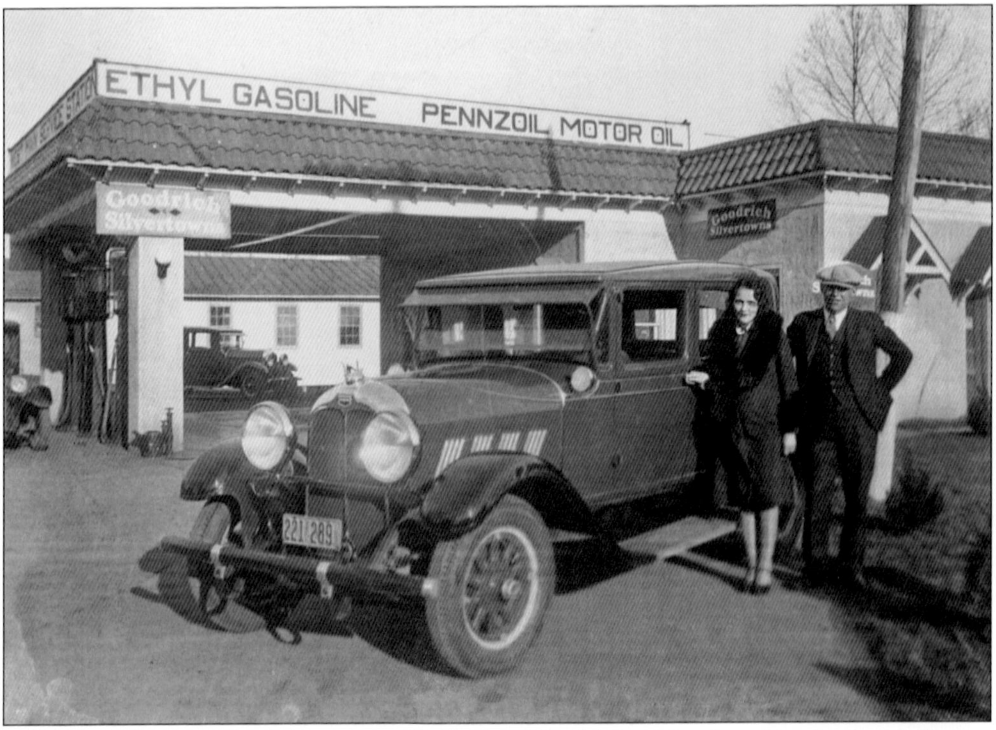

Roadside architecture had character in 1930 when Hazel (Hix) Kirsch and her husband, George T. Kirsch Sr., posed in front of the West Main Service Station (later site of the Gallatin Bakery). Such unique structures, which once dotted the highways of America, were replaced when the interstate system was constructed between the 1950s and 1970. (Courtesy of Allen Haynes.)

Contents

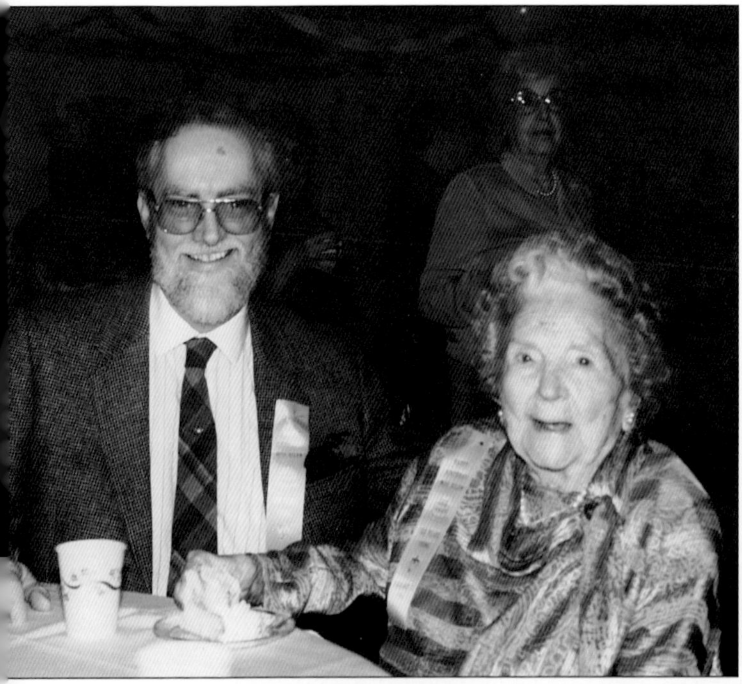

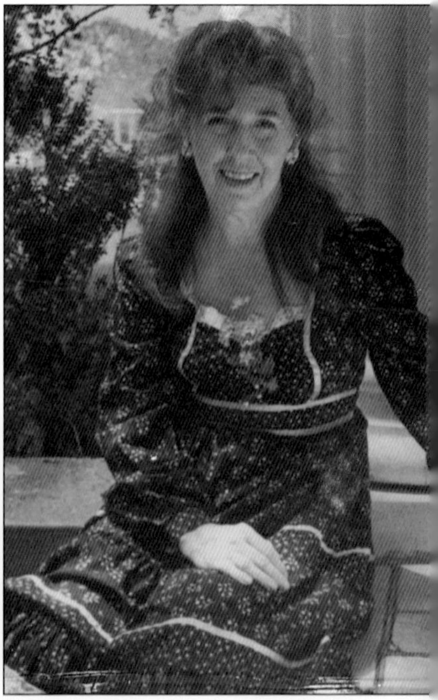

Left: "Miss Ellen" (Stokes) More Wemyss of Gallatin is pictured here with co-author Kenneth C. Thomson Jr. in February 1998 on the occasion of her 103rd birthday. *Right:* Jacalyn "Jackie" Comer Waddell is pictured in 1982 on the front porch of her Monthaven home.

This book is dedicated with love to "Miss Ellen" Wemyss
who has witnessed so much of our history
and in memory of Jackie Comer Waddell
who did so much to keep Hendersonville history alive.

Introduction

Public curiosity about local history, including pictorial histories, often falls off around the 1920s when greater familiarity makes events, people, and places seem commonplace. But the history of the recent past holds its own kind of fascination. The 20th-century history of Sumner County is an example.

Overlapping Volume I, *Around Gallatin and Sumner County*, this book picks up the Sumner story in the 1920s and closes in 1960. Public memory of this period includes the trauma of the Great Depression and World War II. But the towns and rural areas of Sumner County also experienced the impact of the implementation of progressive public policy at all levels of government, the influx of new residents, and the shift from rural to urban domination.

Crucial to these changes were the dramatic improvements in transportation and infrastructure. As railroads replaced rivers as the major channel for trade during the 19th century, Sumner's river towns, such as Cairo, declined in importance, and towns along rail lines, such as Gallatin, Portland, and Westmoreland, became the county's lifeline to trade and economic development. In the early 20th century, the county's lumber industry shipped millions of board feet, while Portland's strawberry industry dominated the national market.

By the 1930s, the county infrastructure also benefited from improvements. With gains in the popularity and availability of automobiles for citizens at nearly all income levels, the old concept of toll roads was abandoned in favor of public roads built and maintained by local or state government. Ownership of automobiles became a sign of success and pride as revealed in period photographs. Whereas earlier family photographs, such as those in Volume I, include the house as a backdrop for the family, photographs in this volume are more likely to include the family car.

The automobile brought change in many areas of community life. Ease of travel by automobile forced the closing of the Interurban Rail Line, a commuter train connecting Gallatin and Nashville. Ease of movement pushed retail beyond the town square and Main Street as home construction on the outskirts brought the need for greater convenience and expanded services. As motels, service stations, tourist camps, and cafes sprang up, roadside architecture reflected the need for speedier service, allowing travelers to quickly get back on the highway.

Although considered slow by today's standards, the faster pace of life shocked older members of the community who reveled in the days of commercial fairs, presentations by the local opera company, and fancy dress balls. Suddenly, quiet malt shops became teen "hangouts," locals chided the opinions of "Old Pop Sumner" while boasting the glories of a new Gallatin and a new Sumner County, and the talents of locals performing in plays and operas were eclipsed by the popularity of Hollywood "stars" at the local movie house.

However, while entertainment from beyond its borders invaded on all sides, locals continued to share the gift of music with the outside world. From participation in the first radio performance of the Grand Ole Opry to the nation's pioneer record mail order house, or the late 20th-century influx of country music star homes, the imprint of Sumner Countians upon the "people's music" has remained strong. Big dance bands, ragtime, jazz, and other music styles include top performers from throughout the county.

Pride in the talents of her citizens, her history, and advantages prompted a surge of Sumner boosterism, beginning in the late 1920s and continuing to the present. Demonstrations of pride can be seen in annual events such as the Portland Strawberry Festival, the 1937 celebration of the sesquicentennial, or the short-lived excitement of hosting an international steeplechase.

Pride was also seen in the local efforts to attract business and manufacturing to the area. The earlier manufacturing dominance by the lumber industry, cotton and flour mills, and distilleries was eclipsed with the successful recruitment of Kraft Cheese and the opening of two Sumner County plants by Jarmen Shoes. The influx of new companies and opportunities for employment attracted new residents to the area. As incomes increased, major retail chains such as J.C. Penney opened stores and began competing with the smaller mom and pop stores. Competition for the consumer dollar changed the store layouts and the quality of goods and services being offered to locals.

None of the changes between 1920 and 1960 matched the dramatic effect of the coming of the Tennessee Valley Authority (TVA) to the region during the 1930s and the creation of both the Interstate Highway System and Old Hickory Lake in the early 1950s. The effects of the TVA and the interstate system expanded the county's ability to attract business and industry and to compete in the national (and later global) marketplace. The 1951 creation of Old Hickory Lake, with its hundreds of miles of shoreline, assured Sumner County's appeal as a residential, recreational, and business location. Situated directly on the lake, the tiny town of Hendersonville became one of the state's fastest growing residential areas. Unincorporated until 1969, Hendersonville's population quickly surpassed its neighbors, including the county seat of Gallatin, as newcomers rushed to newly developed subdivisions and lakeside properties with the convenience of close proximity to Nashville.

This volume, like the previous one, *Around Gallatin and Sumner County*, and Velma Brinkley and Mary Malone's excellent companion volume for Arcadia, *African-American Life in Sumner County*, offers a snapshot of the county's rich history and the contributions of the wonderful people who paved the way for later generations.

One

Homes

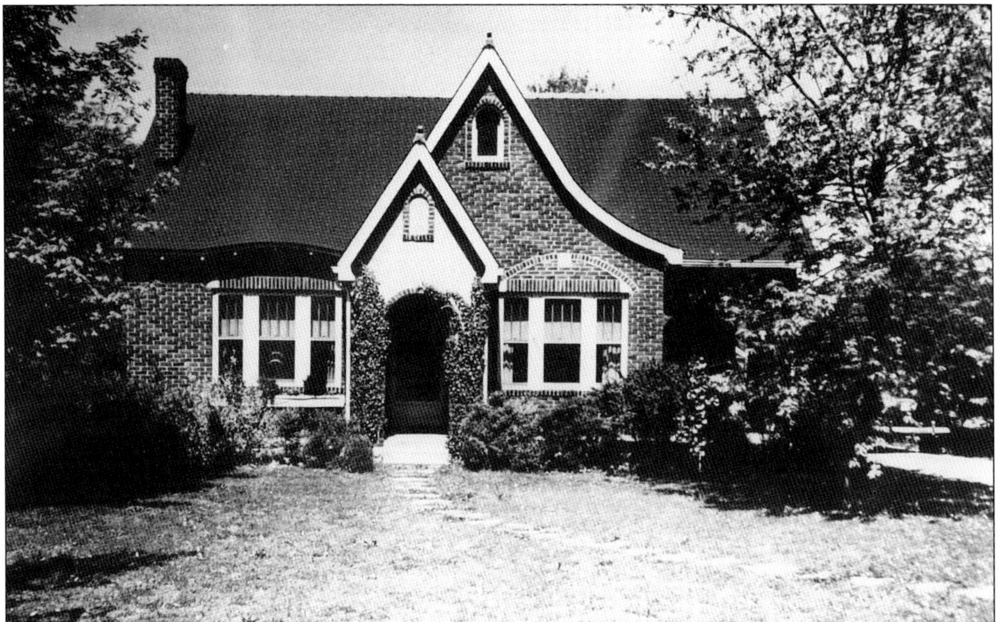

This charming English tudor cottage on East Main Street in Gallatin, known as Seven Gables, was built in 1928 for Mr. and Mrs. Will K. Carr by Robert and Madel Lassiter. Purchased in 1945 by Harold Tillman Hix and his wife, Martha Lorelle (Frakes) Hix, it was their home for 35 years. (1948 photograph courtesy of their grandson, Kenneth C. Thomson Jr.)

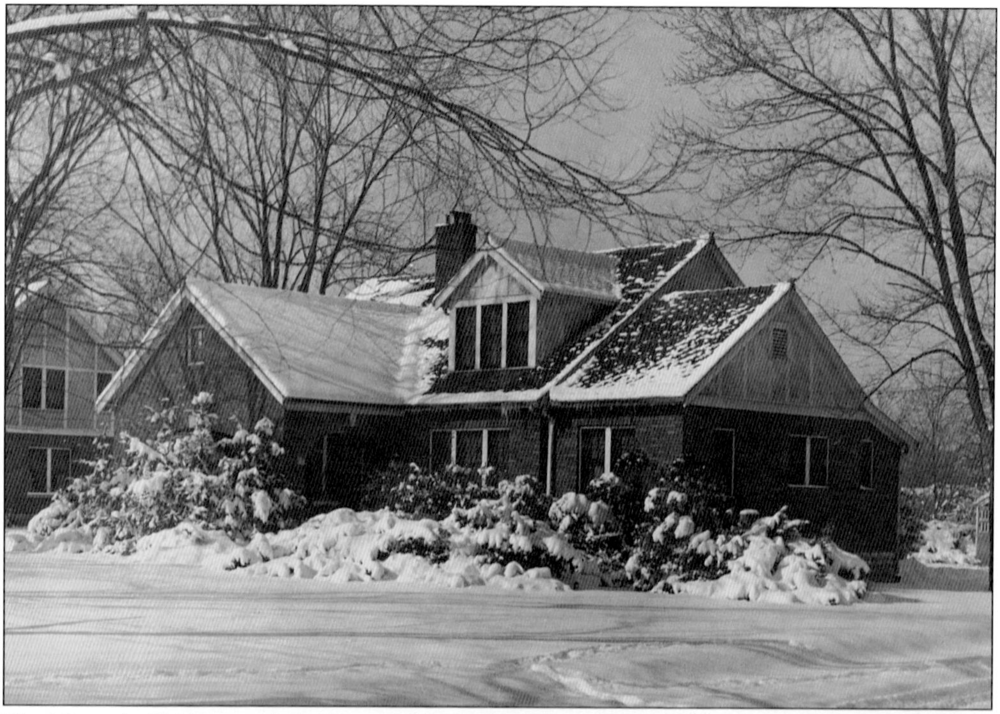

The blizzard of 1951 provided a beautiful background for photographs of many of Gallatin's finest homes, including the lovely home of Mrs. Robert Moore on East Main Street. (Photograph by W.C. Hackett, courtesy of Evelyn Hackett Tuttle.)

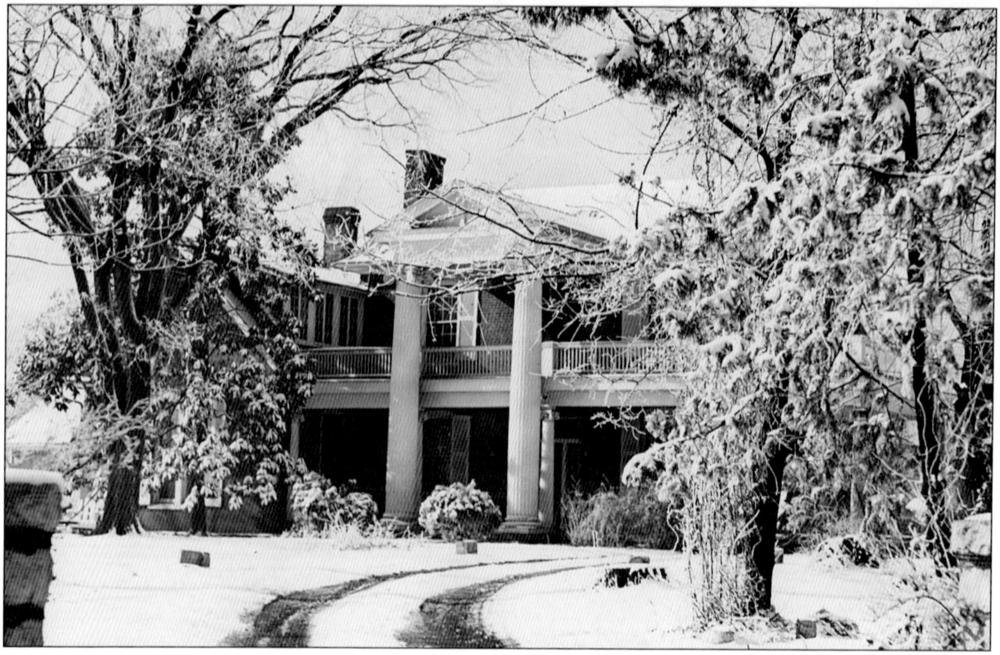

The frozen landscape provides a hauntingly lovely scene in this 1951 photograph of the home of Mrs. Maxine (Dye) Cox of Gallatin. (Photograph by W.C. Hackett, courtesy of Evelyn Hackett Tuttle.)

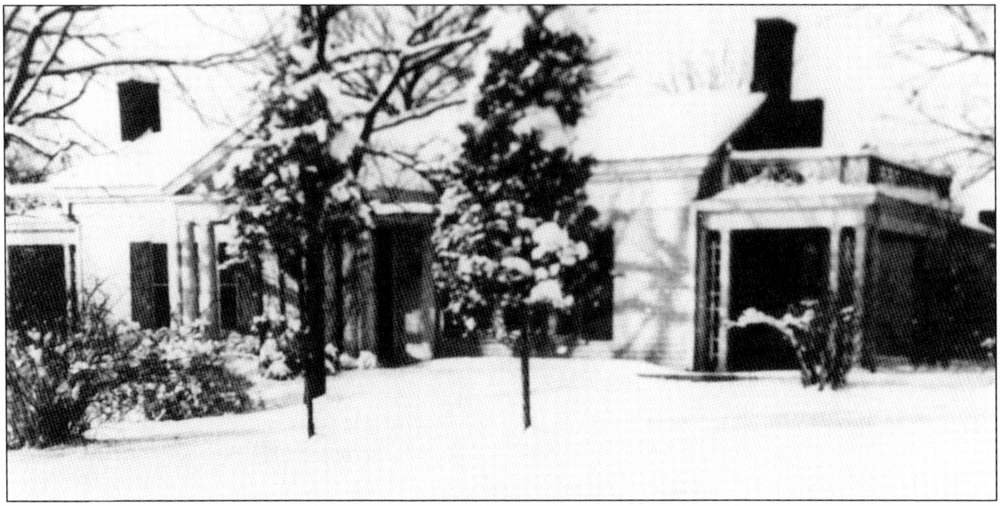

This 19th-century cottage known as Lone Pine was expanded and rebuilt by William B. Conn (c. 1862), who sold it to Mrs. Nannie (Hillman) Franklin in 1885. Through the first half of the 20th century, it passed through the Franklin family before being razed to make way for the Gallatin Nursing Home. (The c. 1940 photograph courtesy of Kenneth C. Thomson Jr.)

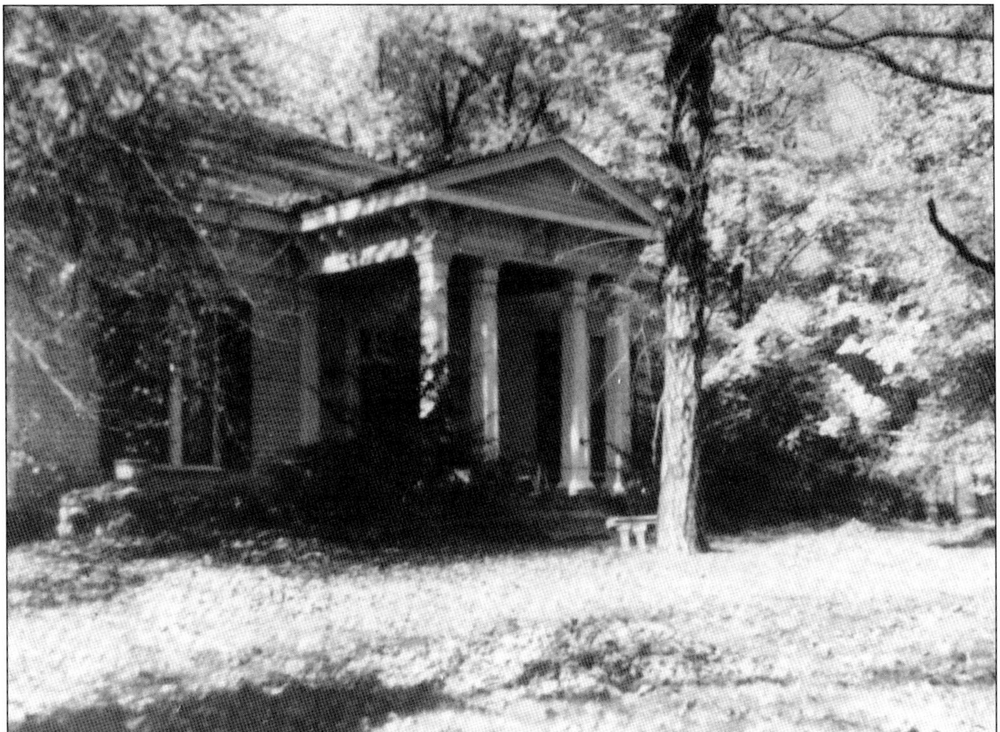

Maple Summit on Gallatin's North Water Street had a similar history. Built in 1868 by Milton Smallwood Elkin and his wife, Martha Conn Moore, on 5 acres of land given to her by her uncle, William B. Conn, the home was purchased by Nannie (Hillman) Franklin in 1901 as a bridal gift for her daughter, Florida (Mrs. Walter Leake) Anderson. She occupied the residence for 60 years. (1960 photograph courtesy of Kenneth C. Thomson Jr.)

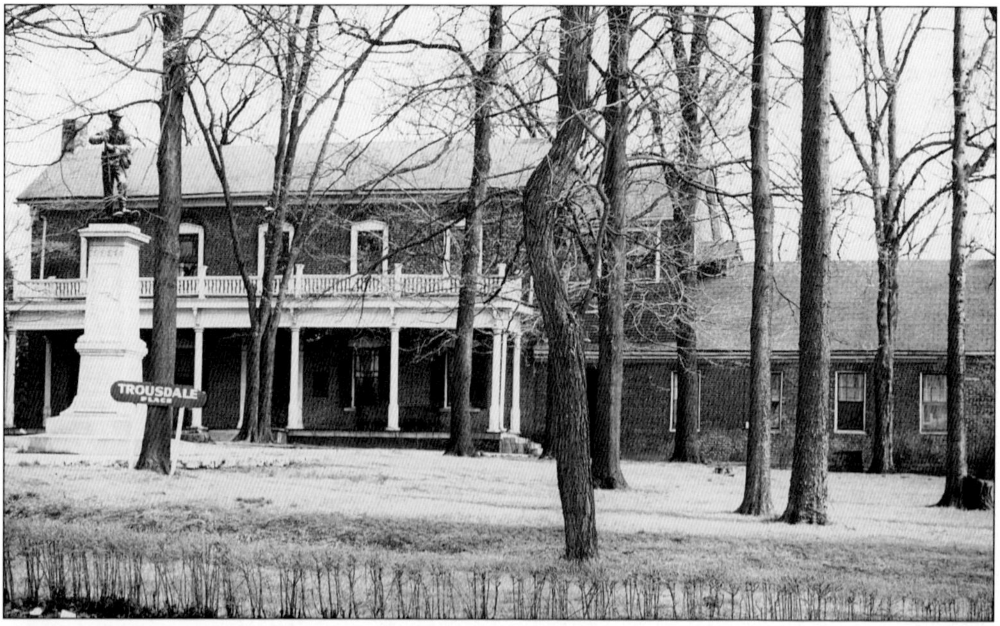

This postcard of Trousdale Place shows the presence of a porch across the front. Built *c.* 1813, the home of Gov. William Trousdale remains a popular historic attraction. The Sumner County Museum is housed behind the home. (Courtesy of Kenneth C. Thomson Jr.)

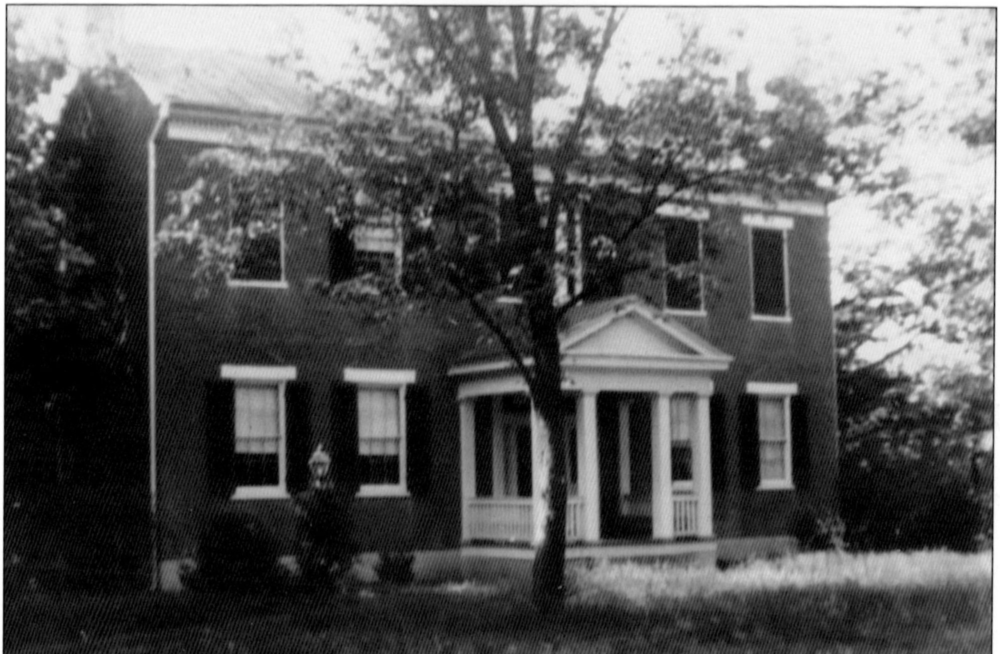

Oakland, located on Hartsville Pike in Gallatin, was built by Dr. Daniel Wade Mentlo and Mary Brandon Alexander (*c.* 1840s). Dr. Mentlo's medical office remained on the grounds well into the 20th century as the property was passed down through his son, James Alexander Mentlo, to his granddaughter, Susie Mentlo Anderson (pictured on page 55). (1955 photograph courtesy of Kenneth C. Thomson Jr.)

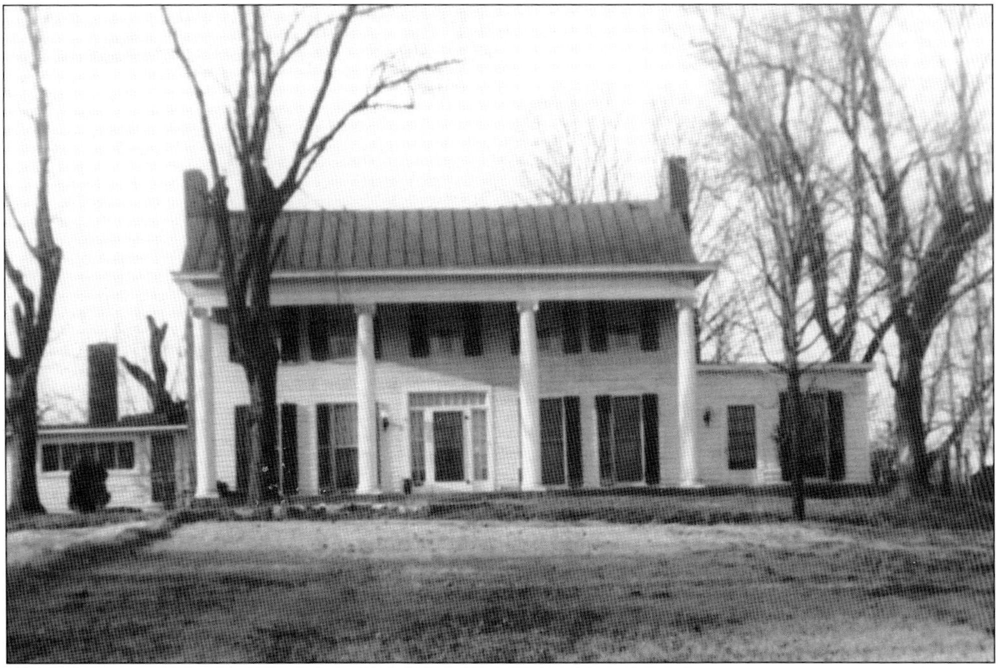

Located on the Franklin Street extension in Gallatin, this handsome home was built (c. 1850) by Henry Barker and his wife, Julia Farnsworth Barker. The home underwent extensive renovations in the early 20th century by Loraine (Sullivan) Gray. (1954 photograph courtesy of Kenneth C. Thomson Jr.)

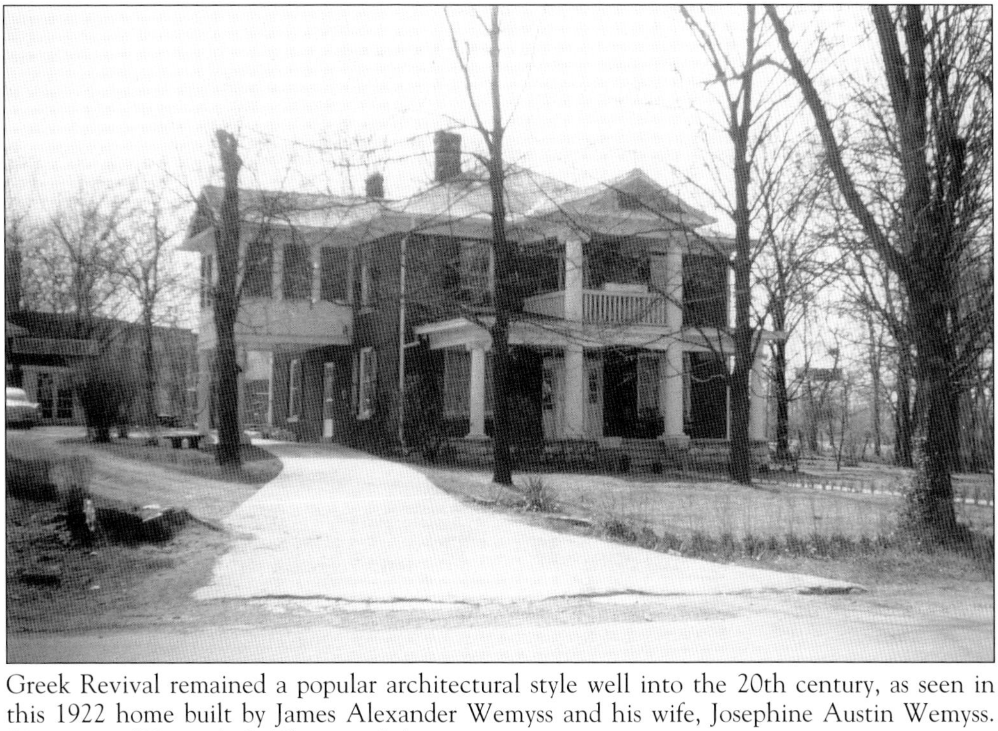

Greek Revival remained a popular architectural style well into the 20th century, as seen in this 1922 home built by James Alexander Wemyss and his wife, Josephine Austin Wemyss. (Courtesy of Kenneth C. Thomson Jr.)

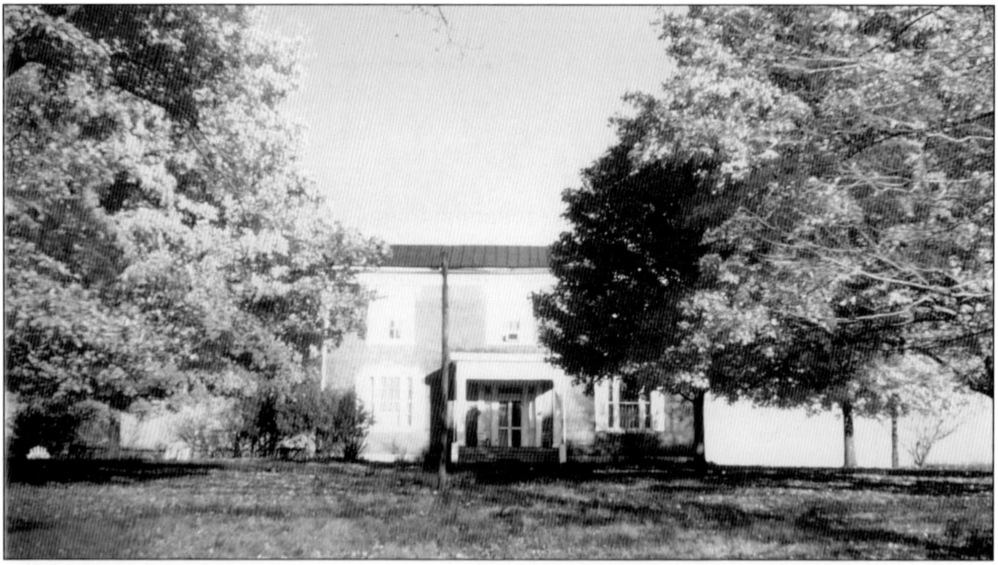

Known as Douglass Heights, this home was constructed by Young Norvel Douglass in 1850 on Douglass Pike, now Highway 109 north, next to the present-day Crestview Cemetery. (Courtesy of Kenneth C. Thomson Jr.)

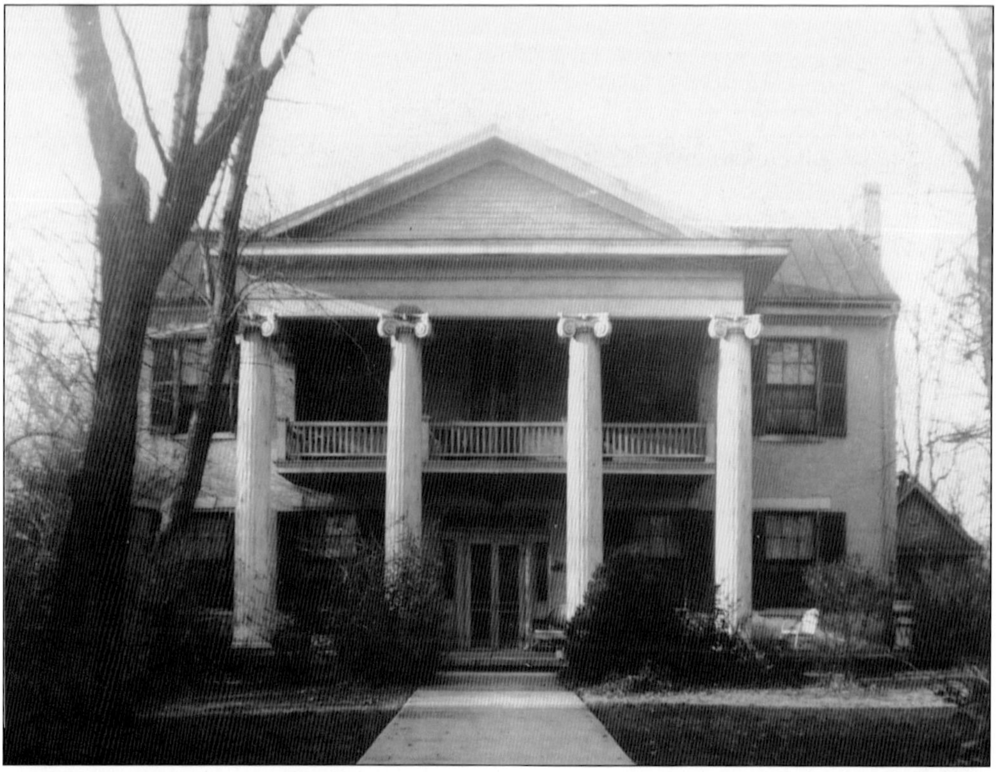

Built in the 1830s by Levy D. Ring, president of Transmontania Academy, this Gallatin home was later used in various capacities by Neophogen College and Howard College. When this photograph was taken in 1954, the home was the Main Street residence of Mrs. Ernest B. House. (Courtesy of Kenneth C. Thomson Jr.)

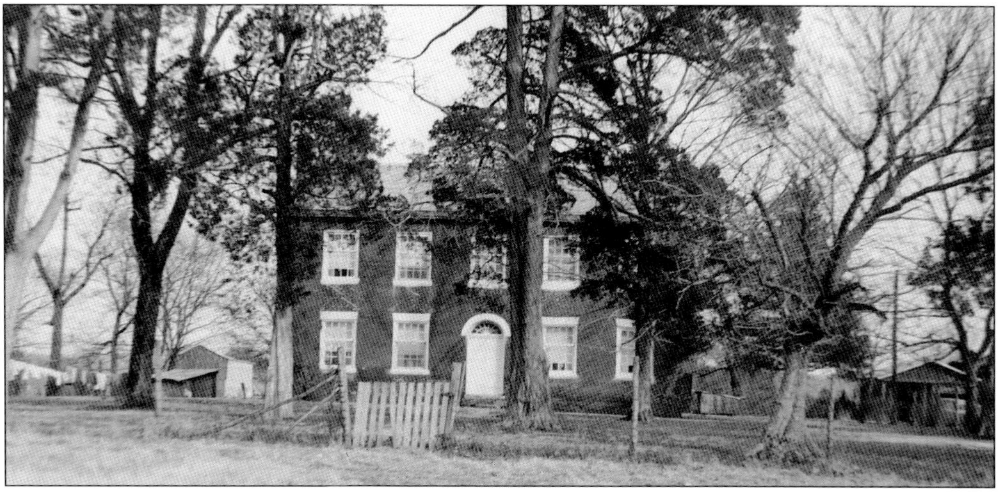

This rural home on Douglas Bend Road was built (*c.* 1824) by William Cantrell and his wife, Jocie Bugg Cantrell, in the popular Federal style. The home's smooth facade and elliptical fanlight over the doorway are elements of Federal architecture, a popular style in the South until it was eclipsed by the grandeur of Greek Revival. (1962 photograph courtesy of Kenneth C. Thomson Jr.)

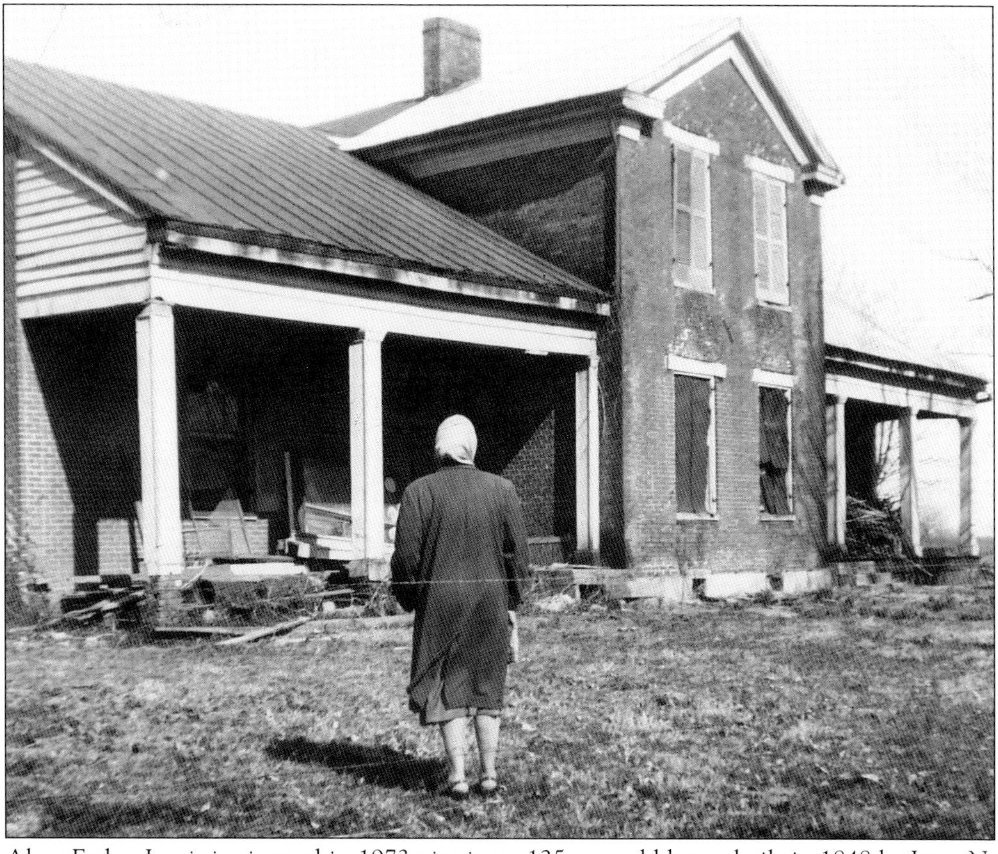

Alma Frakes Lewis is pictured in 1973 viewing a 125-year-old home built in 1848 by Isaac N. Guthrie on St. Blaise Road in Gallatin. (Courtesy of Kenneth C. Thomson Jr.)

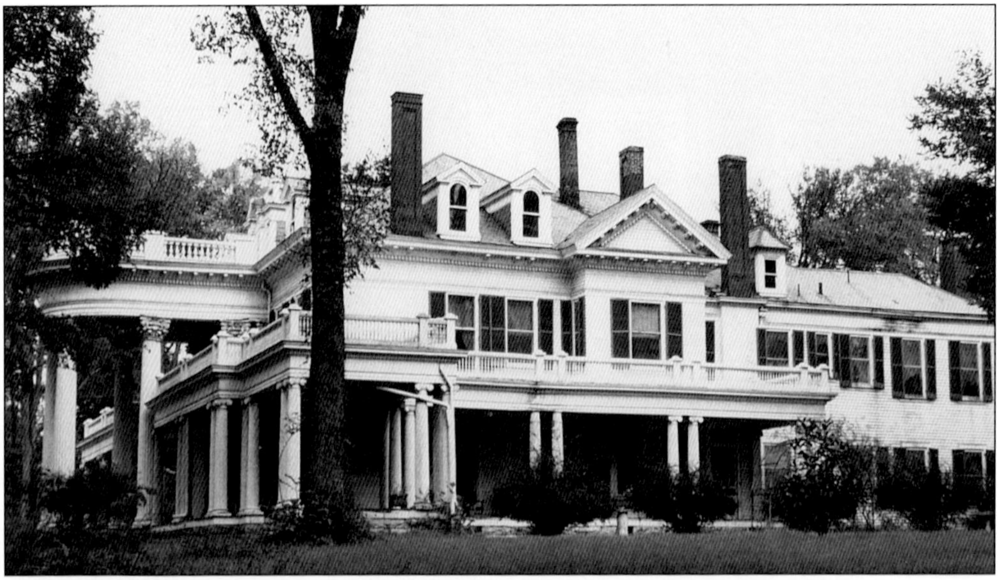

In volume I of *Around Gallatin & Sumner County* (pages 9 and 26), readers saw photographs of Langley Hall under construction in 1903. This photograph provides an excellent view of the completed home located on Coles Ferry Road. Built by a single woman, Eleanor Katherine Trousdale, before her marriage to William Young Allen, the magnificent home was the largest in the county and included a spectacular front porch featuring Corinthian columns. The home was razed in 1965 by Allen Trousdale Guild. (Courtesy of the Bob Perry Collection, Sumner County Archives.)

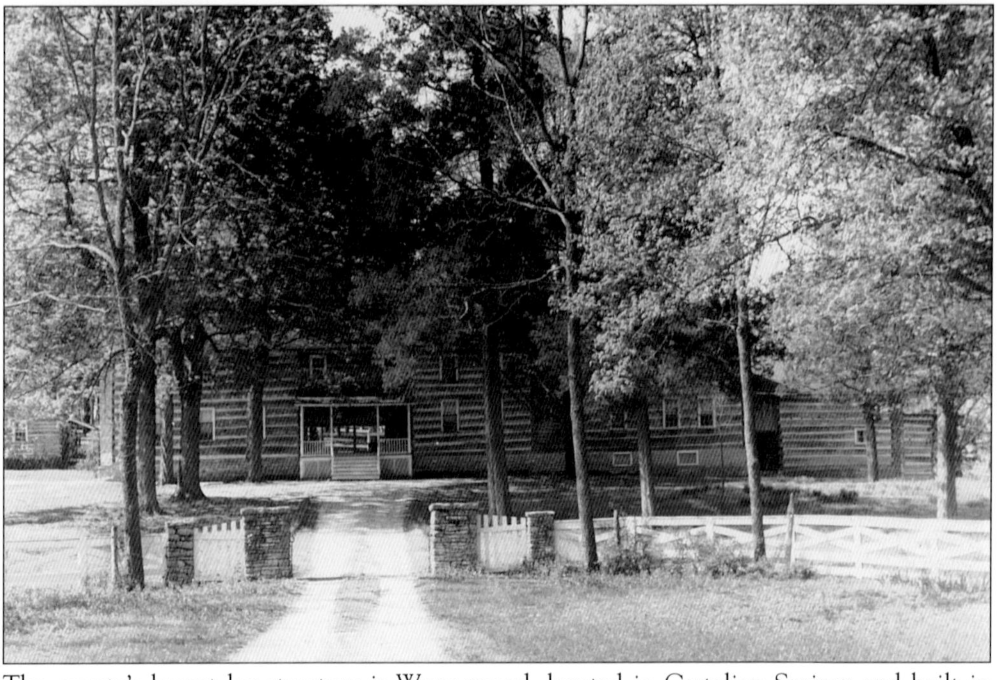

The county's largest log structure is Wynnewood, located in Castalian Springs and built in 1828. The former stagecoach inn is now a popular Sumner County tourist attraction. (Courtesy of the Bob Perry Collection, Sumner County Archives.)

The distinguished man pictured here is Robert H. Miers (1813–1892), builder of the Miers-Roseal Home (below) on Red River Road near Gallatin. (Courtesy of the E.A. Green Collection.)

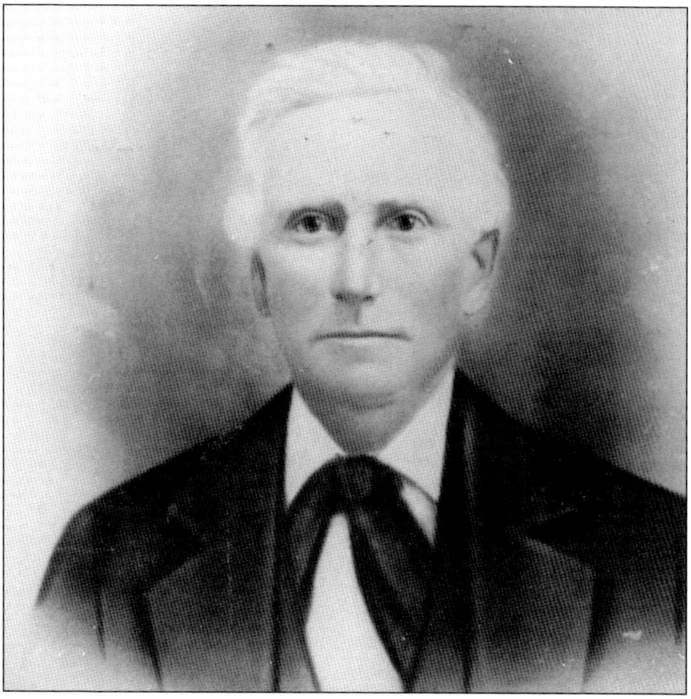

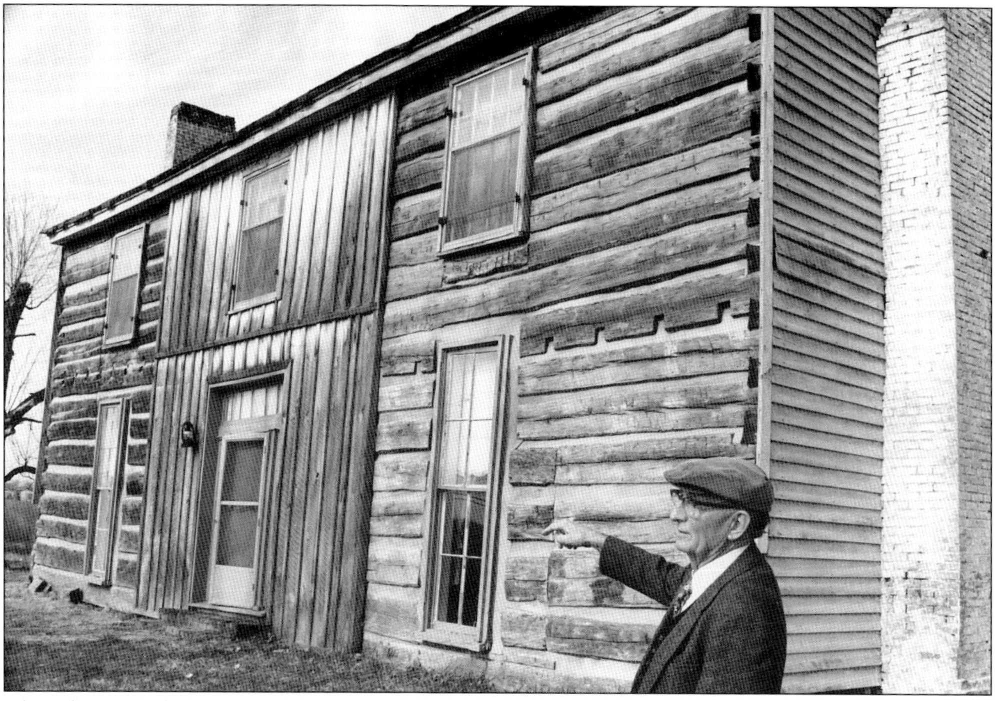

This photograph shows the various building styles incorporated in the long history of the Miers-Roscoe Home. The original log construction can be seen across the front of the building with the later board-and-batton finish associated with the Gothic Revival styles surrounding the doorway. Clapboard siding can be seen on the end of the house beside the chimney. (Courtesy of the E.A. Green Collection.)

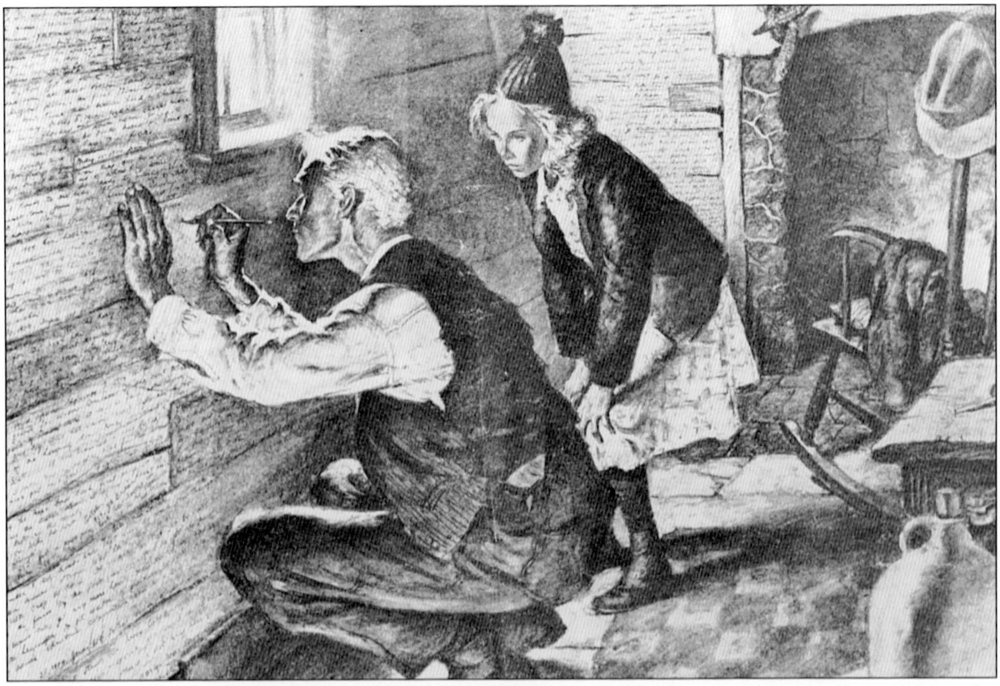

This drawing by Amos Sowell accompanied an August 17, 1940 article by Lucretia Penny for the *Saturday Evening Post*. The article was about the life of Mr. Claire Parker whose Sumner County home was called The Ranch. Parker, a bachelor, depicted here with a little girl named Tennessee Woodson, wrote his daily journal on the walls of his home. (1976 copy by Dalton Studio of Scottsville, Kentucky; courtesy of Kenneth C. Thomson Jr.)

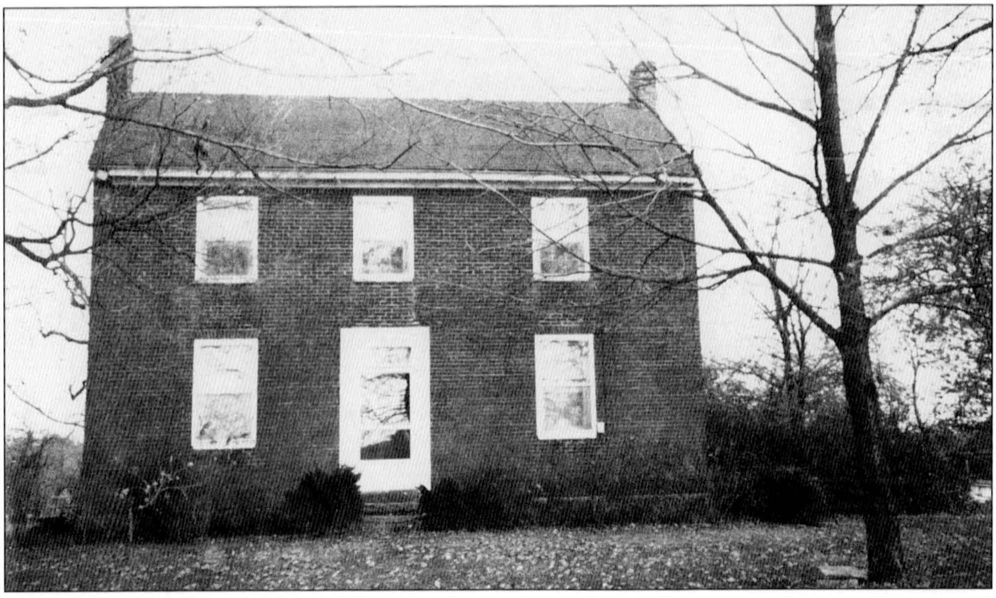

Built in 1823 by John McNeal, The Ranch was located near Rogana in Sumner County and received national notoriety for the wall journal of Mr. Claire Parker, who lived there from 1881 to 1916. Later owners sought more appealing interiors, covering the wall journal and giving the home a more traditional look. (Courtesy of Kenneth C. Thomson Jr.)

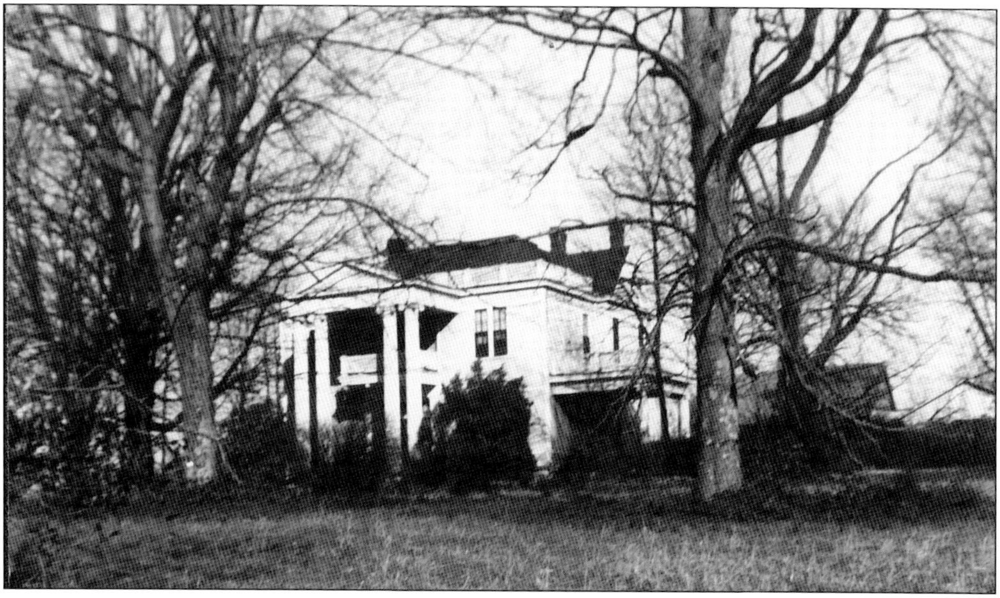

The Victorian cottage known as Idelwilde was built in 1872 by Judge Josephus Conn Guild for his daughter Kittie, when she married her first husband, J.M. McKee. In 1916, John G. Witherspoon renovated the home before his marriage to Kathrine (McKee) Brown, Kittie's widowed daughter. Photographed in 1955 by Ken Thomson, the home is no longer standing. (Courtesy of Kenneth C. Thomson Jr.)

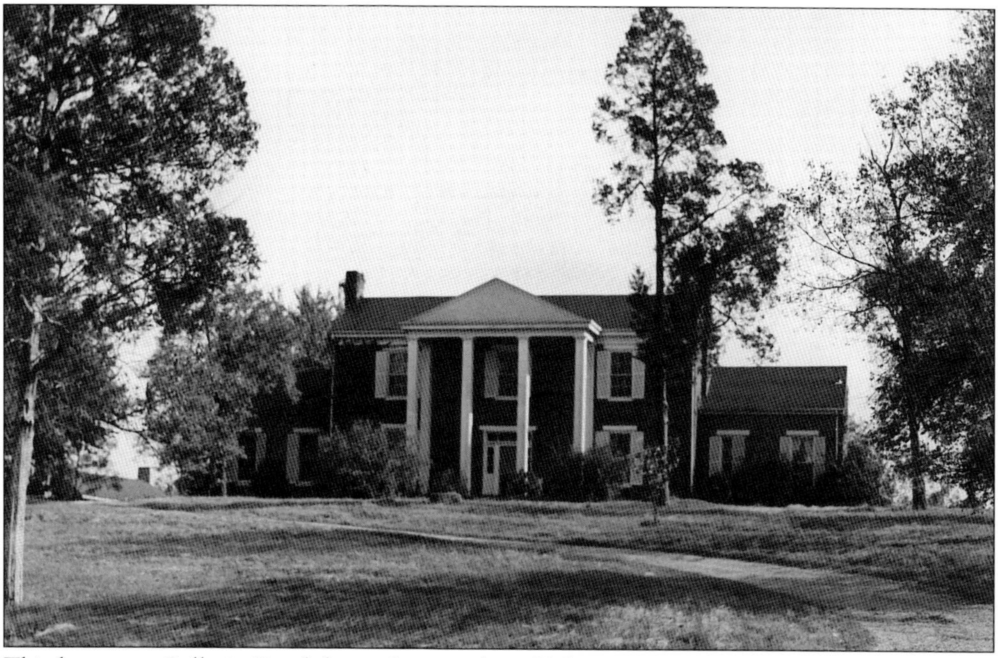

This home on Gallatin Road, located across from Volunteer State Community College, is the home of Gallatin entrepreneur Randy Woods, the founder of Dot Records. A pioneer in the national mail order business, Woods founded the famous Randy's Record Shop, which mailed records throughout the United States into the mid-1990s. (Photograph by W.C. Hackett, courtesy of Evelyn Hackett Tuttle.)

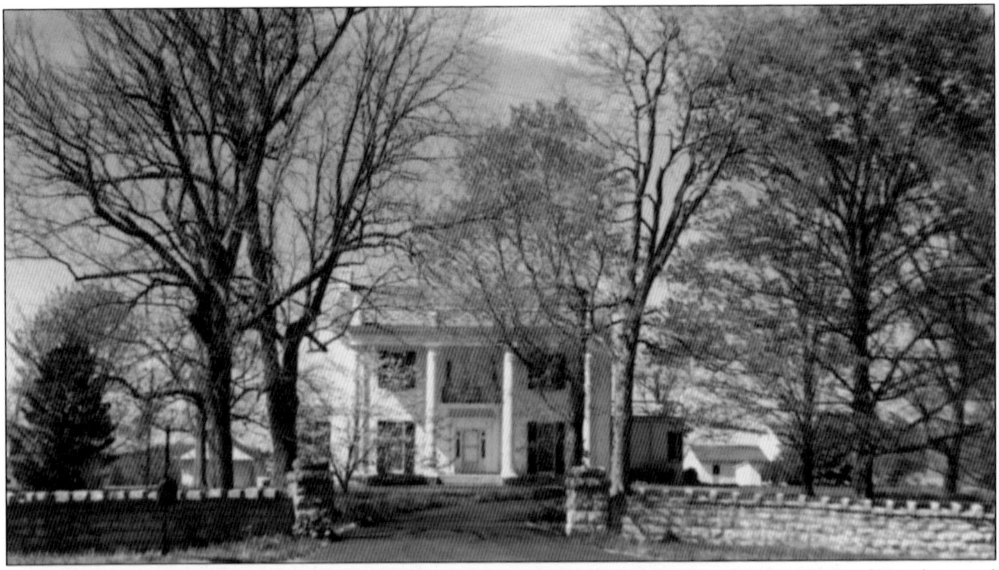

Originally called Woodlawn when built by John Franklin in 1807, this majestic farm located midway between Hendersonville and Gallatin is now called Wilson Farms. The Greek Revival architecture of the home, the rock walls and attractive fencing, and the handsome horse barn visible from Gallatin Road, combine to give the property a look reminiscent of the "Old South." (Courtesy of Kenneth C. Thomson Jr.)

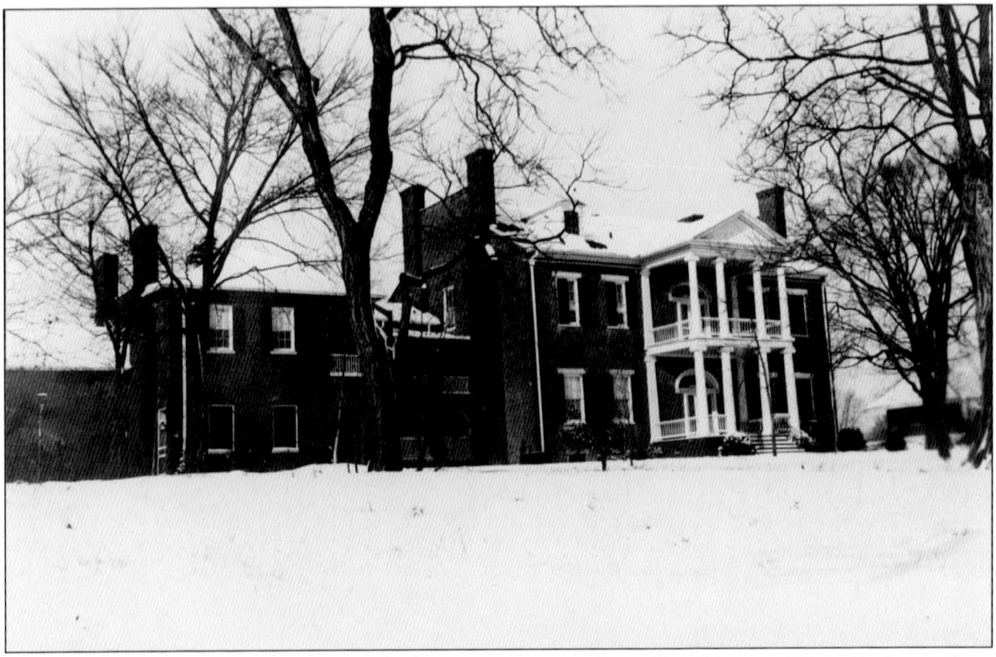

Fairvue was built by slave trader and plantation owner Isaac Franklin in 1832. A show place throughout its history, the loss of slave labor following the Civil War shifted the site's focus to the breeding of thoroughbred horses. This 1940 photograph shows the home following its restoration by William Hatch Wemyss and his second wife, Ellen (Stokes) More Wemyss. (Courtesy of the collection of the late Sterling Beaumont Updyke of New York City, a descendant of the Franklin family.)

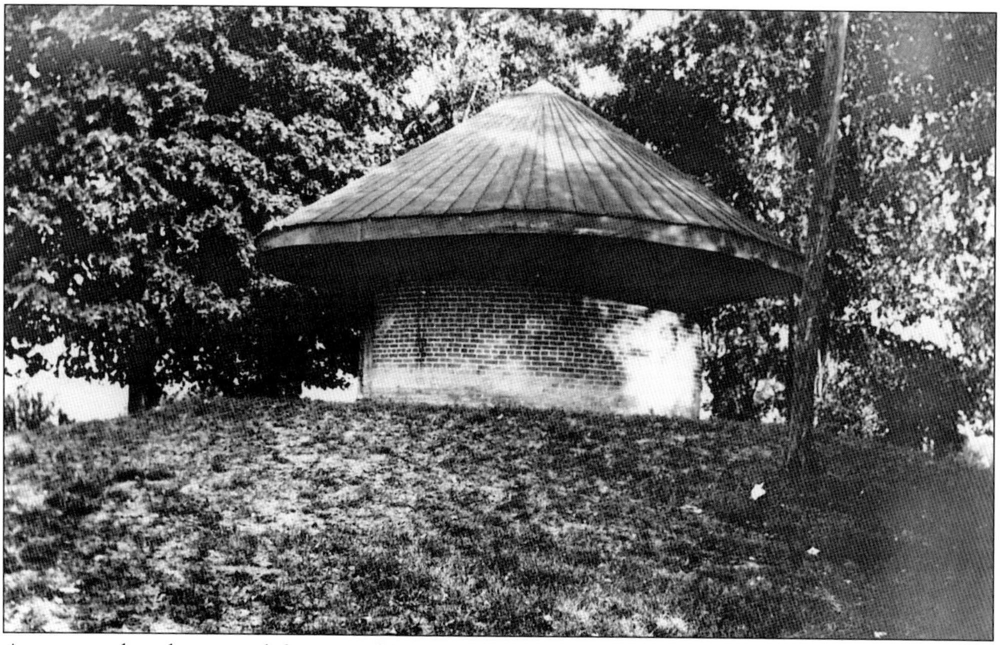

An unusual architectural feature of Fairvue can be found in this mushroom-shaped brick ice house built in 1840. (Courtesy of Sterling Beaumont Updyke.)

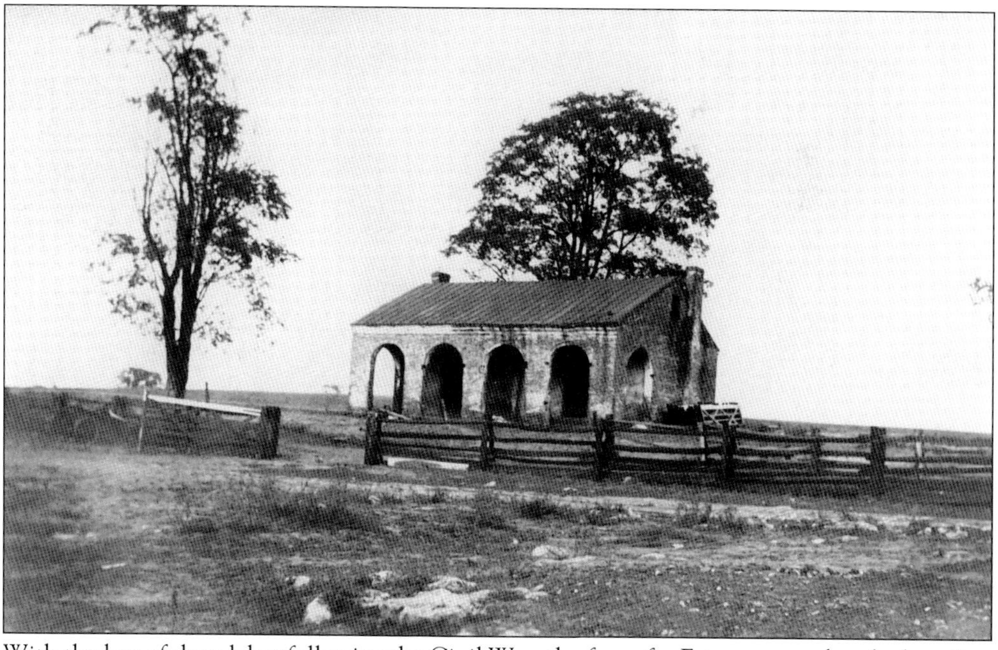

With the loss of slave labor following the Civil War, the focus for Fairvue turned to the breeding of thoroughbred horses. In the late 1920s and early 1930s, a portion of the property along Gallatin Road was used by the Southern Grasslands Hunt and Racing Foundation as the site of the prestigious Grasslands Downs steeplechase course. (Courtesy of Sterling Beaumont Updyke.)

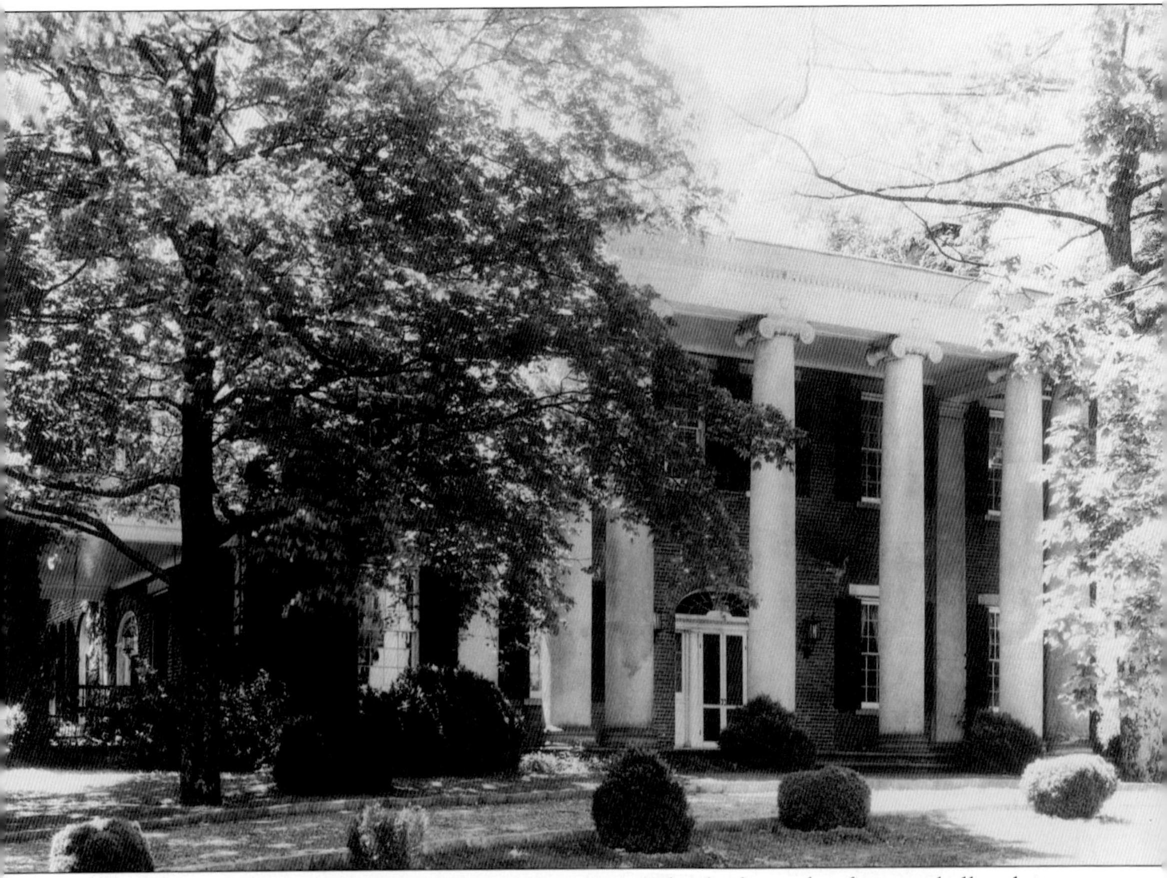

Across Station Camp Creek from Fairvue, Thomas A. Baber built another fine antebellum home, Bellemont, that featured massive Ionic columns. A century later, it was called Foxland Hall. The residence of John and Laura (Stratton) Branham, the home was noted for its thoroughbred horses. (Photograph by Wiles of Nashville, 1975 copy courtesy of Kenneth C. Thomson Jr.)

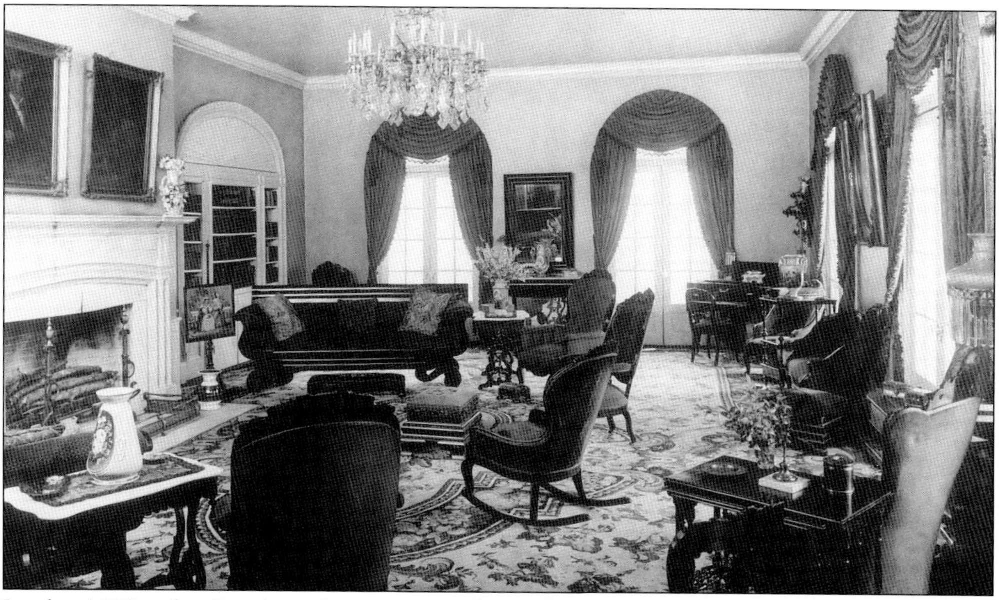

In the 1930s, the Branham home was a show place. Here the living room of the home features antiques and excellent craftsmanship comparable to any home throughout the South. (Photograph by Wiles of Nashville, 1975 copy courtesy of Kenneth C. Thomson Jr.)

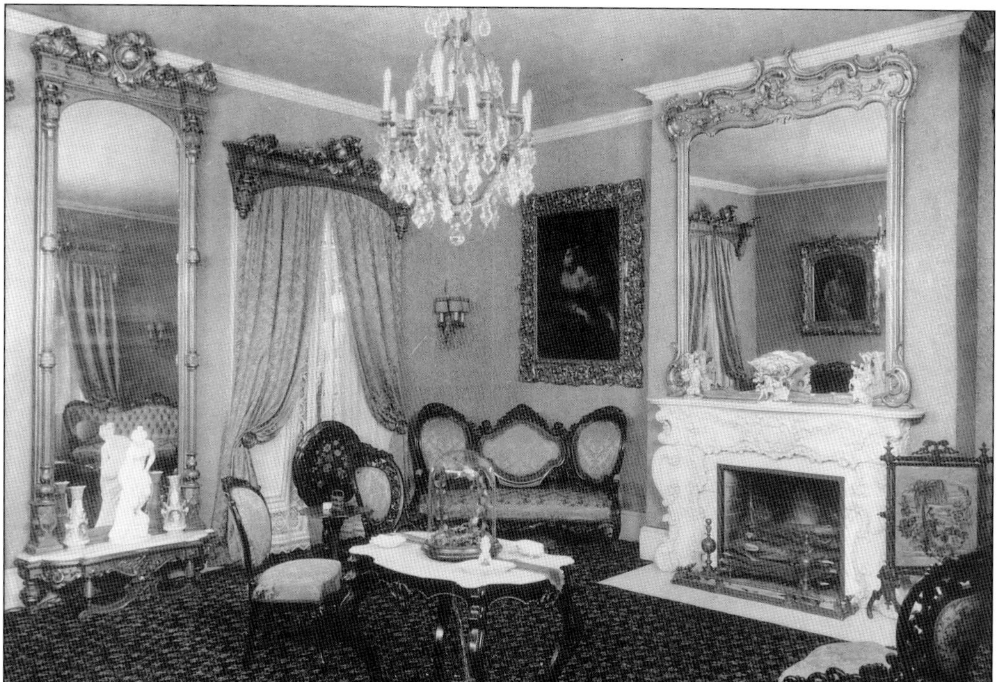

The music room of Foxland Hall features grand touches that include the carved mantel, crystal chandeliers, and enormous gilded mirrors. (Photograph by Wiles of Nashville, 1975 copy courtesy of Kenneth C. Thomson Jr.)

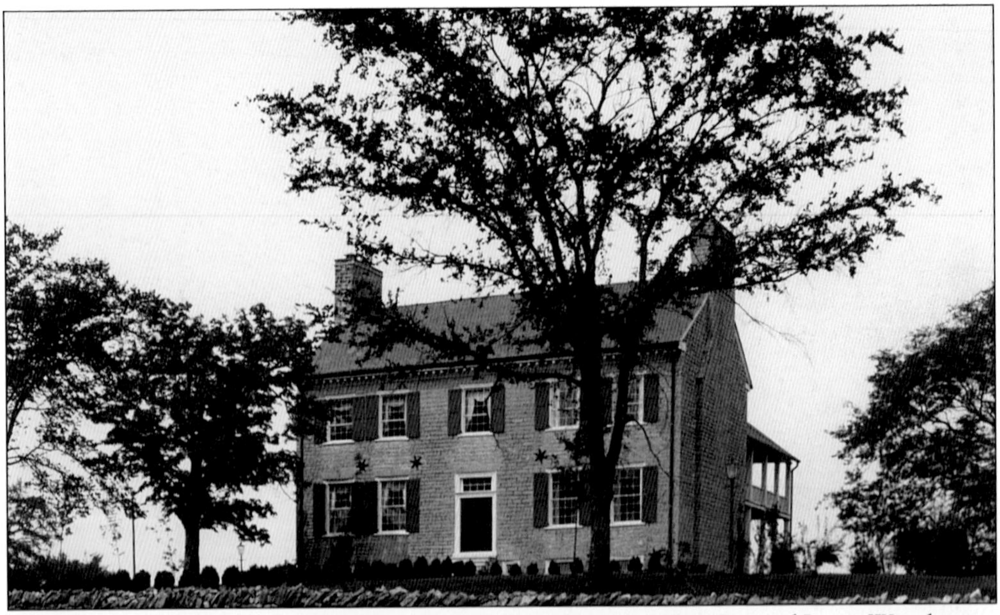

Cragfont, the home constructed (1798–1802) by Revolutionary War General James Winchester, remains a major Sumner County attraction. Compare this photograph with those on page 11 of the first volume of *Around Gallatin & Sumner County*. Here the old tree-lined entrance has been replaced by a neat stone wall, while the addition of shutters gives a neat, formal appearance. Still visible are the star-shaped coverings of the earthquake rods. (Courtesy of the Bob Perry Collection, Sumner County Archives.)

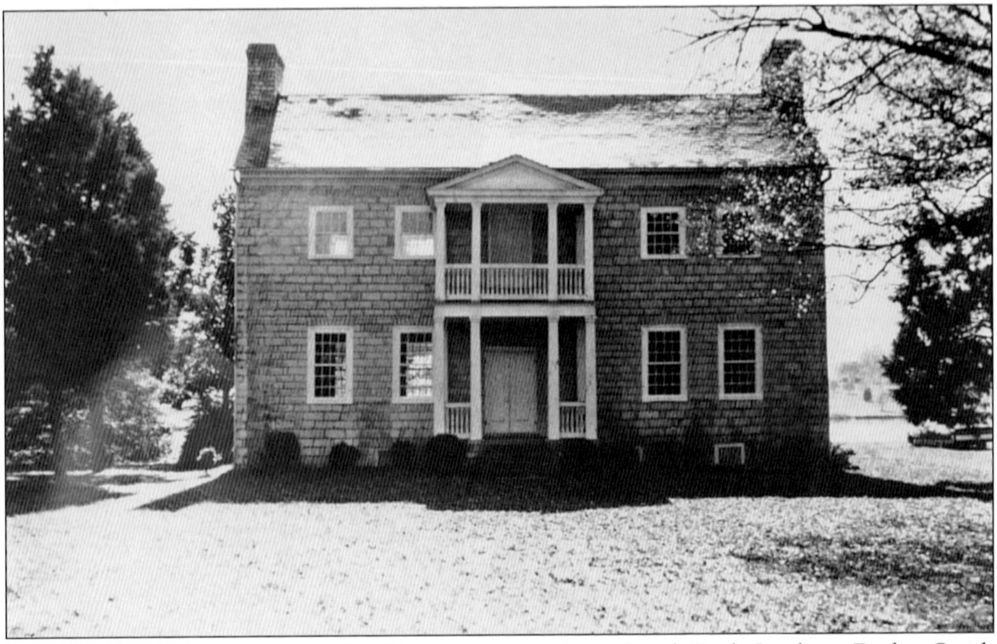

Completed in 1794, two years before Tennessee gained statehood, Rock Castle on Drakes Creek was built in sections covering seven levels by Daniel Smith. The historic home barely escaped inundation when Old Hickory Lake was created in 1953 and rising waters halted within yards of the house. (Courtesy of the Bob Perry Collection, Sumner County Archives.)

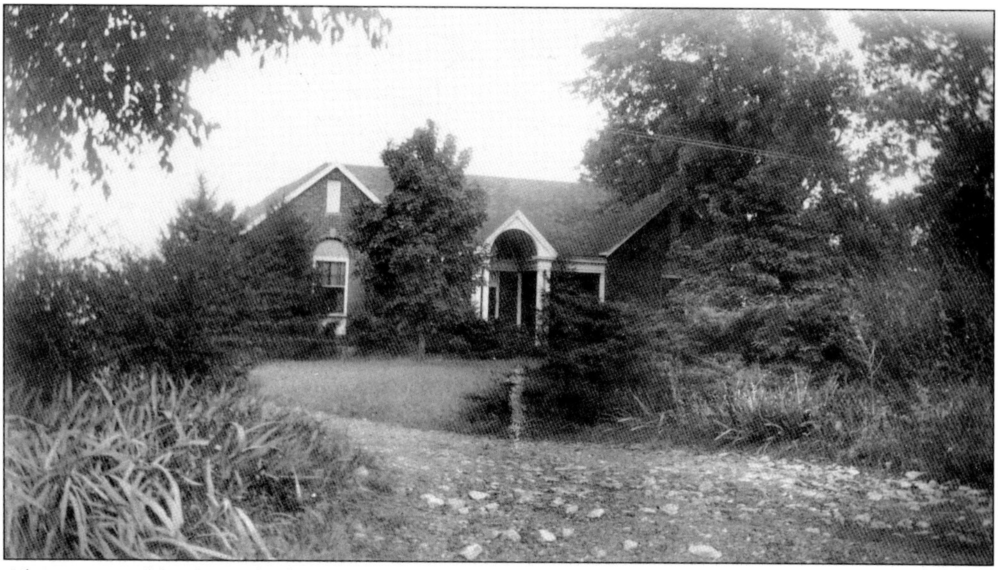

Almost invisible through the trees is the charming J.B. Shute cottage on Old Shackle Island Road in Hendersonville. (Courtesy of Quinton Coppage.)

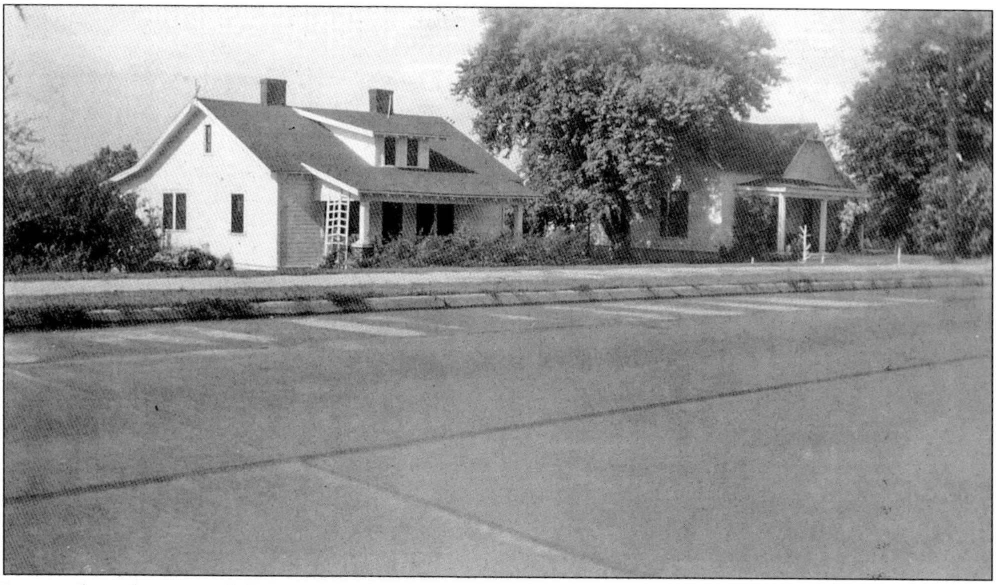

Located at the site of the present Captain D's in Hendersonville, were the Thomson homes. The home on the left was built by Emily Ann Bridgwater Thomson for her son, Horatio Berry Thomson, upon his marriage to Margaret Polk. To the right, the home of William Parrish Thomson and his wife, Emily Bridgwater, was built in the 1890s. (Courtesy of Quinton Coppage.)

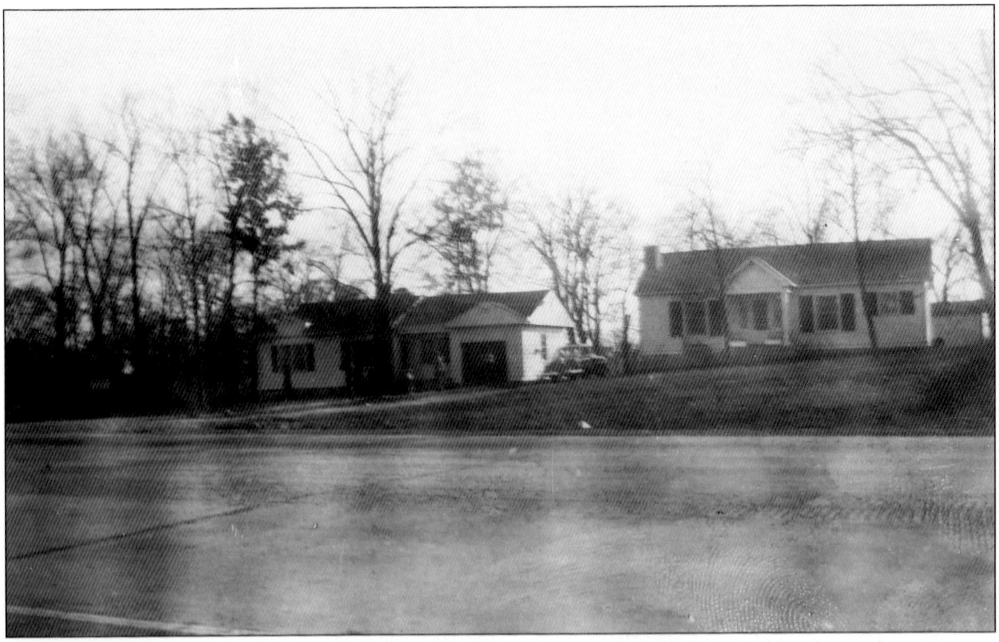

Homes once lined Hendersonville's Main Street. These two houses across from the present-day location of the animal clinic on West Main were built by Horatio Thomson. (Courtesy of Quinton Coppage.)

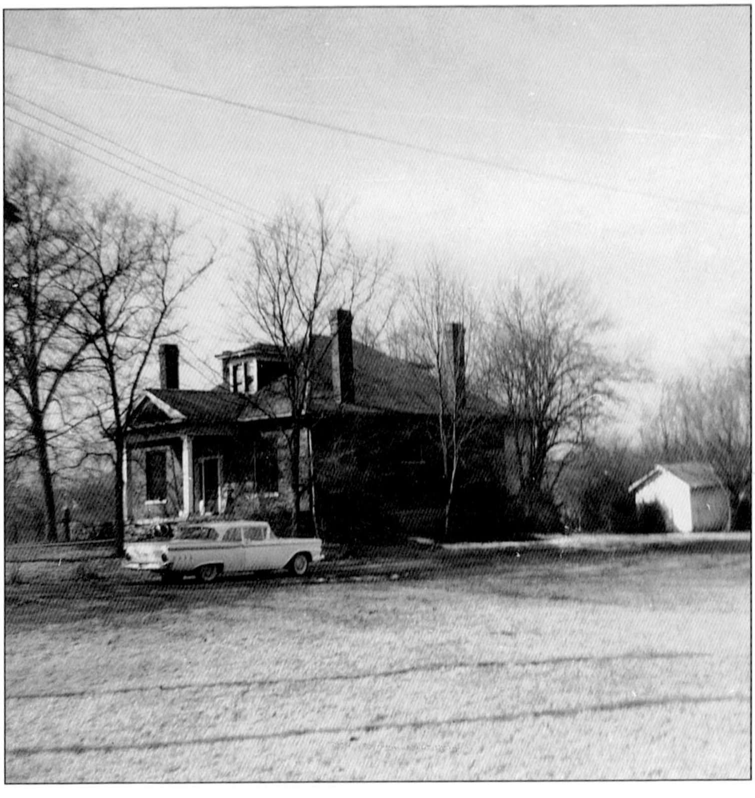

Today, Bush Jewelers is located on property that was the site of the Waller Pierce home on Main Street in Hendersonville. Sitting back from the highway, the home enjoyed a wide expanse of lawn which today is covered by the City Square shopping center parking lot. (Courtesy of Quinton Coppage.)

Further east, near the site of today's Papa John's Pizza in the City Square shopping center, was the small frame home known as the Lawrence House. (Courtesy of Quinton Coppage.)

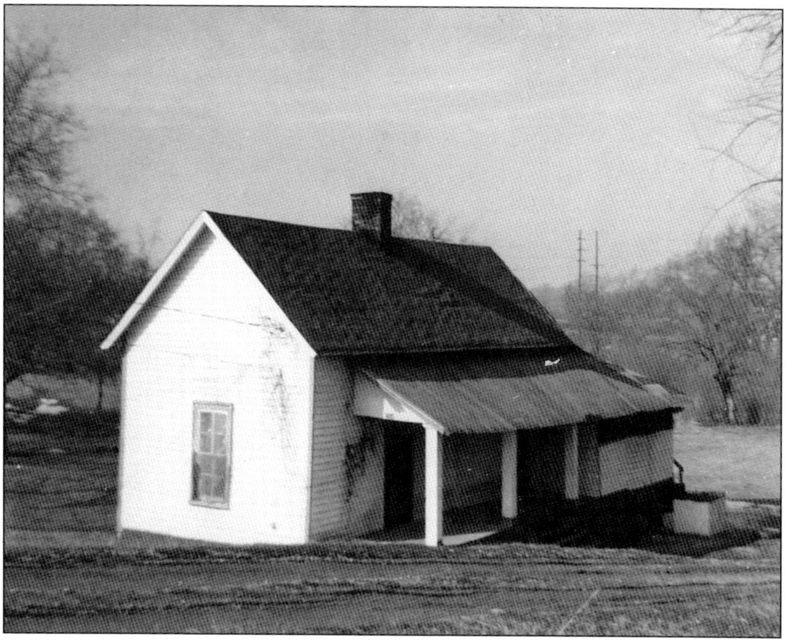

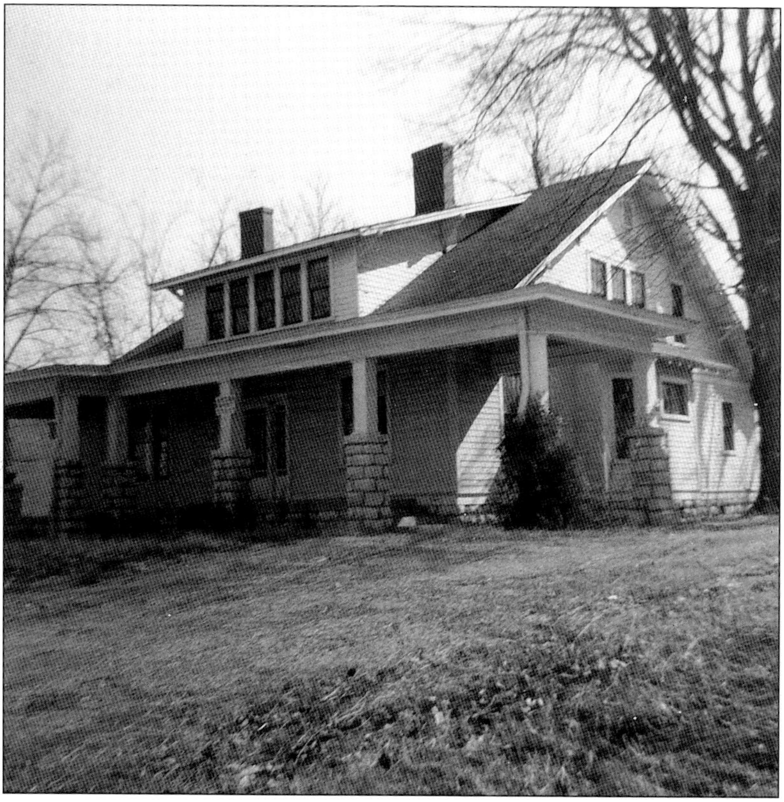

The Mann home stood at the site of the present-day parking lot between Volunteer State Bank and Phillips-Robinson Funeral Home. (Courtesy of Quinton Coppage.)

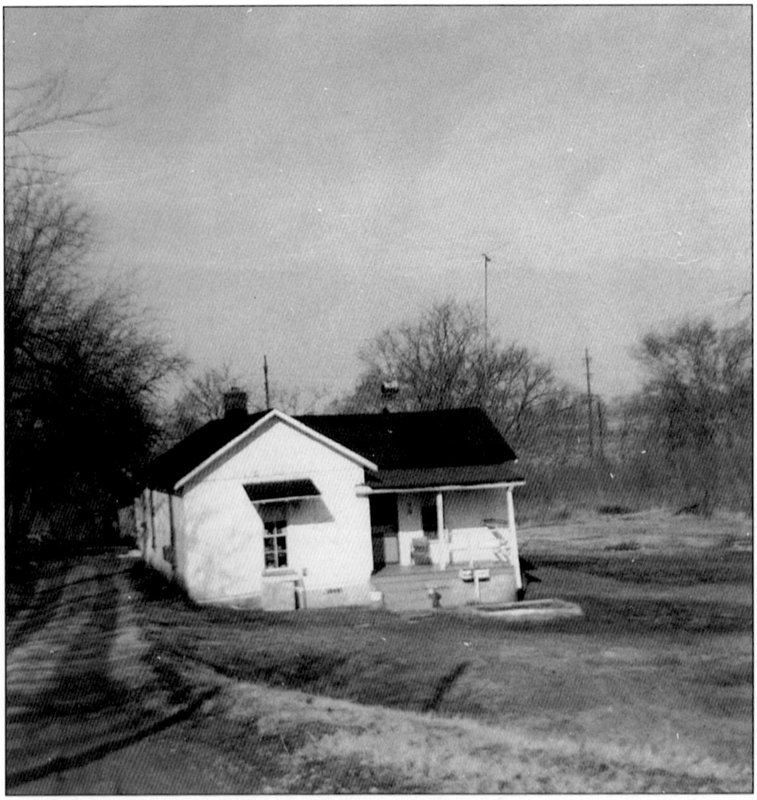

This small house in Hendersonville served as a private school, which was established by local people who were upset with county schools. (Courtesy of Quinton Coppage.)

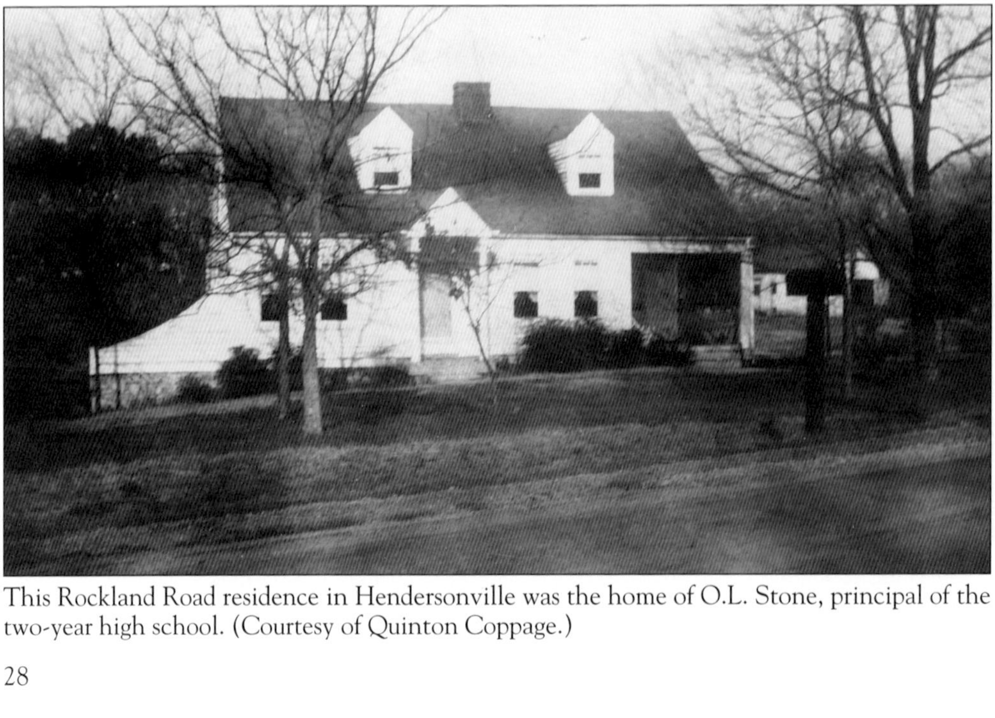

This Rockland Road residence in Hendersonville was the home of O.L. Stone, principal of the two-year high school. (Courtesy of Quinton Coppage.)

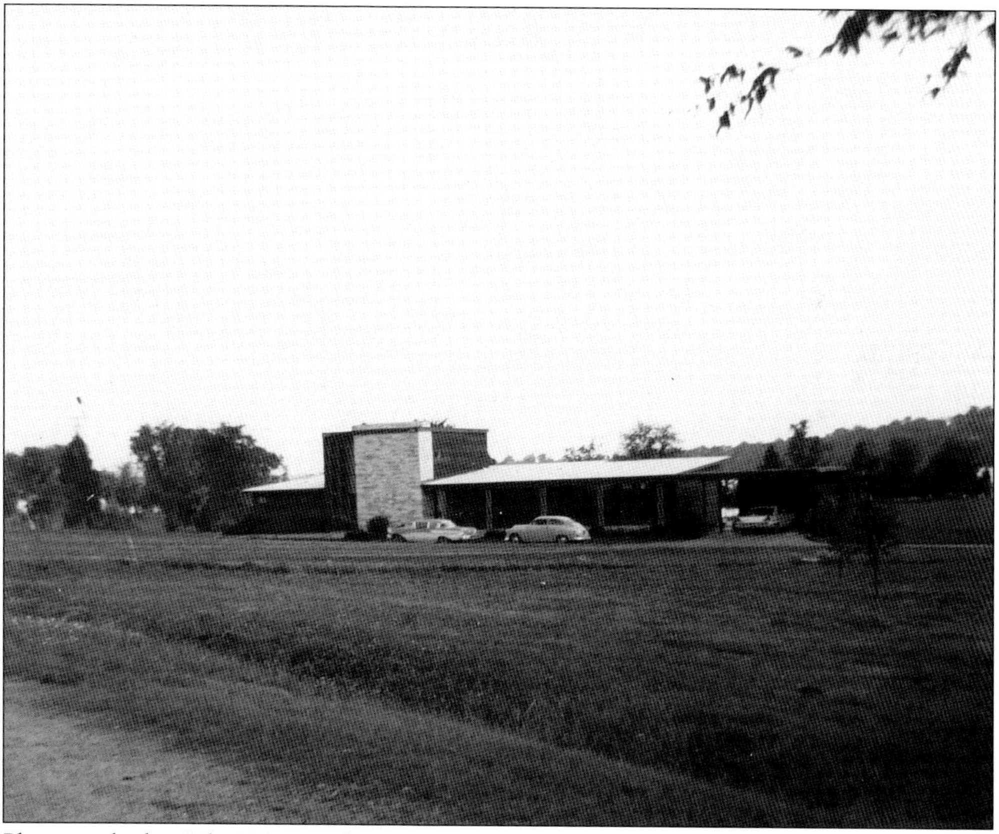

Photographed in July 1959 was the Hendersonville home of Gov. Frank Clement in Bluegrass. The home burned after Clement's death. (Courtesy of Quinton Coppage.)

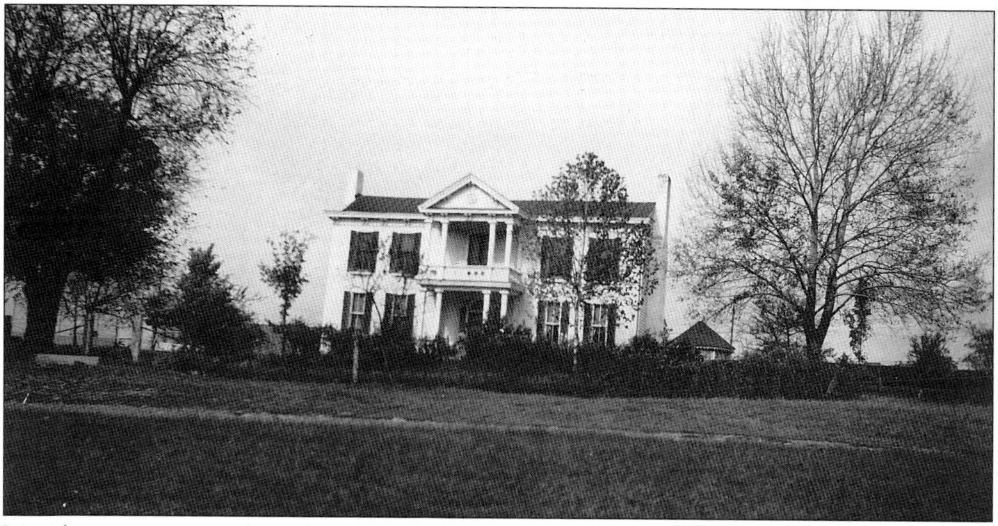

Monthaven is pictured in the 1930s before the addition of trees along the entrance. The longtime home of the Comer-Waddell families, the building today houses Hendersonville's Arts Council. (Courtesy of Lee Waddell Curtis.)

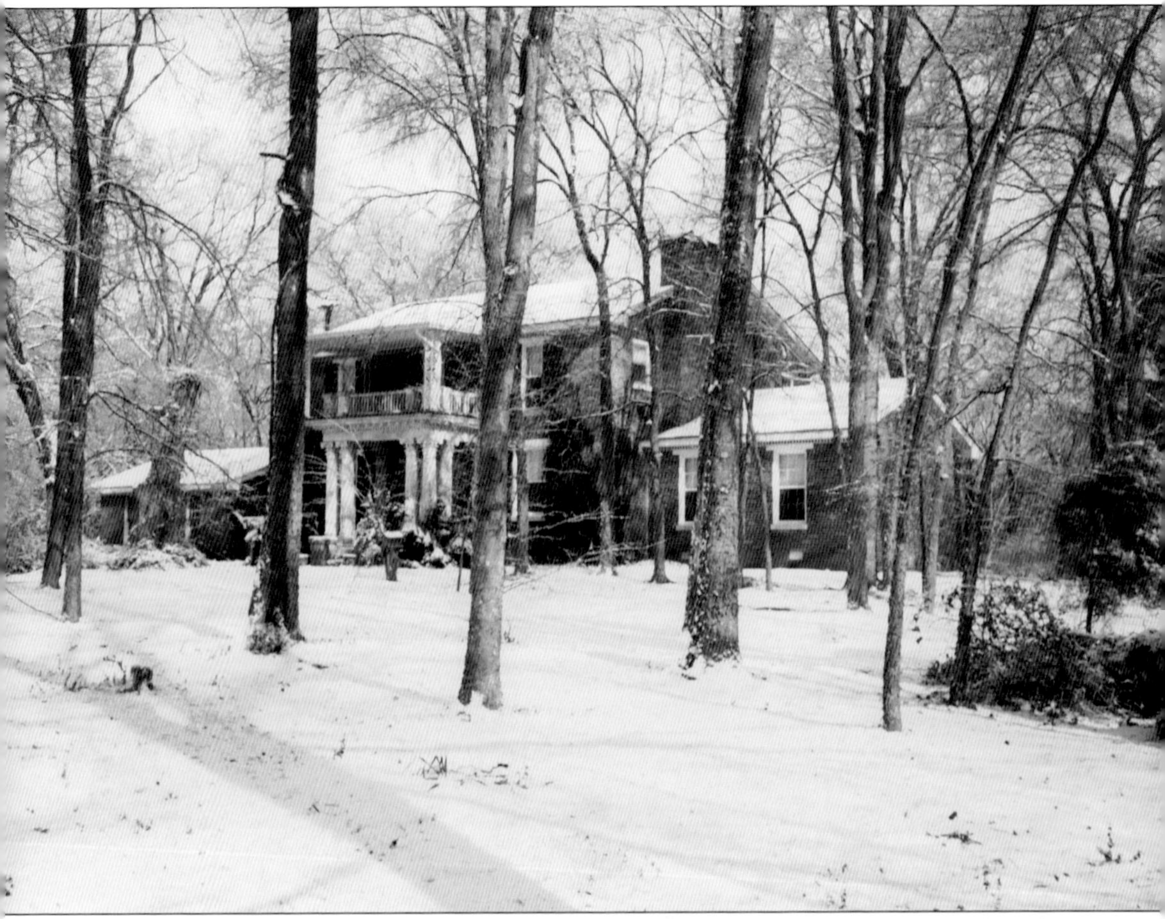

Located along New Shackle Island Road, Carrview is the home of Quinton and Pauline Coppage. This historic restored property includes a cedar tree given by Pres. Andrew Jackson. The home is adjacent to the popular Coppage Creek Driving Range which was formerly part of the property. (Courtesy of Quinton Coppage.)

Two

PEOPLE

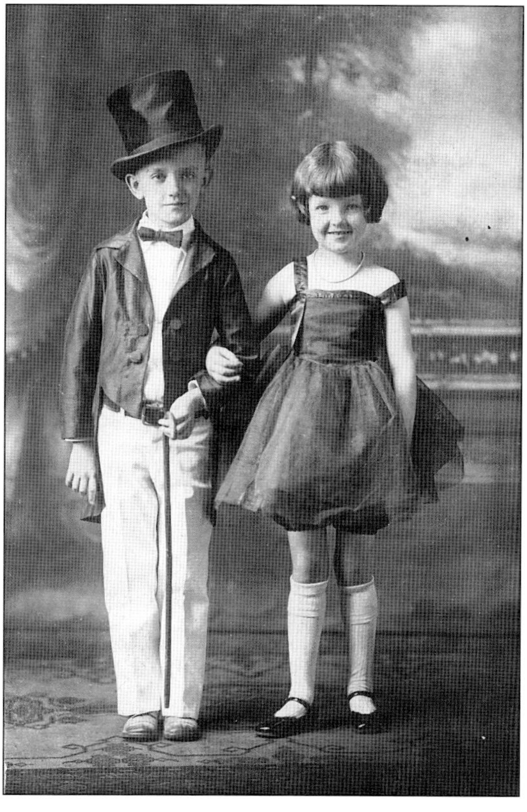

Reminiscent of the Hollywood musicals of the 1930s and 1940s, youthful dancers Cameron Bundy "Tippy" Crutcher and Mary Reese look spiffy as they pose for the camera. (Postcard courtesy of Kenneth C. Thomson Jr.)

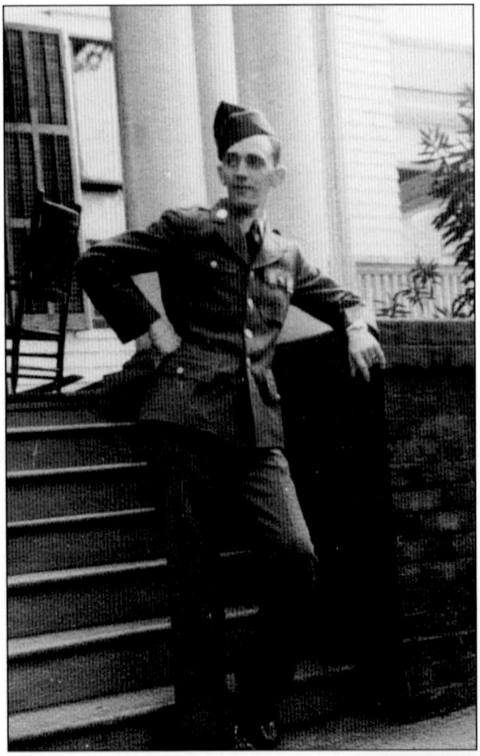

As an adult, Cameron Bundy "Tippy" Crutcher continued his career as a professional dancer and movie stand-in for the great Fred Astaire. (Courtesy of Mary St. Charles Boniol.)

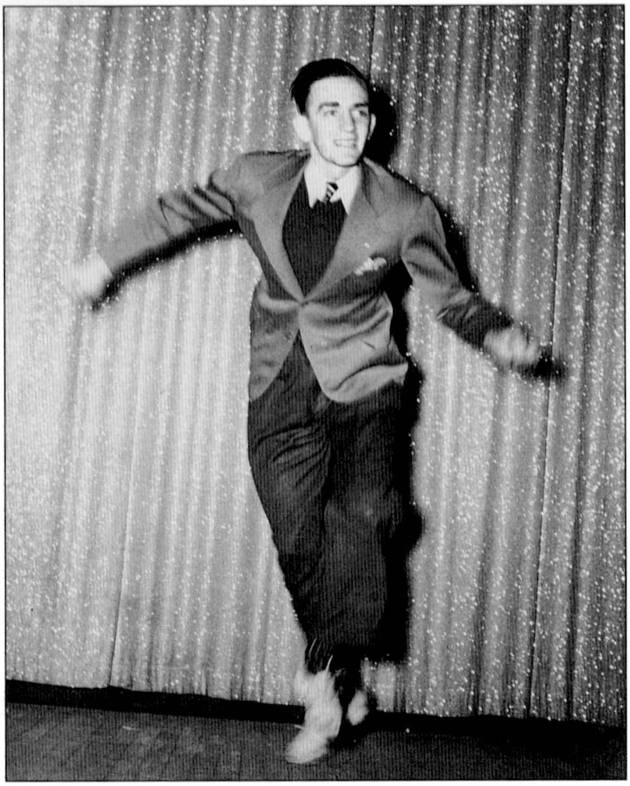

"Tippy" Crutcher played vaudeville stages in the 1930s and performed at Rockefeller Center in New York. He later worked as a professional photographer with a studio in Gallatin. (Courtesy of Cameron Crutcher.)

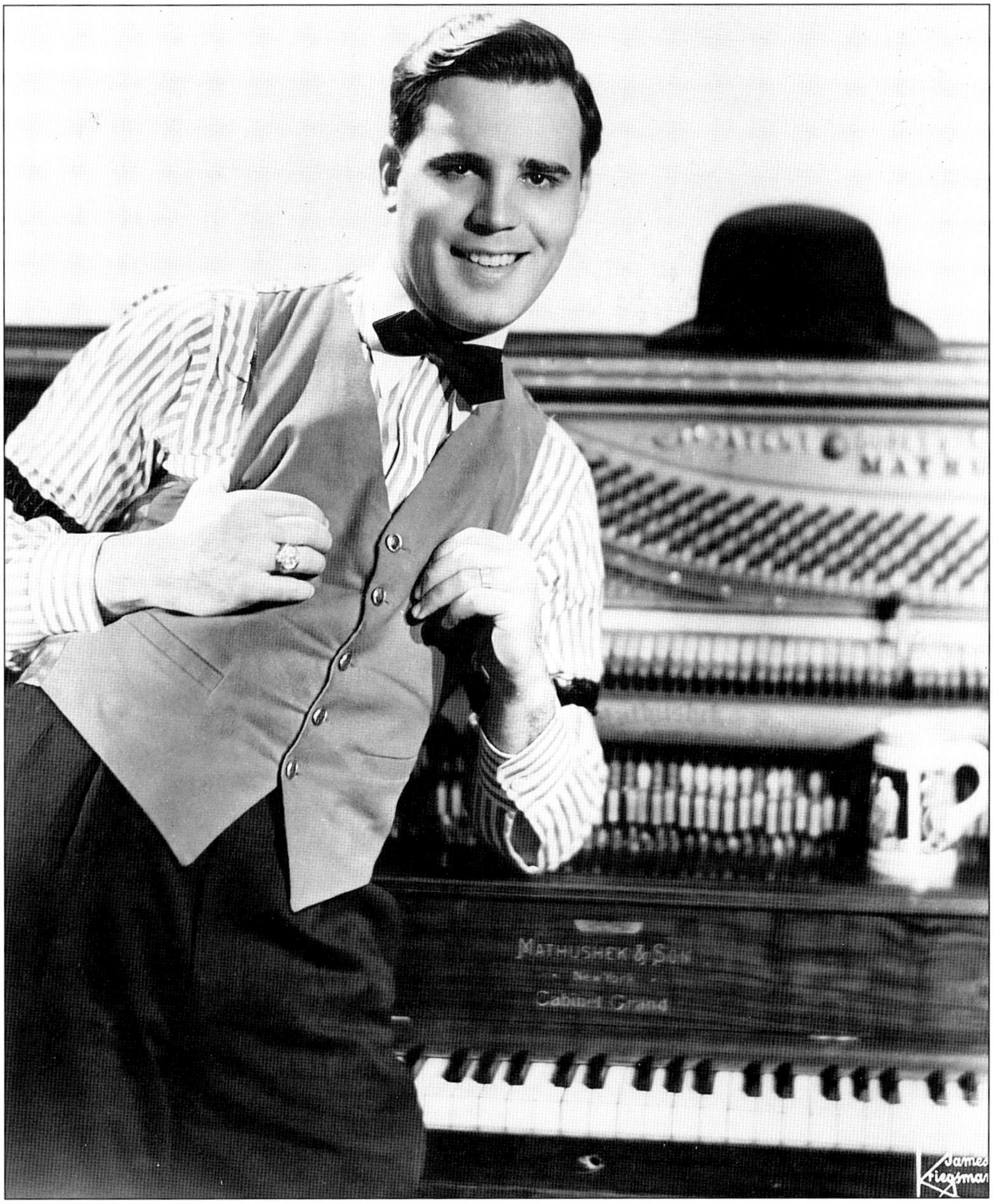

Sumner County provided a number of stars to the entertainment world, including ragtime piano player Johnny Maddox of Gallatin, the first recording artist for Dot Records. Maddox's talent has charmed audiences around the world. (Courtesy of the Johnny Maddox Collection.)

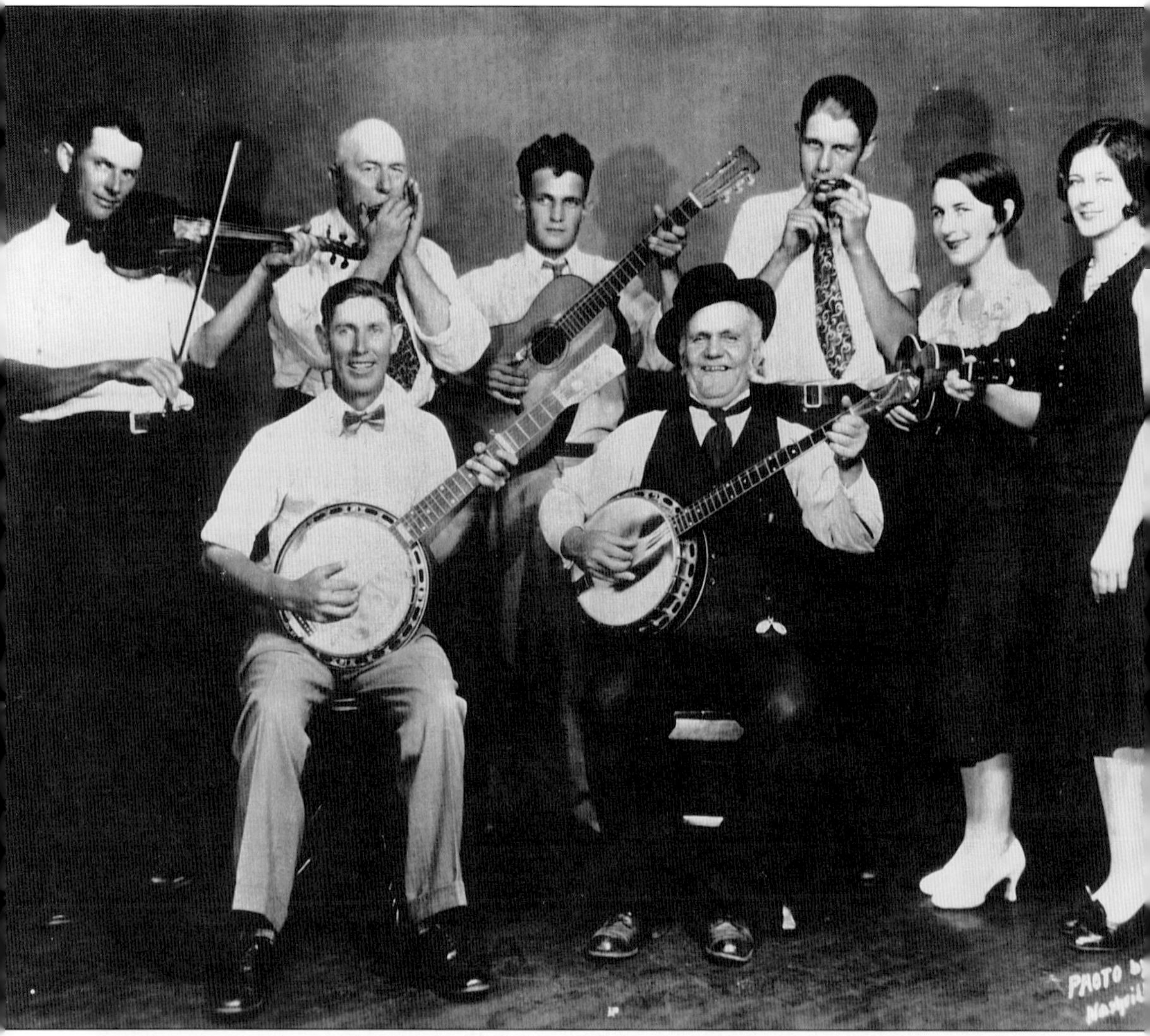

Sumner County's musical traditions run the gamut. Here, country music legend Uncle Dave Macon (front row, center) performs with a group including Gallatin's Dr. Humphrey Bate (back row, second from left) and Alcyone Bate, the first woman to perform at the Grand Ole Opry (front row, second from right). (Courtesy of the Bob Perry Collection, Sumner County Archives.)

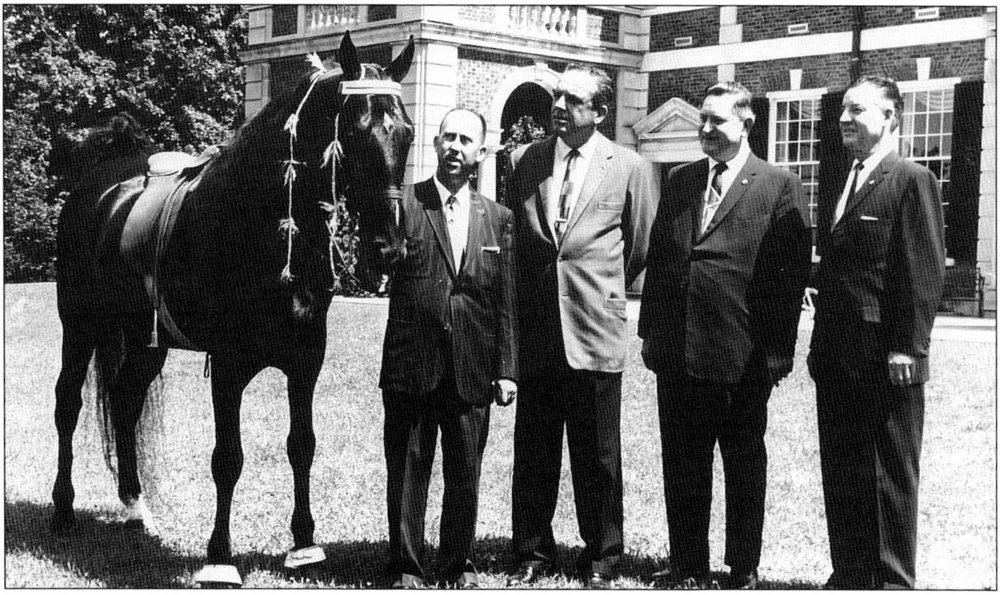

On the grounds of the Governor's Mansion in Nashville, a group including William K. Hale (left) and Gov. Frank G. Clement (second from left) admire Hale's Ebony Masterpiece, the world's champion from the 1962 Tennessee Walking Horse National Celebration. (Courtesy of the Bob Perry Collection, Sumner County Archives.)

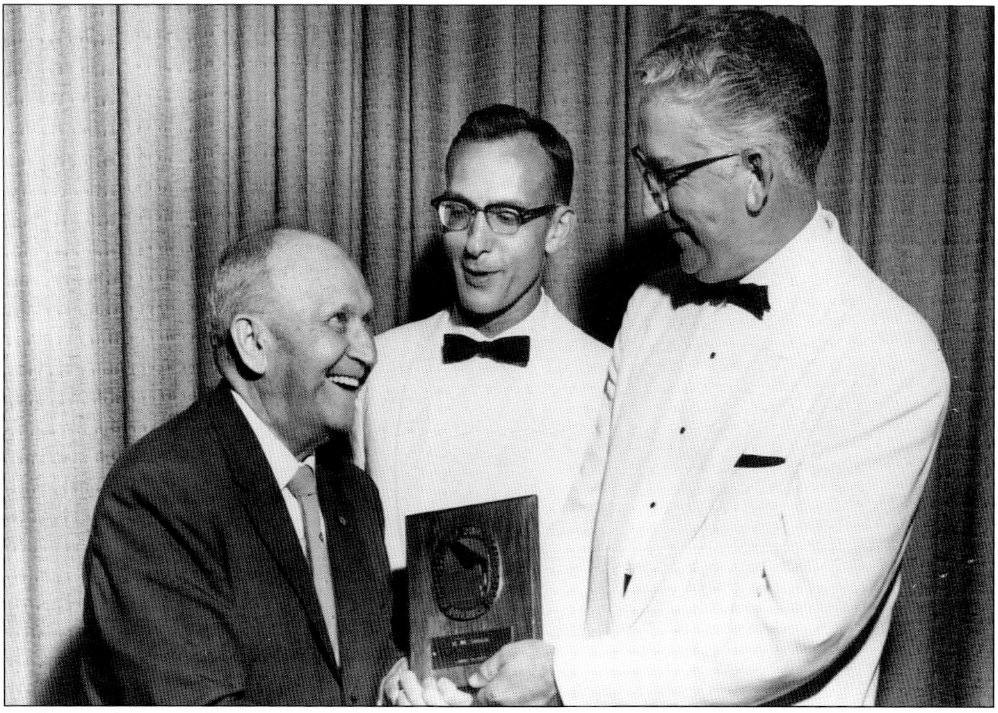

Gallatin photographer E.M. Stark is pictured at a photography convention receiving one of his many awards. Many of the charming photographs in this volume as well as the first volume of *Around Gallatin and Sumner County* were made by Mr. Stark. (Courtesy of Kenneth C. Thomson Jr.)

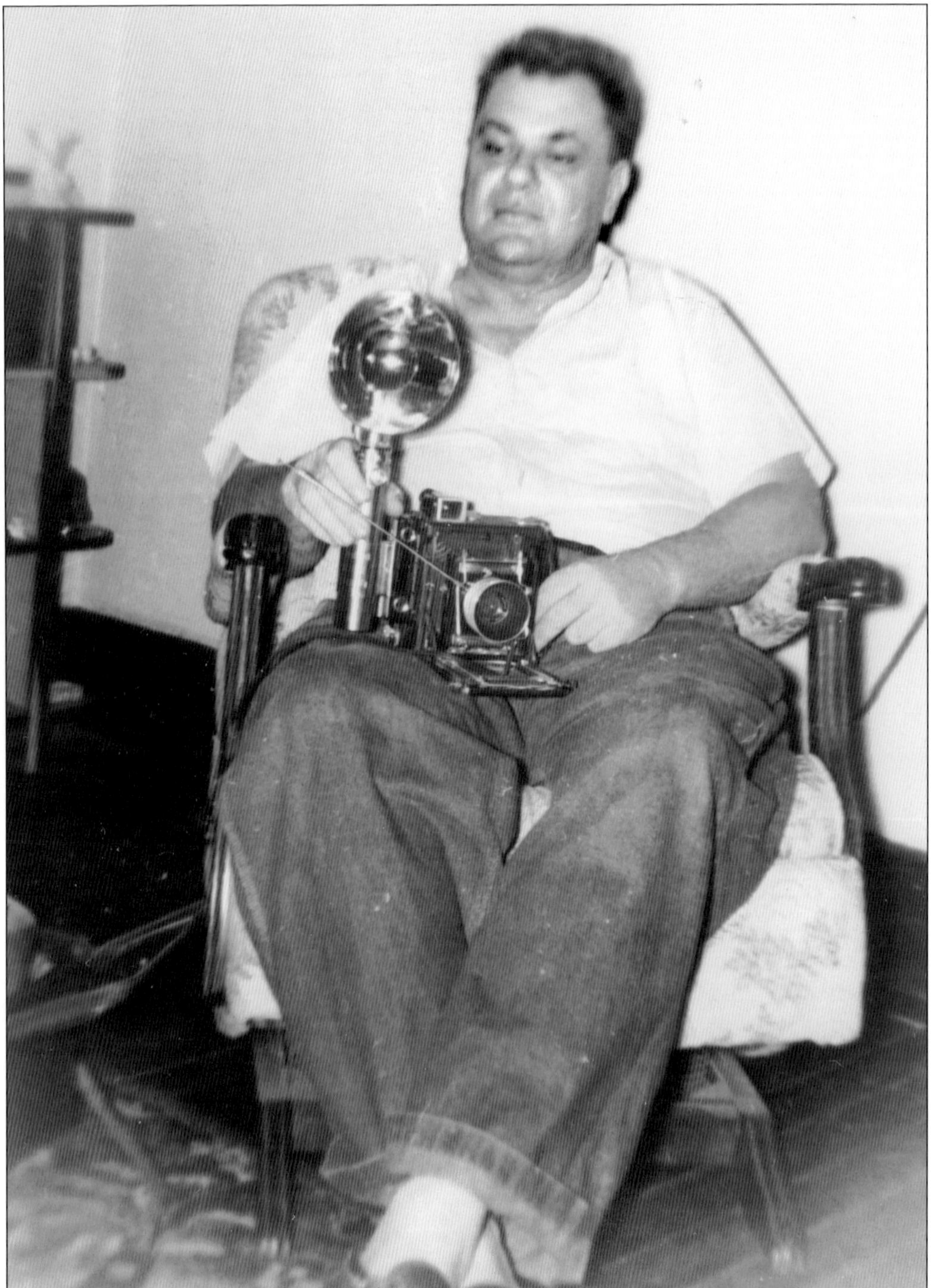

Portland's Elmer Hinton was the editor of the *Upper Sumner Press* before becoming a noted reporter and photographer for the Nashville *Tennessean*. Over the years, Hinton reported major stories and wrote a column of home-spun humor called "Down to Earth." He also served as Portland's mayor. His contributions to the community were recognized when the city library was named in his honor. (Courtesy of Allen Haynes.)

Sumner County heroes were not limited to the arts community. Norman Leo Plant (left) is pictured here with one of Gallatin's favorite sons, Staff Sgt. David Brown Parrish, in Tokyo, Japan with the army of occupation in 1945. Parrish, now a retired teacher, is known throughout the county for his community service and wonderful sense of humor. (Courtesy of David Brown Parrish.)

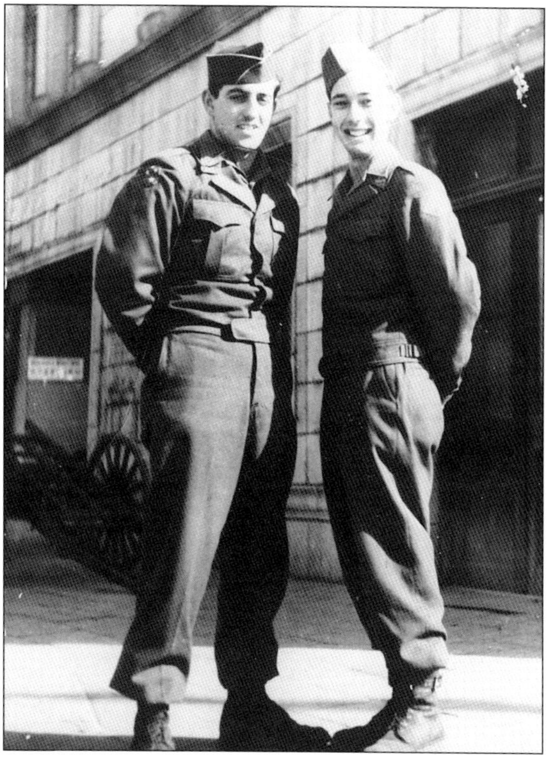

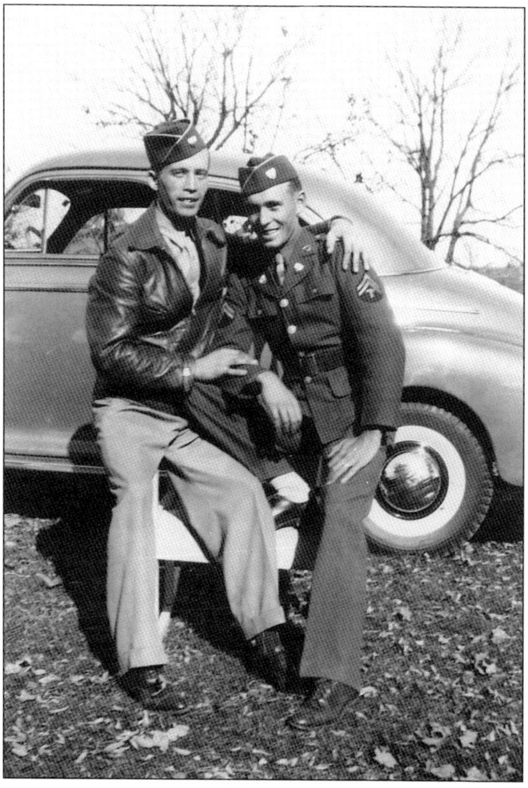

Brothers Harold and William A. Haynes pause for this photograph before heading off to World War II. William was killed during the war. (Courtesy of Allen Haynes.)

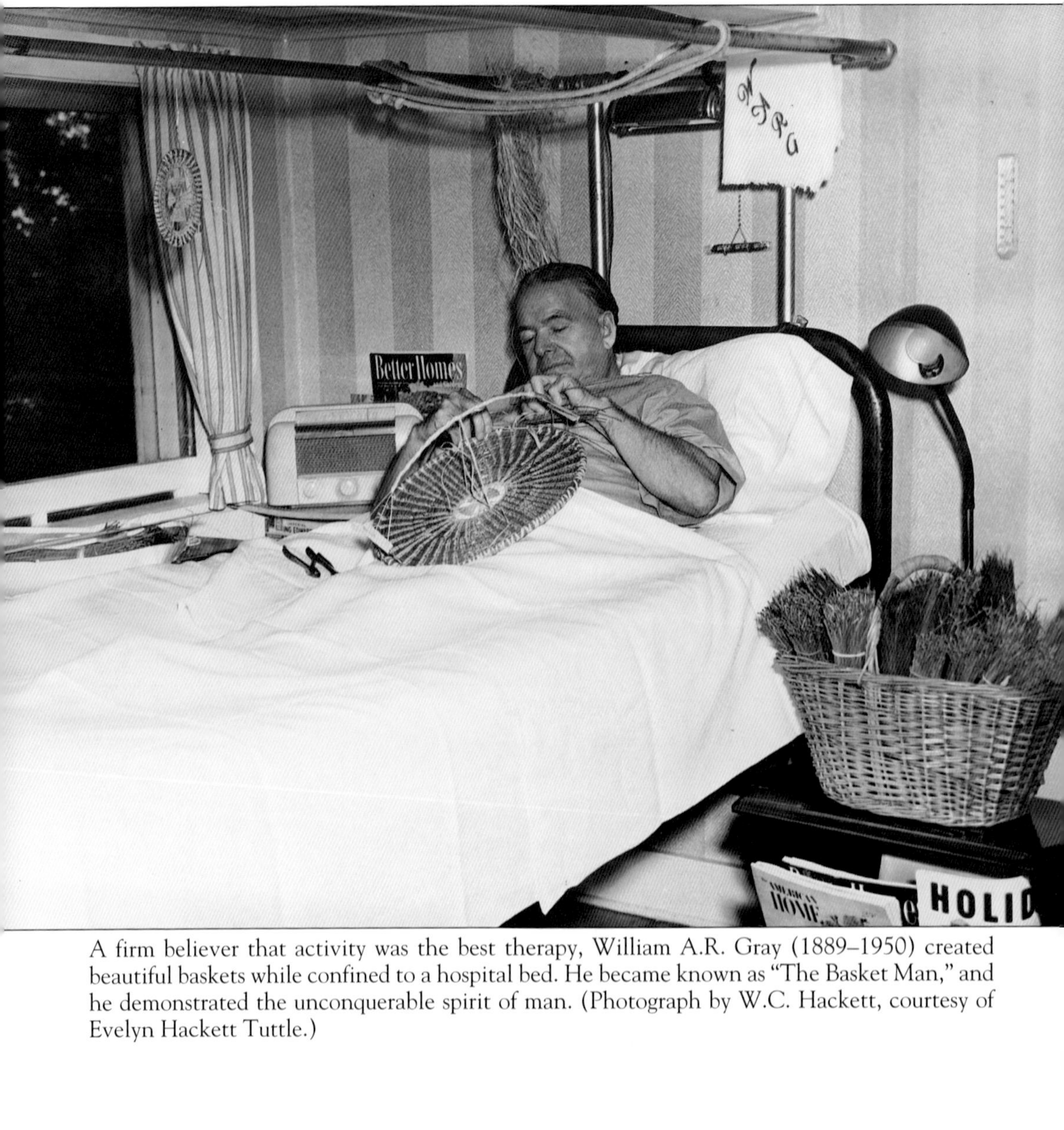

A firm believer that activity was the best therapy, William A.R. Gray (1889–1950) created beautiful baskets while confined to a hospital bed. He became known as "The Basket Man," and he demonstrated the unconquerable spirit of man. (Photograph by W.C. Hackett, courtesy of Evelyn Hackett Tuttle.)

Gallatin fire chief Joseph Anthony St. Charles poses beside the flag-bedecked windows of his business, St. Charles Grocery, across from the Old Howard School. (Courtesy of Mary St. Charles Boniol.)

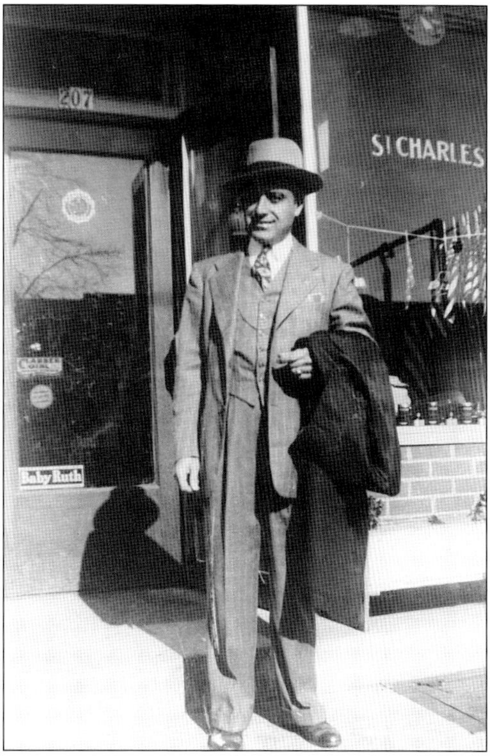

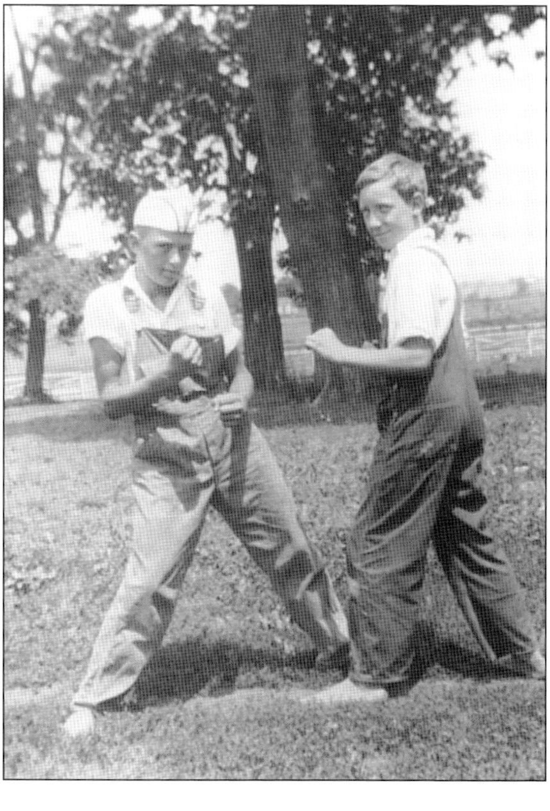

Boys will be boys! Kenneth Calvin Thomson (Sr.) and Billy Dick Brown battle each other on the grounds of Cloverdale Farm on Harris Lane in Gallatin. (Reprint courtesy of Kenneth C. Thomson Jr.)

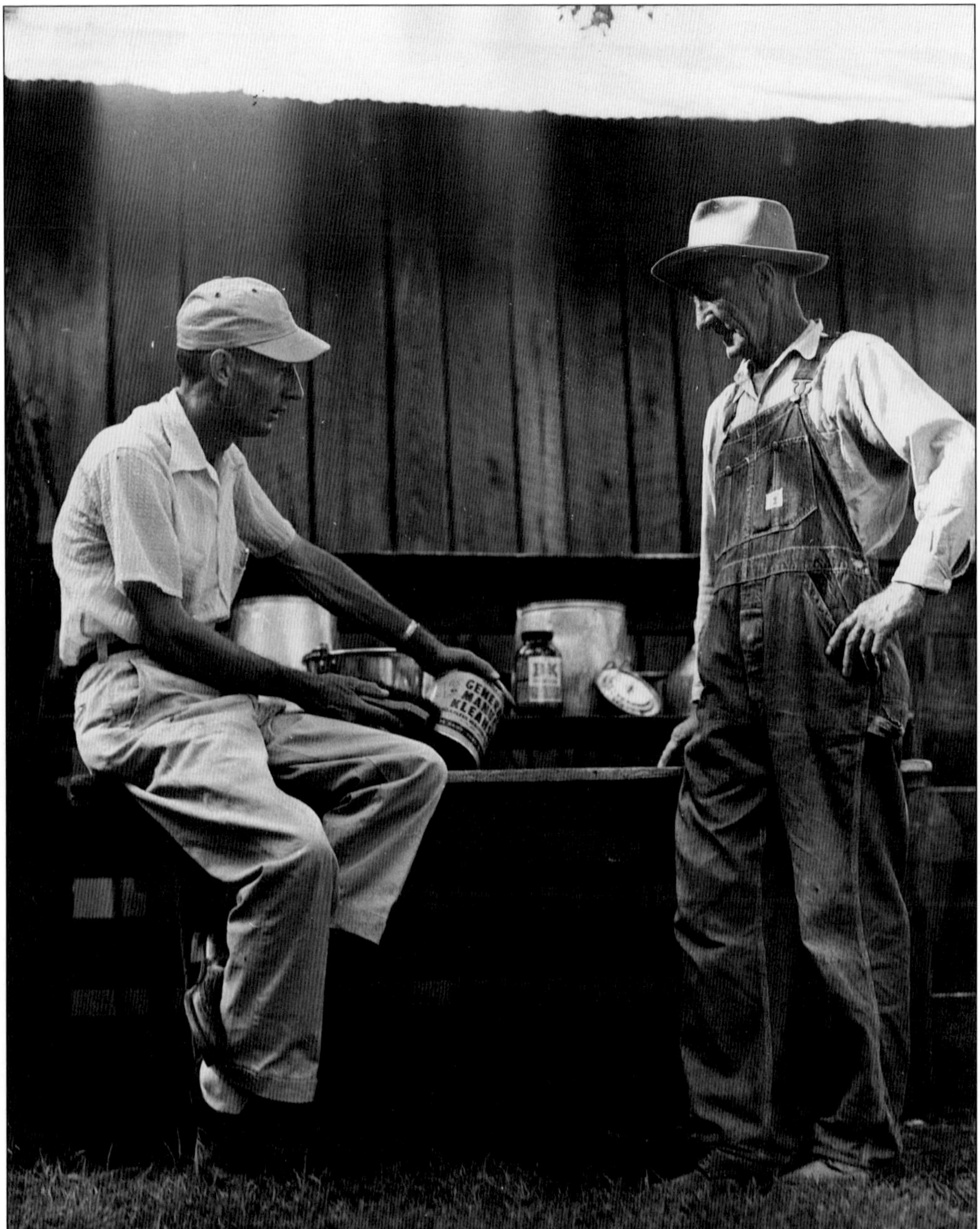

Before the rush of modern life, men customarily took time from their busy days to sit and chat about work, politics, and the weather. Here, John Prosser (left) visits with a friend. (Courtesy of the Bob Perry Collection, Sumner County Archives.)

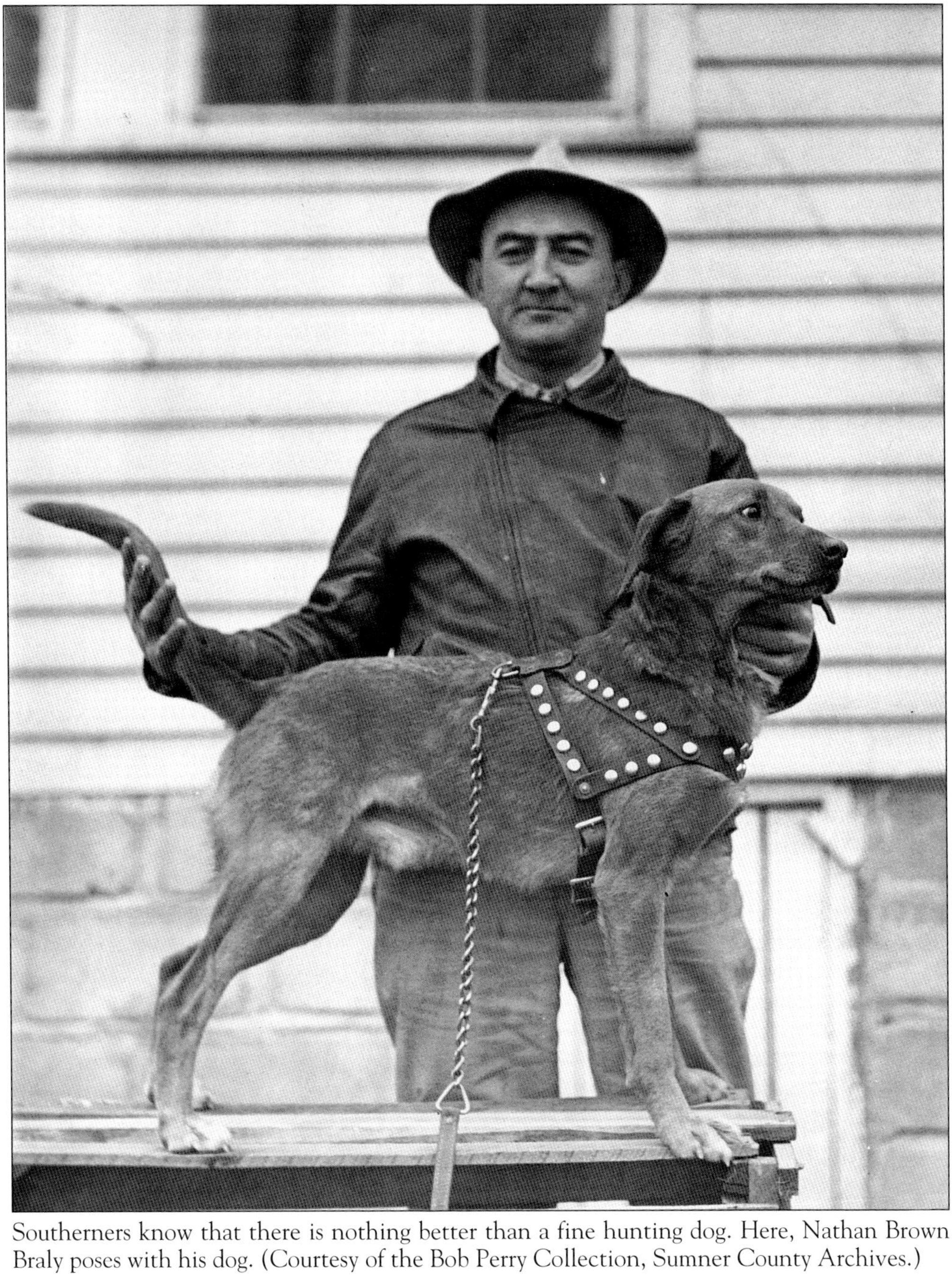

Southerners know that there is nothing better than a fine hunting dog. Here, Nathan Brown Braly poses with his dog. (Courtesy of the Bob Perry Collection, Sumner County Archives.)

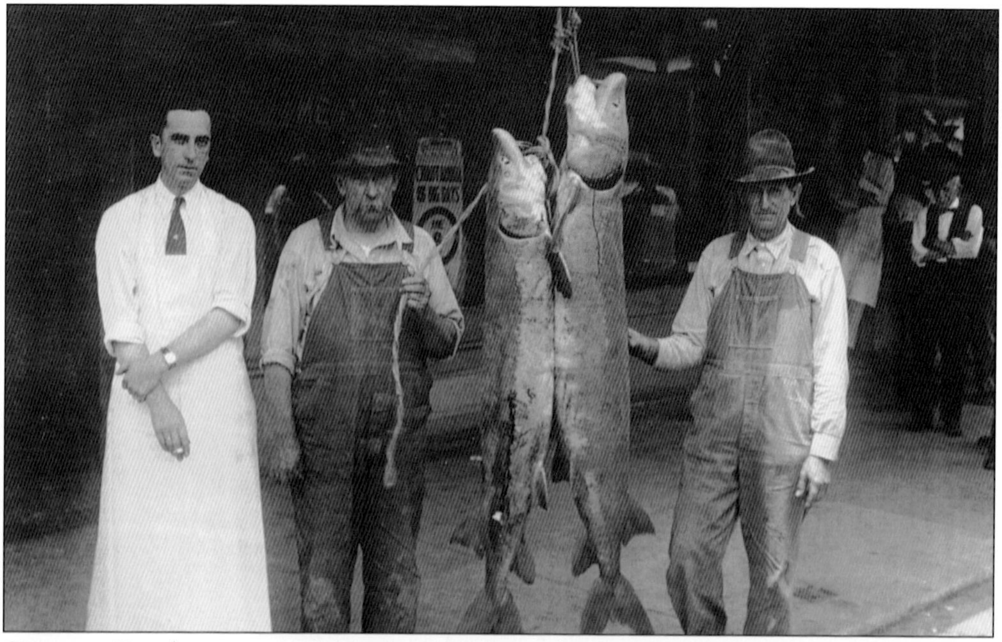

Cameron Crutcher, owner of Crutcher's Meat Market, is pictured here with Eli and Clate Corum and a couple of sturgeon fish (68 lbs and 94 lbs) caught in the Cumberland River along Seven Mile Bluff in 1930. (Original owned by Mary Woodrow Corum Pendaris.)

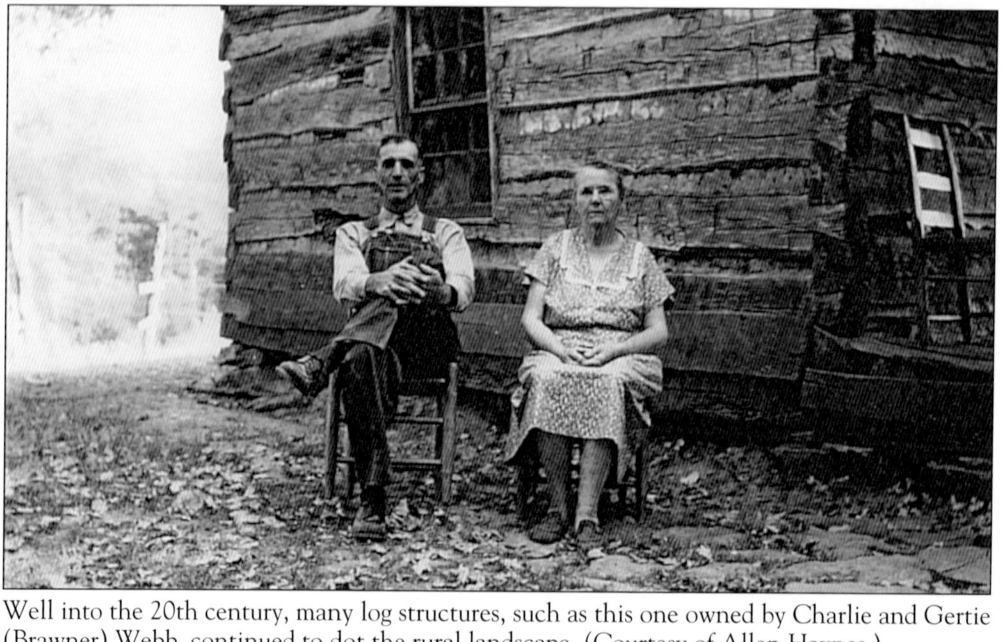

Well into the 20th century, many log structures, such as this one owned by Charlie and Gertie (Brawner) Webb, continued to dot the rural landscape. (Courtesy of Allen Haynes.)

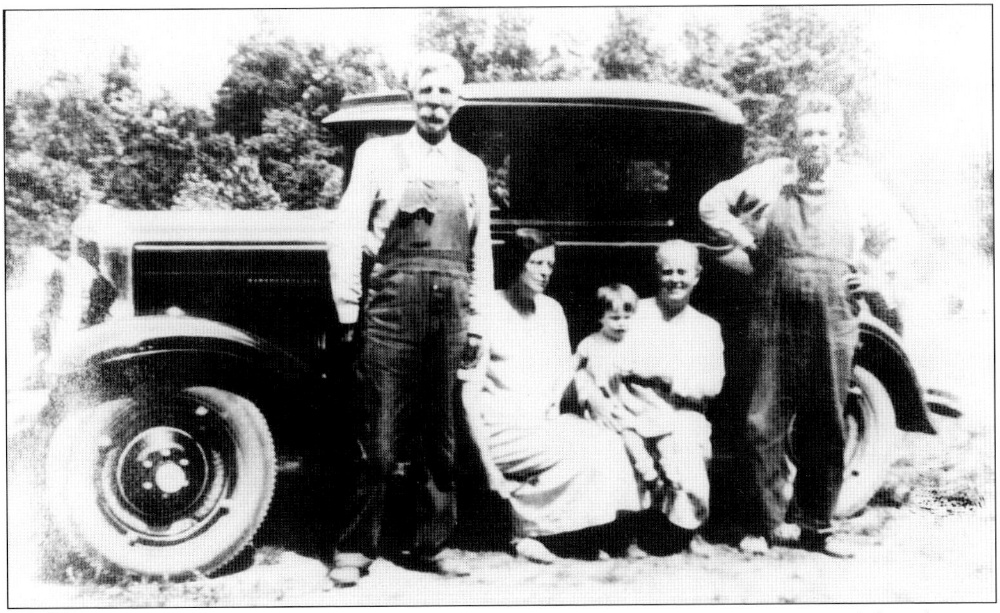

You may recall from Volume I the trend of earlier generations posing in front of their homes. As the automobile became a status symbol in American society, many individuals and families were proudly photographed beside their automobiles. Posing with their Model A are members of the Wilson and Pirkle families. (Courtesy of Denise Wilson.)

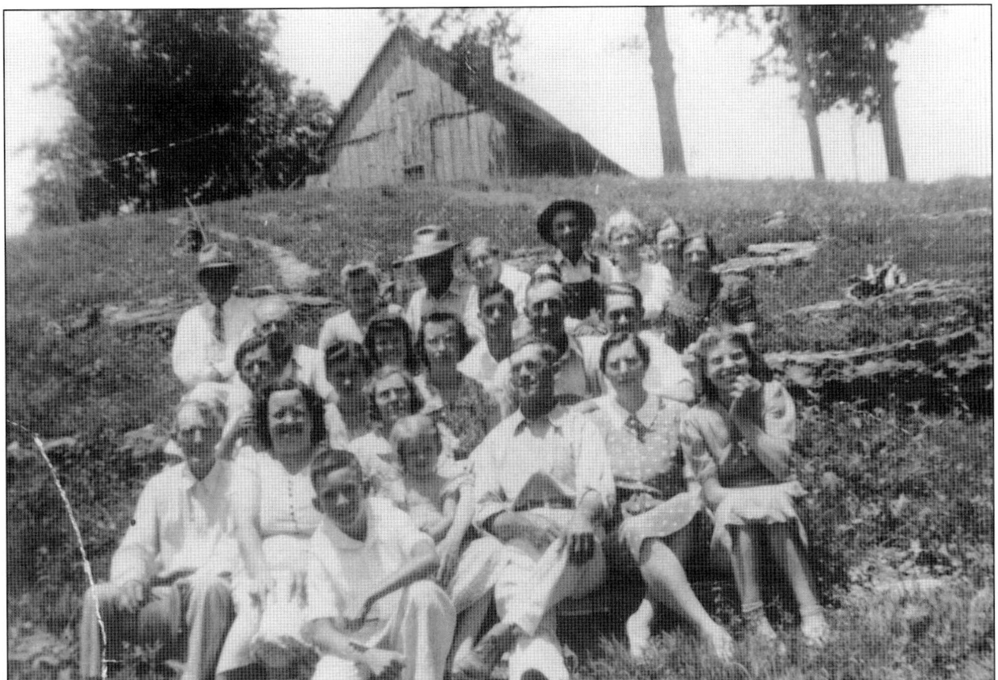

You can almost feel the summer heat and smell the fried chicken while viewing this photograph. A stony, rural hillside near Portland was the site of the Harper family reunion where about two dozen members of the family gathered, *c.* 1940s. (Courtesy of Denise Wilson.)

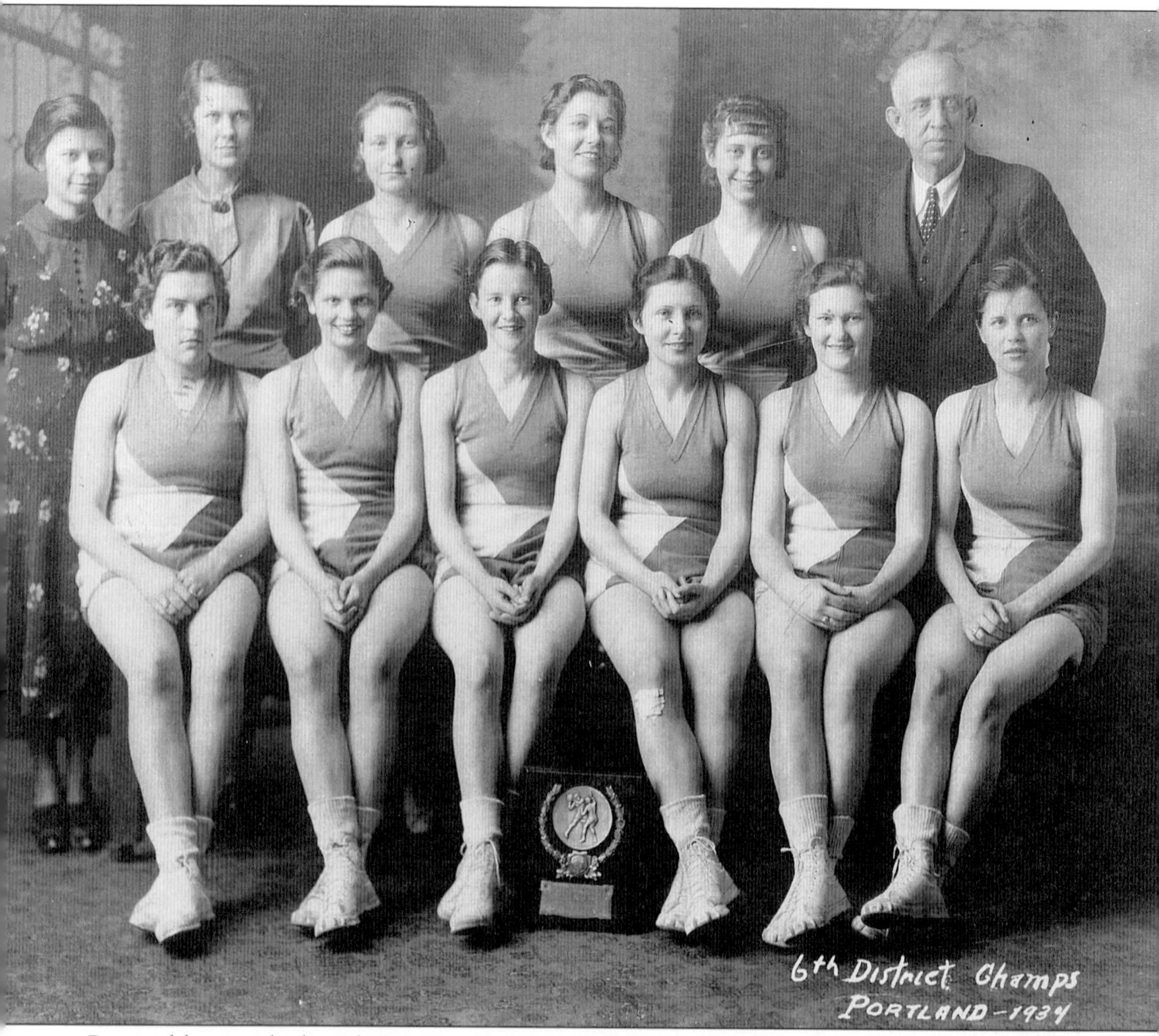

Pictured here with the 6th District Championship trophy are members of the 1934 women's basketball team from Sumner County High School in Portland. Not until the late 1970s were high school women in Tennessee allowed to play full court basketball, but the half court game also honed the women's skills as forwards played only offense and guards focused solely on defense. Members of the team, from left to right, are as follows: (front row) Edna Kirkham, Lenora (Hardison) Alden, Sarah (McNeil) Payne, Ruth (Link) Hessey, Pauline (Suttle) Elliott, and Marguarite (Carter) Caudill; (back row) Christine (Lane) West (manager of the team), Coach Ora (Jones) Miller, Marjorie Groves, Euna Mae (Lambert) Gregory, Eleanor (Moore) White, and Professor C.F. Alden. (Original photograph by E.M. Stark, courtesy of Mrs. Pauline Elliott.)

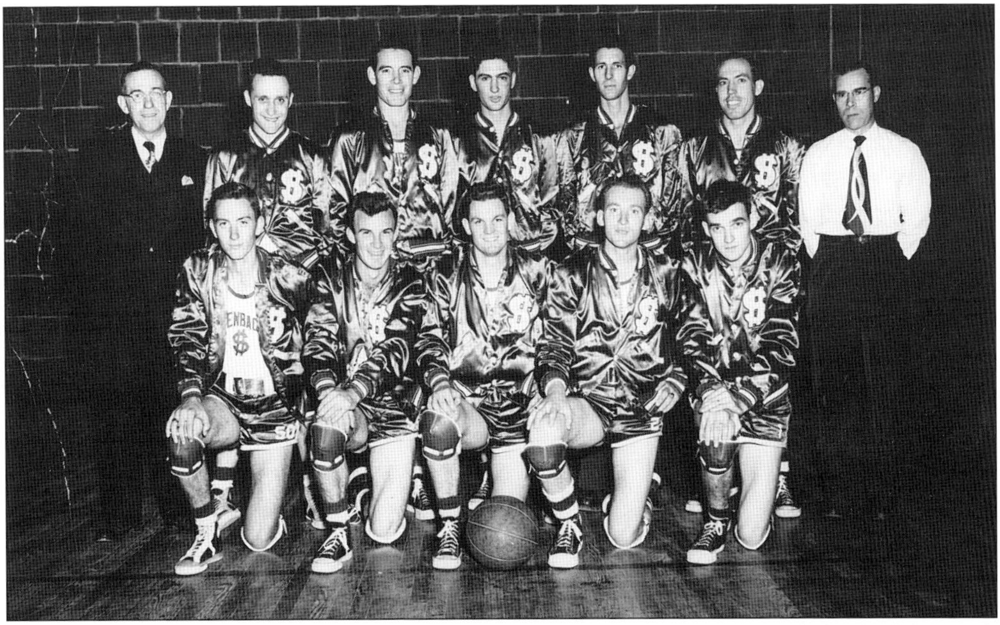

The prominent dollar signs on their uniforms and satin warm-ups were a trademark of the Bank of Hendersonville's Greenbacks basketball team. (Courtesy of Lee Curtis.)

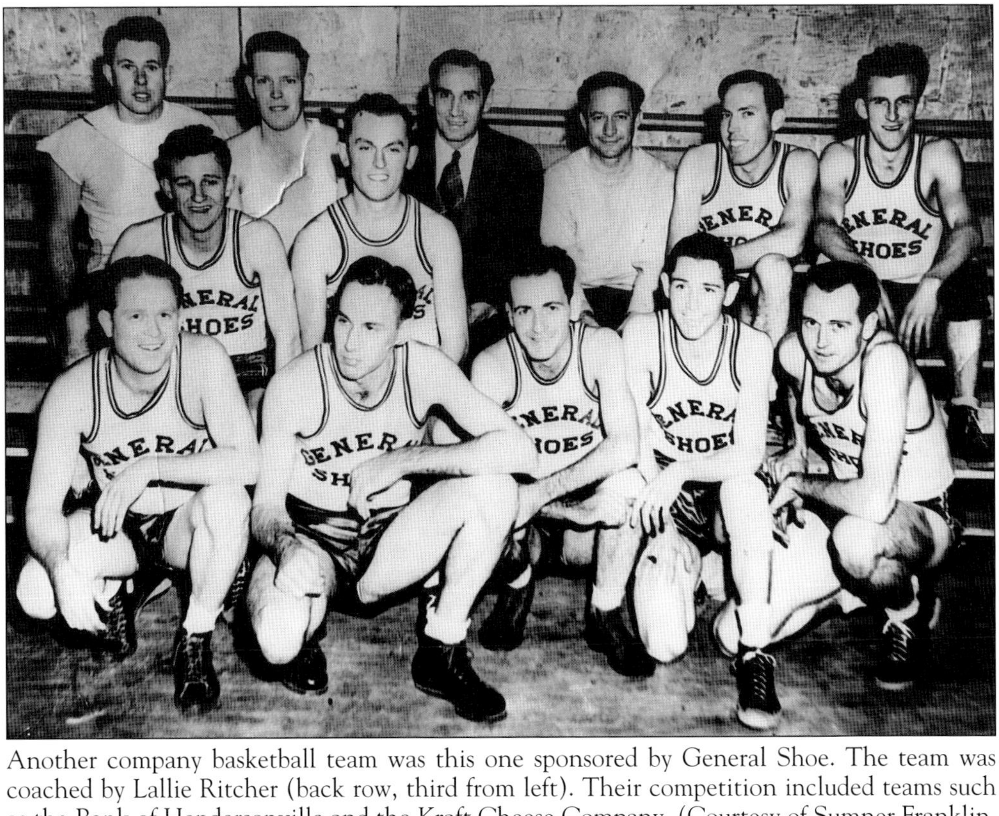

Another company basketball team was this one sponsored by General Shoe. The team was coached by Lallie Ritcher (back row, third from left). Their competition included teams such as the Bank of Hendersonville and the Kraft Cheese Company. (Courtesy of Sumner Franklin, pictured back row, far left.)

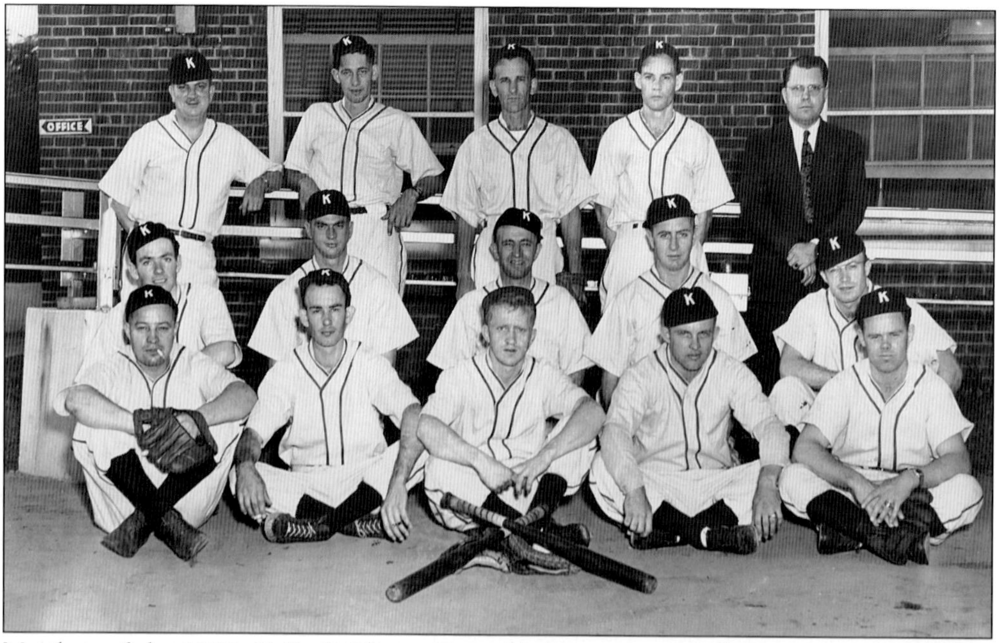

Members of the 1946–47 Kraft Cheese Co. softball team pose with plant manager Willard Huffman (back row, far right). Louis Teissler, owner of this photograph, is pictured in the second row, far right. (Courtesy of Louis Teissler.)

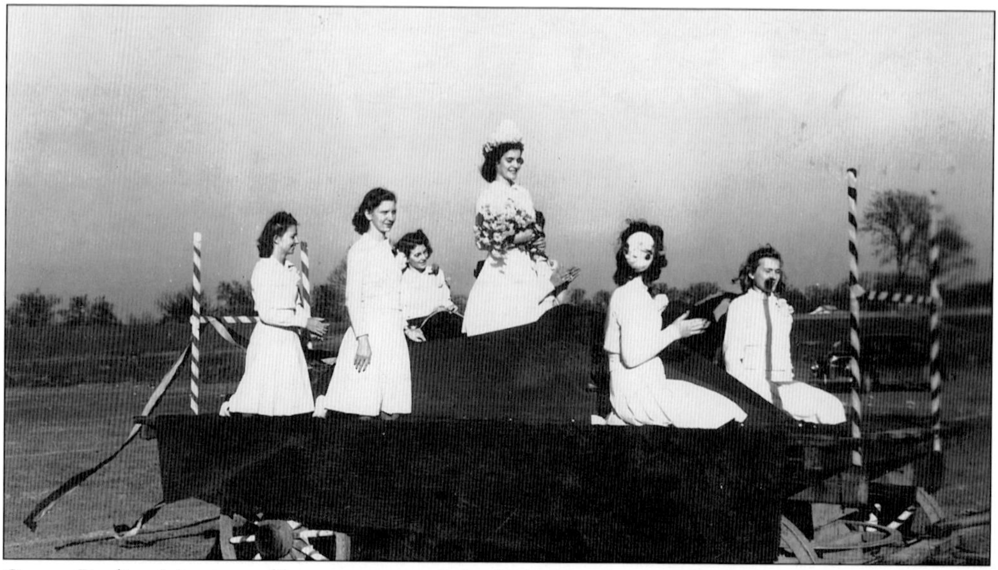

Queen Pauline Martin and her court graced the 1942 Hendersonville High School homecoming festivities. Members of the football team pulled the wagon around the field, and team captain Roy Davis crowned the lovely queen. (Courtesy of Quinton Coppage.)

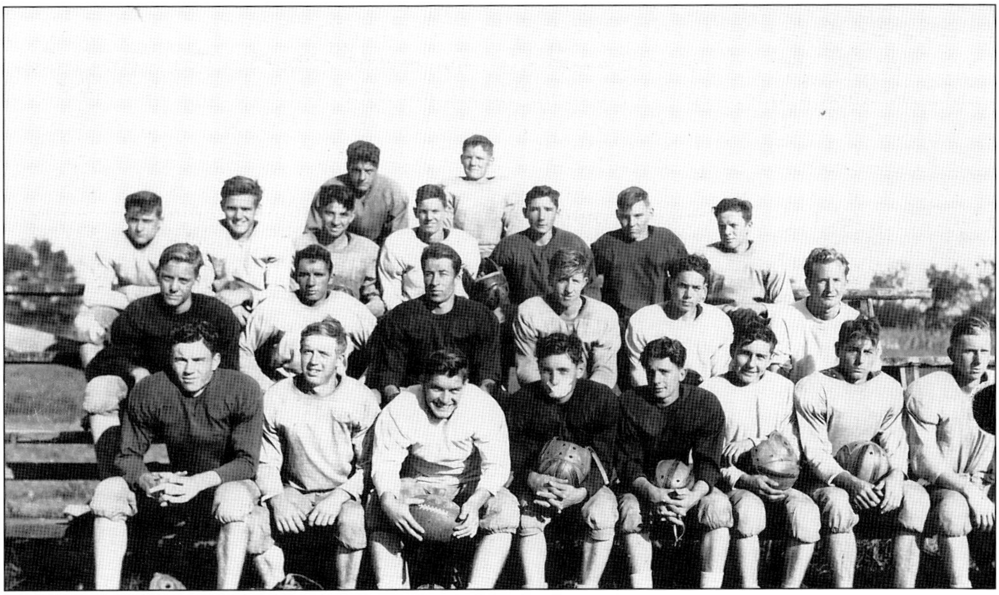

When members of the Hendersonville football team (c. 1941) suited up, their uniform headgear was made of leather and did not include a protective face mask. (Courtesy of Quinton Coppage.)

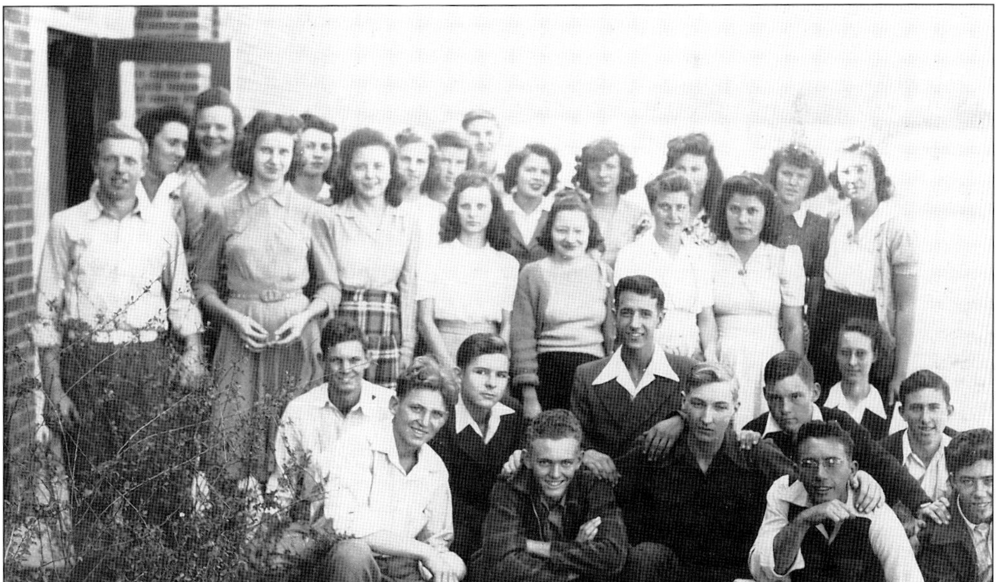

During WW II, Hendersonville High School sophomores gathered for this class photograph in 1942–43. Photograph owner Quinton Coppage is pictured in the front row, third from the left. (Courtesy of Quinton Coppage.)

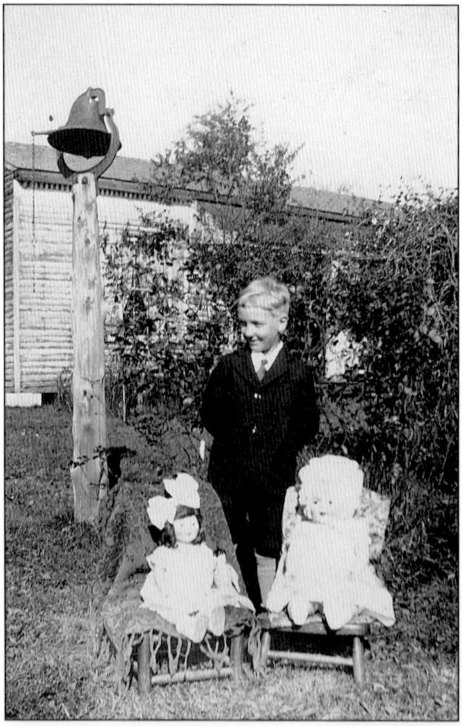

In his best Sunday short pants, coat, and tie, six-year-old Quinton Coppage poses with dolls beneath the dinner bell. (Courtesy of Quinton Coppage.)

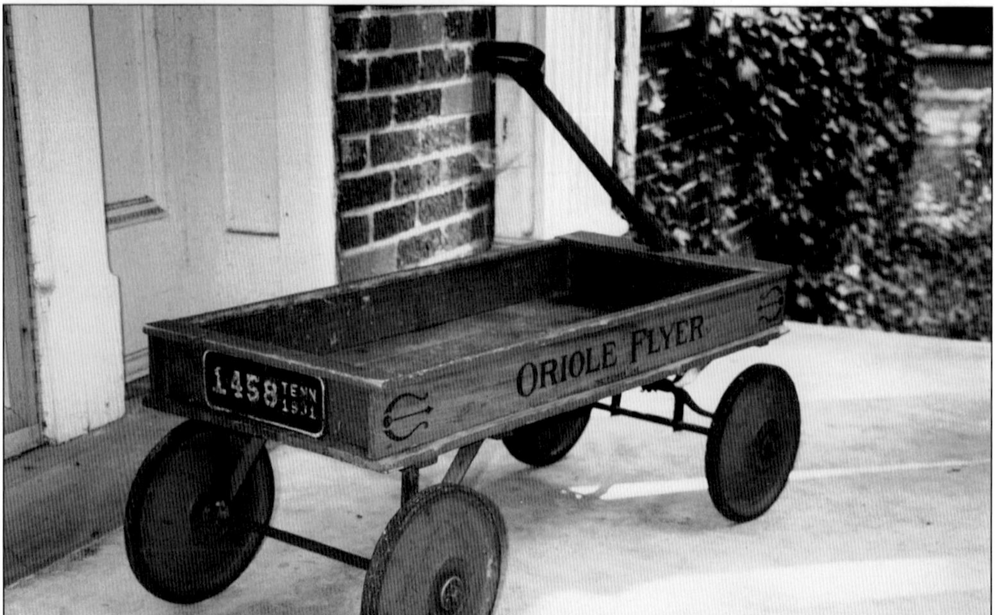

Simple in comparison to the elaborate toys of today, few toys gave as many hours of pleasure as this wagon presented to Quinton Coppage on the day he was born. The boy and his wagon became a familiar sight around Shackle Island as he played or hauled feed for the chickens. While changing license plates on a motorcycle in 1925, local garage owner Roy Hunt attached a plate to young Quinton's wagon. (Courtesy of Quinton Coppage.)

Quinton Coppage's next pair of "wheels" was this 1955 Oldsmobile. (Courtesy of Quinton Coppage.)

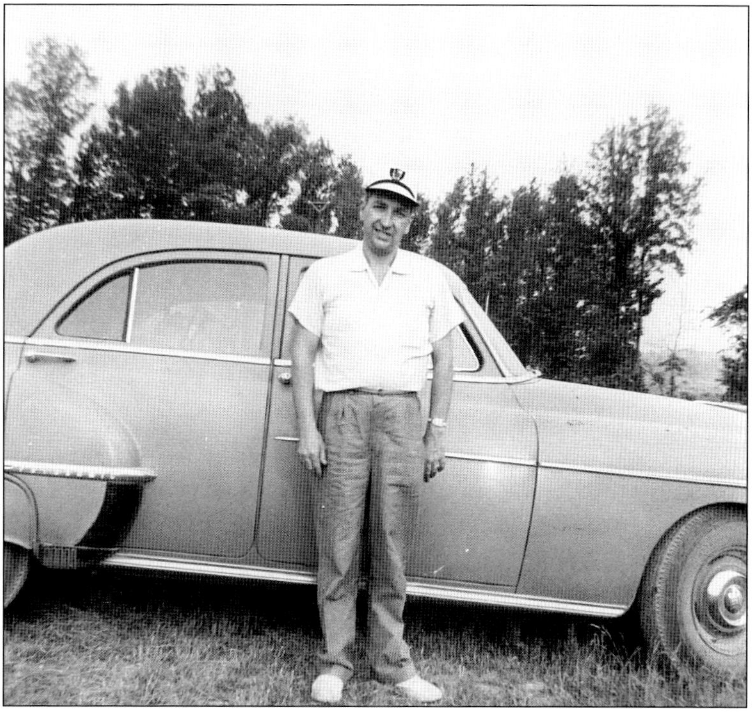

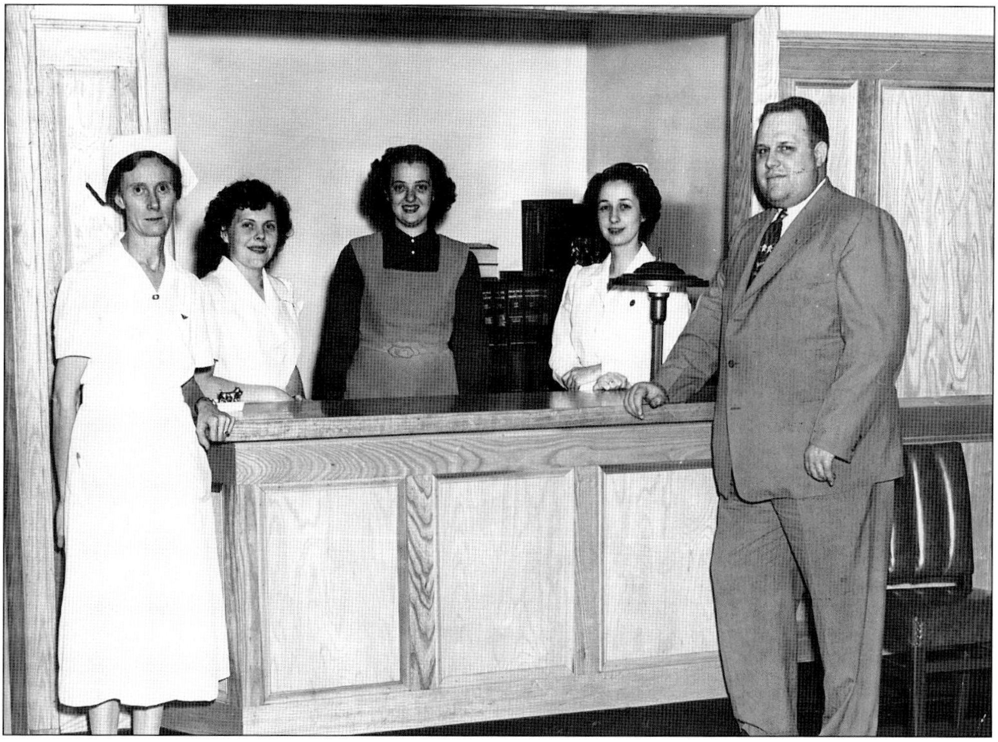

Dr. Robert Moore served the county for over a quarter of a century. In this photograph by W.C. Hackett of Gallatin, Dr. Moore poses with members of his clinic staff. (Courtesy of Evelyn Hackett Tuttle.)

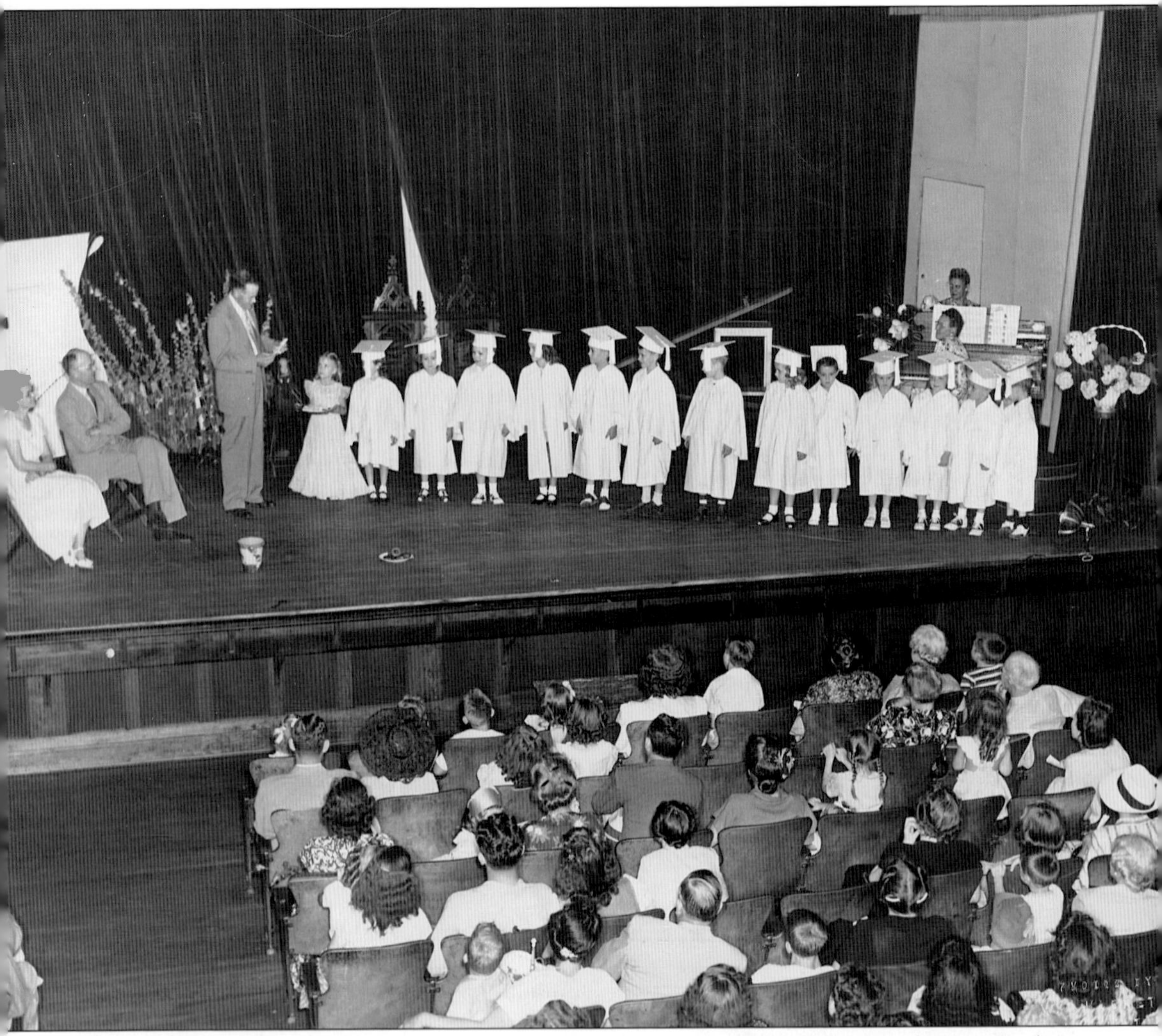

Photographer W.C. Hackett of Gallatin captured the pomp and ceremony of Wee Wisdom graduation (*c.* 1947). Adults on stage include Vernie G. Hawkins (sitting, second from left) and noted Sumner County educator Knox Doss (standing at microphone). One of the graduates is Harold Rogers Thomson (sixth student from the left), the brother of photograph owner Kenneth C. Thomson Jr., who is seated in the audience, in the front row on the far right.

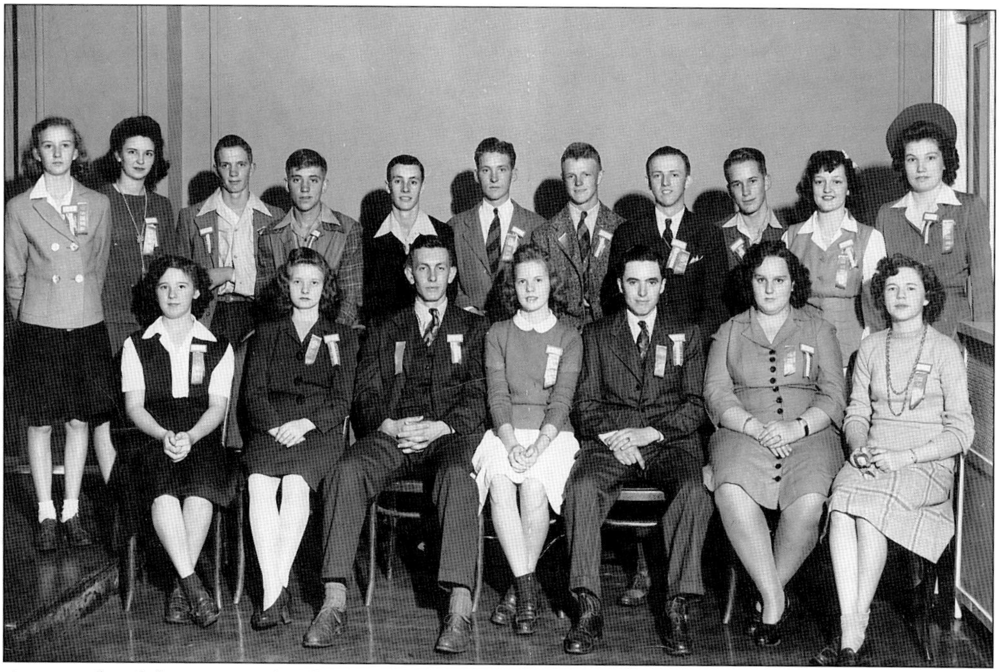

Among the delegates to the State Farm Bureau convention at the War Memorial Building in Nashville (*c.* 1946) were two Sumner County residents: Donald Curtis (back row, sixth from left) and Ann Curtis (front row, left). (Courtesy of Lee Curtis.)

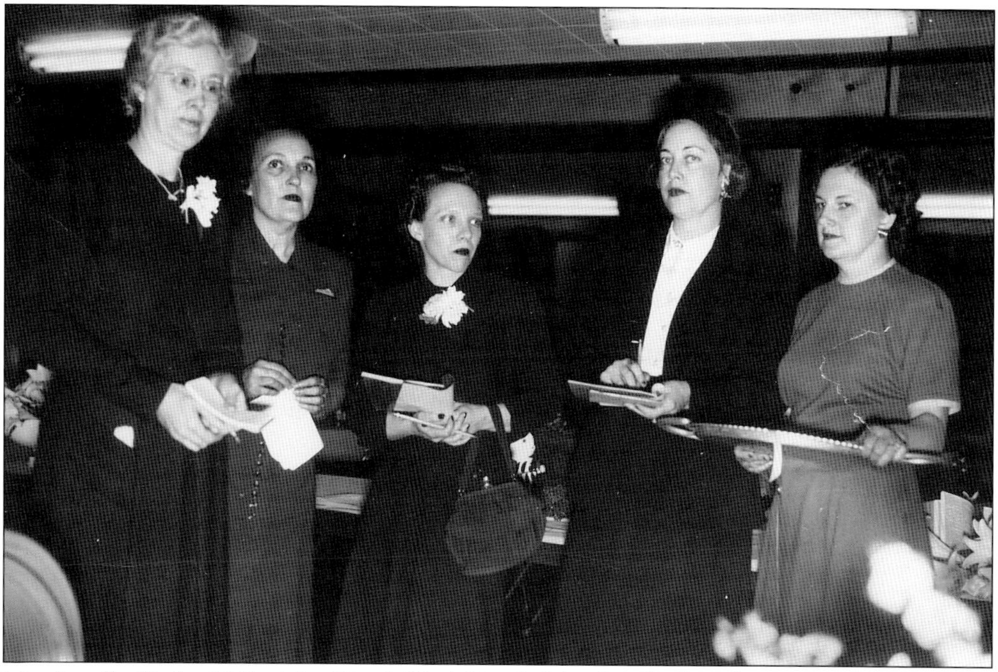

Mrs. Lorelle (Frakes) Hix, Mrs. Hazel (Hix) Kirsch, Mrs. Lucille (Ford) Arrendale, Mrs. Fannie (Puryear) Gillespie, and Mrs. Ann (Wemyss) John attend the annual flower show in the 1950s, held in the basement of the First Presbyterian Church in Gallatin. (Courtesy of Kenneth C. Thomson Jr.)

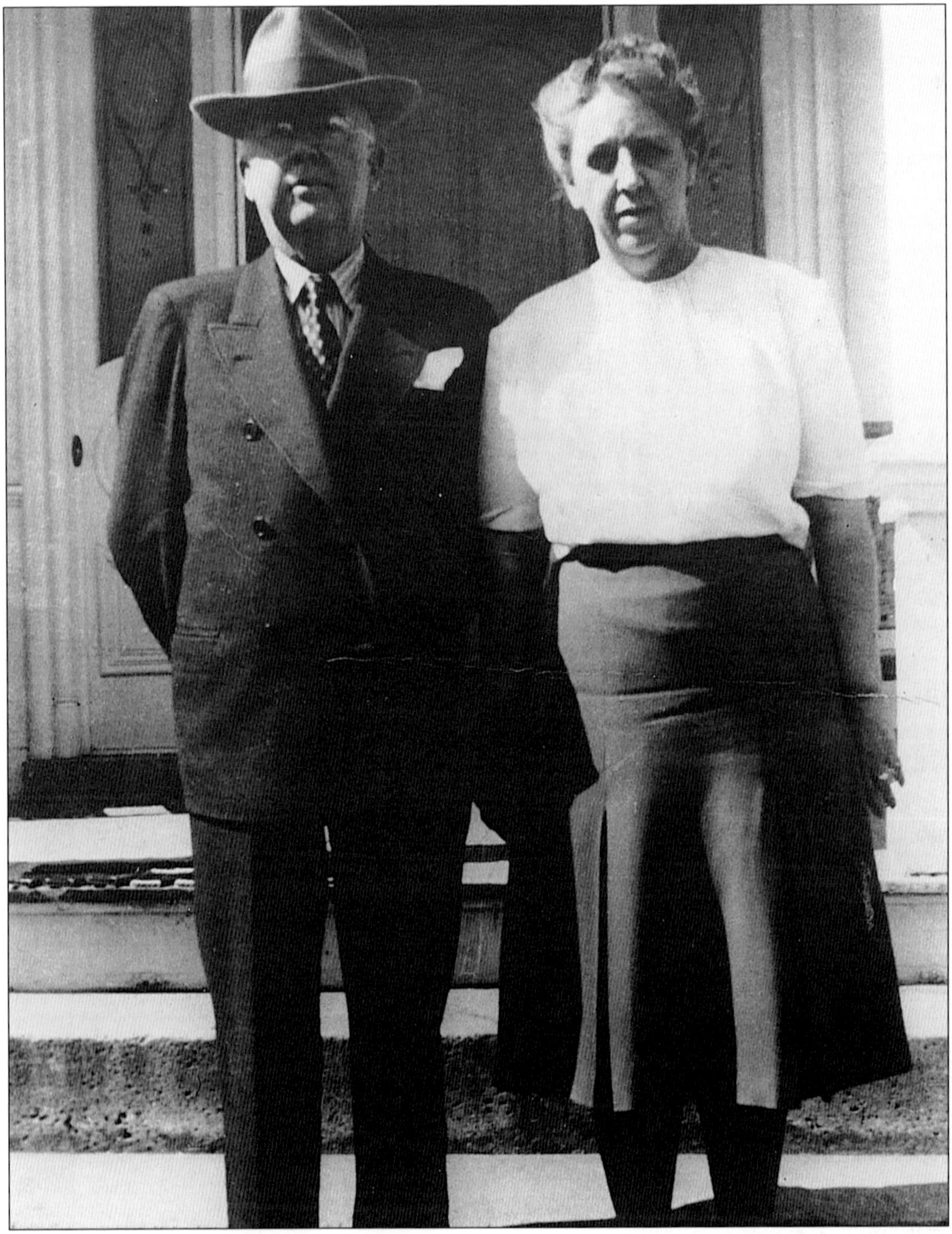

In a rare photograph, Mont B. Comer poses with his wife Marie on the steps of Monthaven, *c.* late 1940s. (Courtesy of Lee Curtis.)

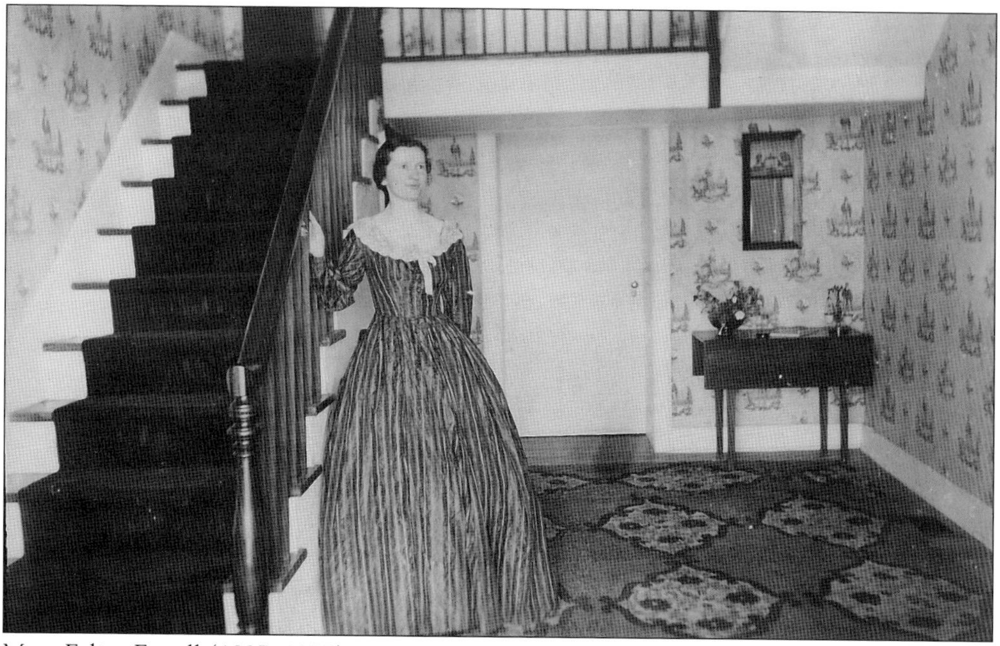

Mary Felice Ferrell (1897–1977) poses in an antique dress in the foyer of Log Cabin Antiques on the Nashville Pike in the community of Number One. "Miss Felice" owned the business for 60 years. Today, the beautifully restored two-story log structure is a popular and successful bed and breakfast called Hancock House. (Courtesy of Kenneth C. Thomson Jr.)

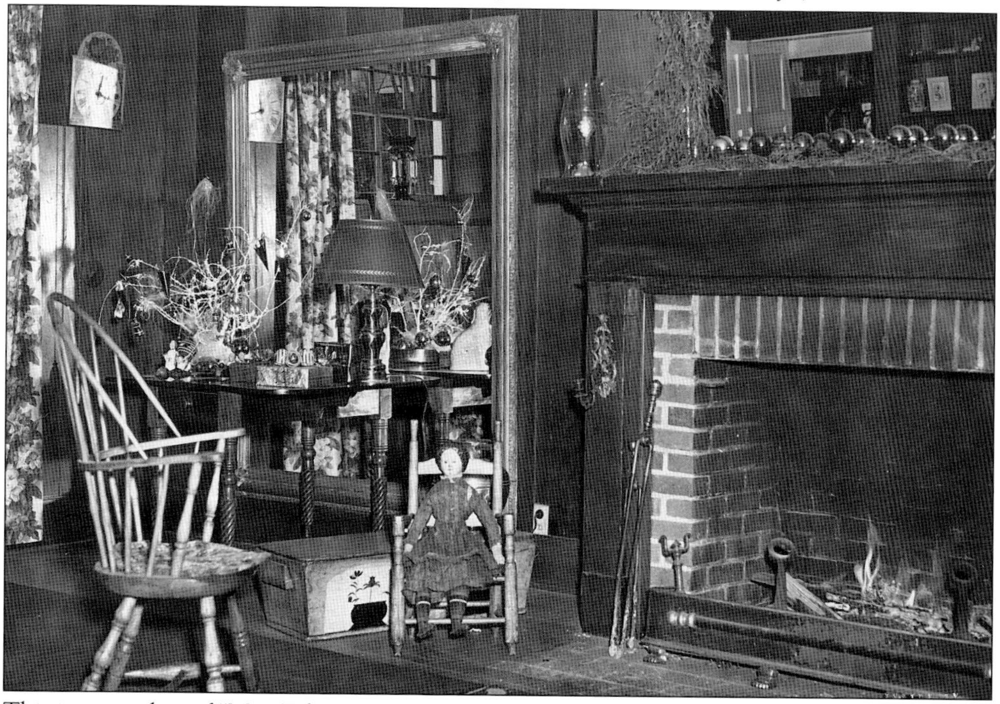

This interior shot of "Miss Felice's" Log Cabin Antiques reveals the owner's attention to detail. Over its 60 years of business, the shop provided local homes with beautiful antiques. (Courtesy of Kenneth C. Thomson Jr.)

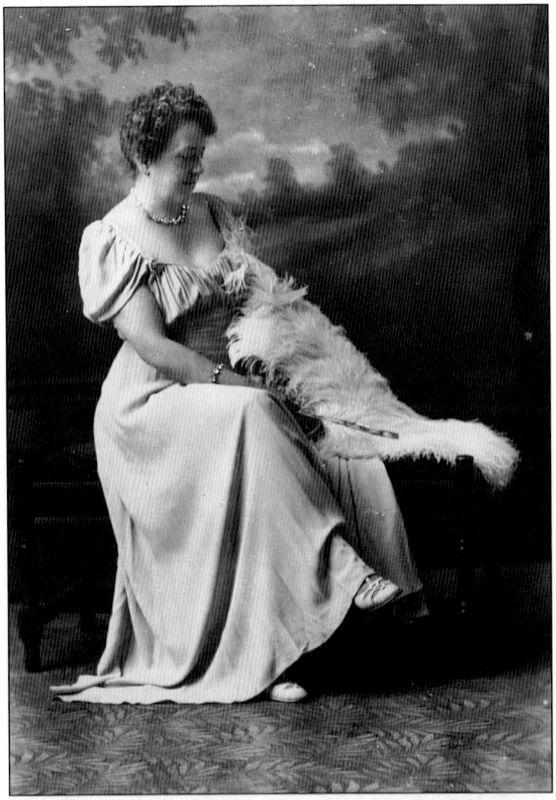

The gracious lady pictured here is Mrs. Lucy (Haynie) Doyle, wife of Capt. Stafford Doyle, and the daughter of Dr. X.B. Haynie and Fannie Young Allen Haynie. (Courtesy of Kenneth C. Thomson Jr.)

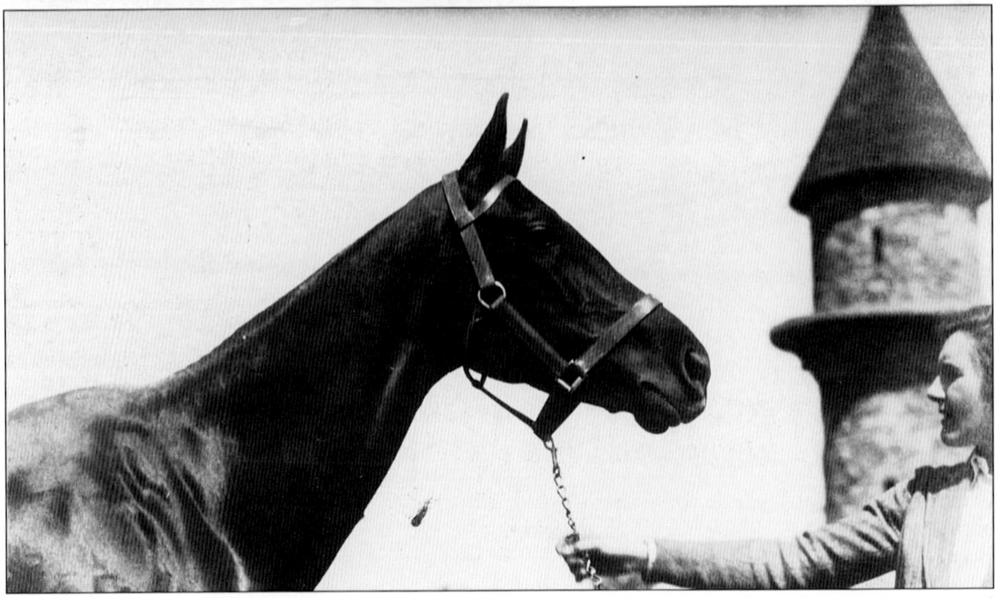

Red Gold, owned by Byron Hilliard of Louisville, Kentucky, ran at the celebrated inaugural steeplechase at Grasslands in 1931. The king of Spain provided the trophy for the race, and hopes were high that this would become a premiere event. However, the Great Depression and the financial disaster that struck many of the original investors dealt a death blow to the future of Grassland Downs. (Courtesy of Kenneth C. Thomson Jr.)

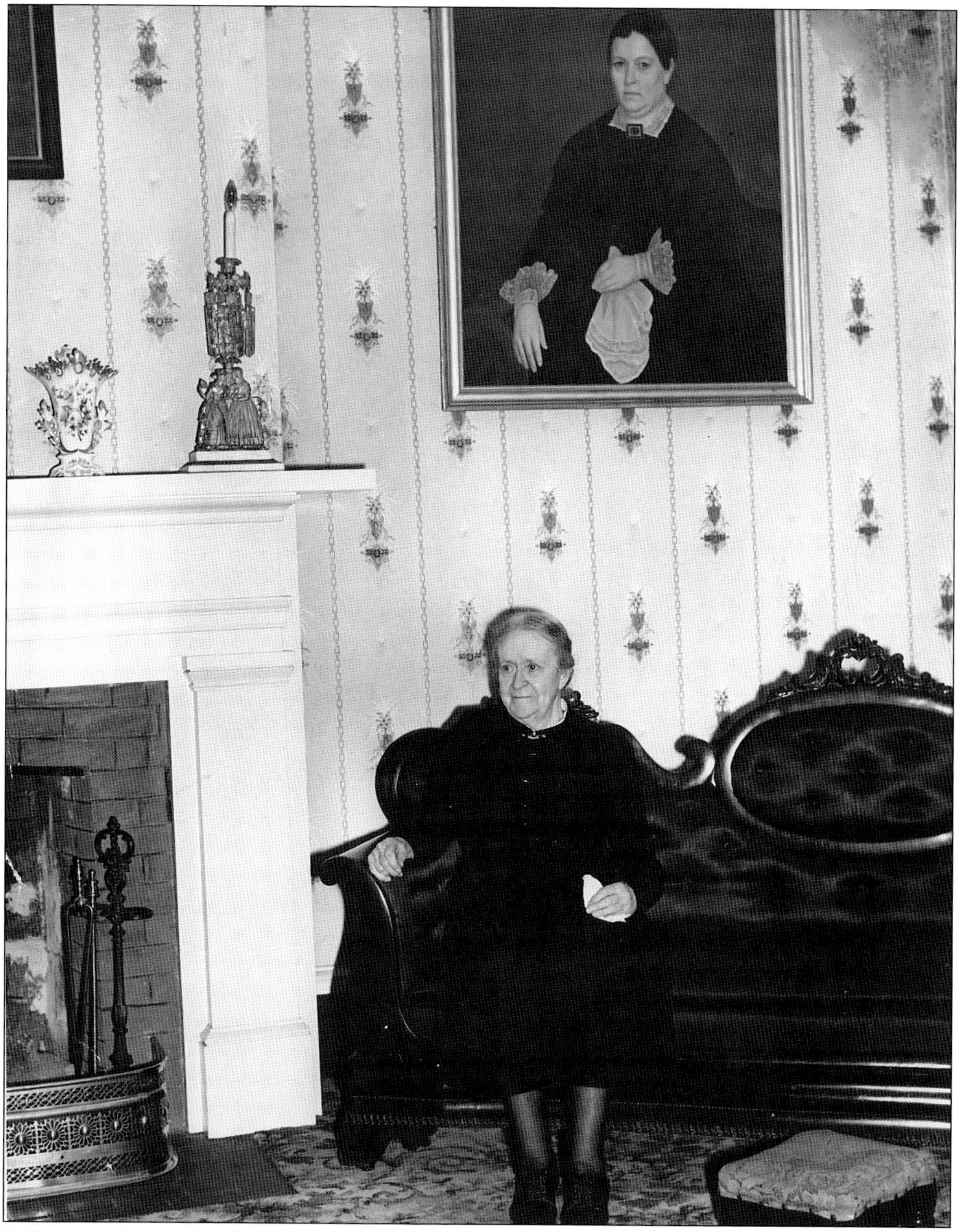

"Miss Susie" Mentlo Anderson (1867–1961) mirrors her grandmother's pose in the portrait above her at Oakland in 1950. The daughter of Capt. James Alexander Mentlo and Susan Branham Mentlo, she married Samuel Mullins Anderson of Richmond, Kentucky in 1886. (Photograph by Gordon Turner, courtesy of Kenneth C. Thomson Jr.)

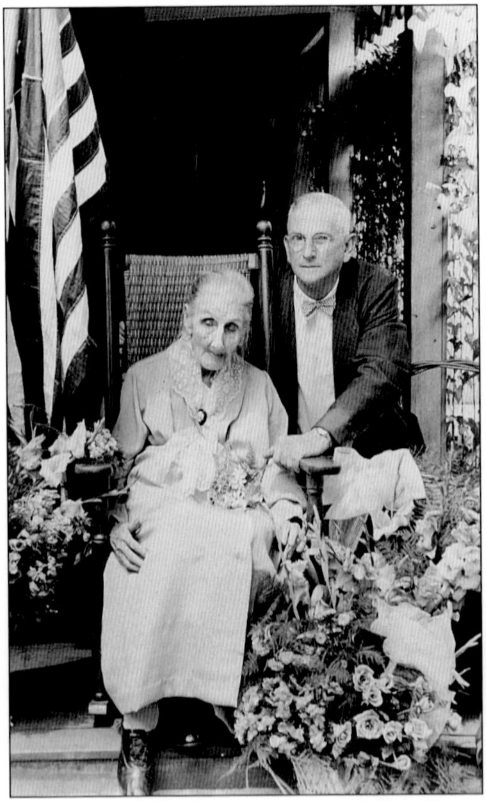

Mary "Mollie" Jane (Gardner) Herring is photographed with her physician, Dr. Lewis Miller Woodson, on the occasion of her 100th birthday on August 11, 1934. She was the widow of David Grant Herring, a Civil War veteran. Her own family's distinguished record of military service included veterans of the Revolutionary War (her grandfather), the War of 1812 (her father), and the Mexican War (her brother). (Courtesy of Kenneth C. Thomson Jr.)

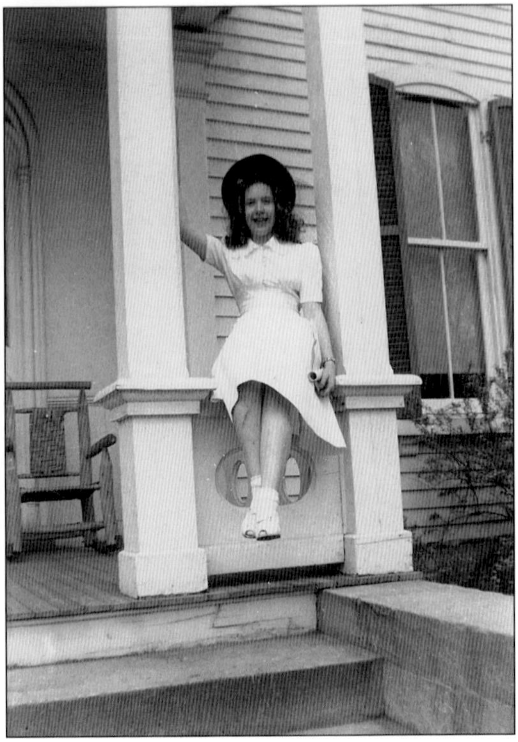

As a young girl, Jackie Comer posed on the front porch of Monthaven in Hendersonville (*c.* 1940–41). As an adult, her enthusiasm and love for Hendersonville was reflected in newspaper writings and her collection of Hendersonville history. (Courtesy of Lee Waddell Curtis.)

Jane Rogers Hix is pictured at her eighth grade graduation in 1936. In the years before caps and gowns, young ladies traditionally wore white dresses and carried flowers during graduation ceremonies, while young men wore suits and ties. (Photograph by E.M. Stark, courtesy of Kenneth C. Thomson Jr.)

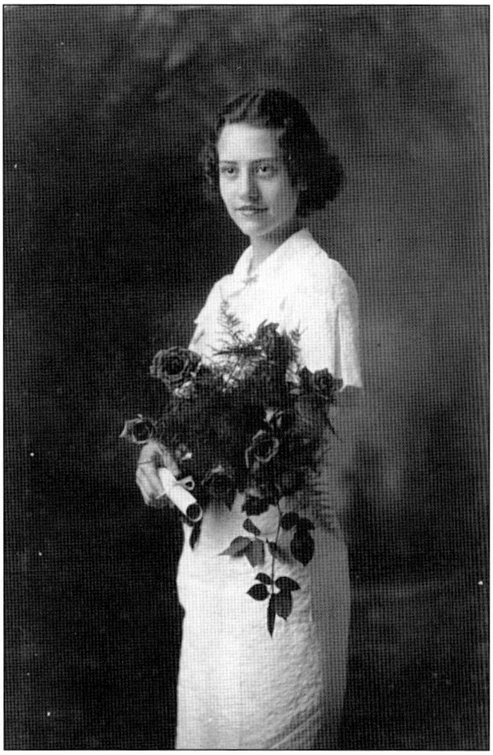

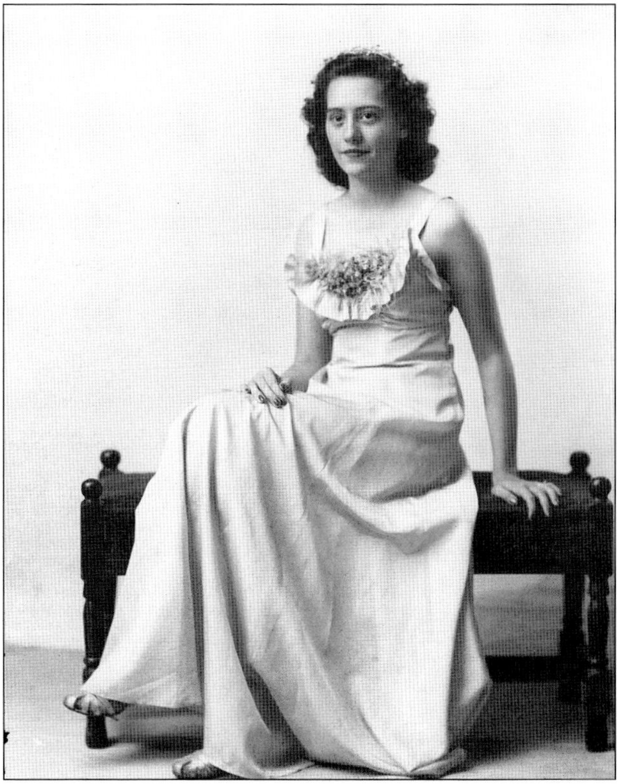

Three years later, Jane, the daughter of Harold Tillman Hix and Martha Lorelle (Frakes) Hix, again posed for E.M. Stark on the occasion of the 1939 Cotillion. From the 1800s through the middle of the 20th century, a wide range of glamorous events such as balls, operas, and cotillions, offered Gallatin residents opportunities seldom enjoyed today—the chance to dress up. (Photograph by E.M. Stark, courtesy of Kenneth C. Thomson Jr., the son of Jane.)

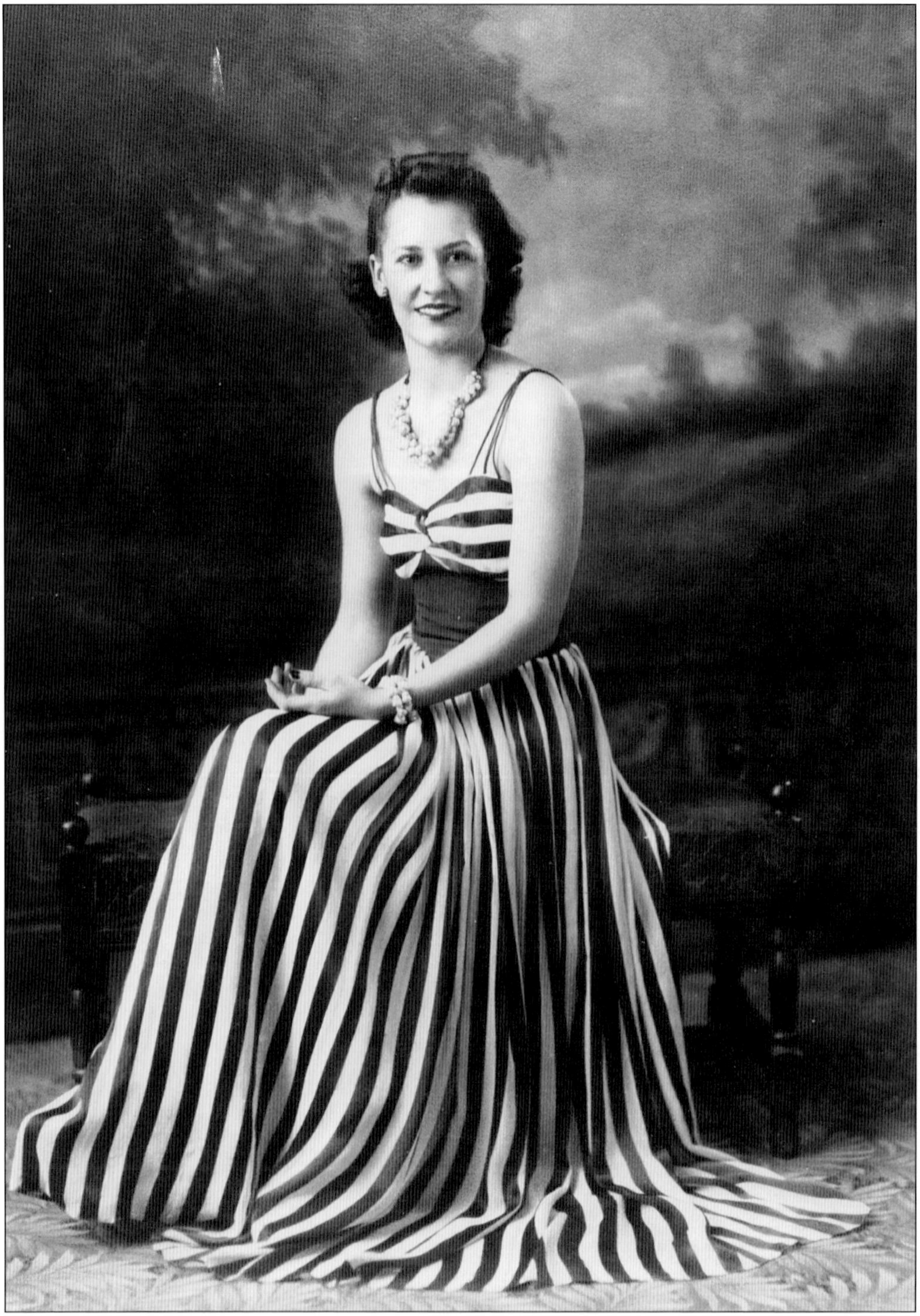

Grace, beauty, and poise are apparent qualities that contributed to the awarding of the Miss Tennessee title to Gallatin's Miss Elvera Moore in 1934. (Original owned by Elvera M.G. Neal, print courtesy of Kenneth C. Thomson Jr.)

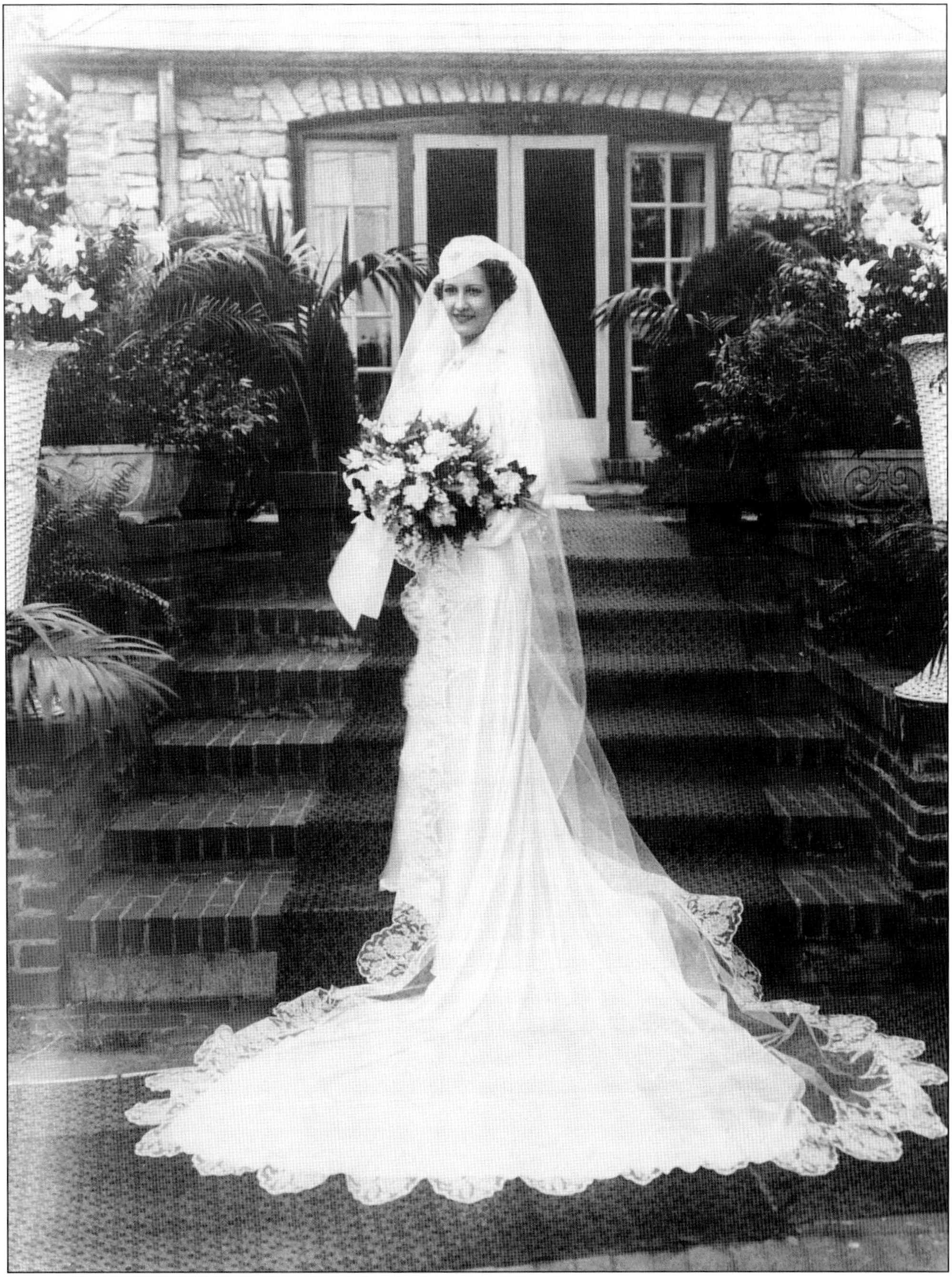

In a rare photograph of beautiful Maple Row, the Hendersonville home of Mr. and Mrs. B.W. Graves, former Miss Tennessee, Mrs. Byron Wilsley Graves Jr. (nee Elvera Moore), poses beside the pool at her 1936 wedding. Today, the Maple Row name is familiar to Hendersonville residents as a planned community located behind the Wal Mart shopping center. (Original owned by Elvera M.G. Neal, print courtesy of Kenneth C. Thomson Jr.)

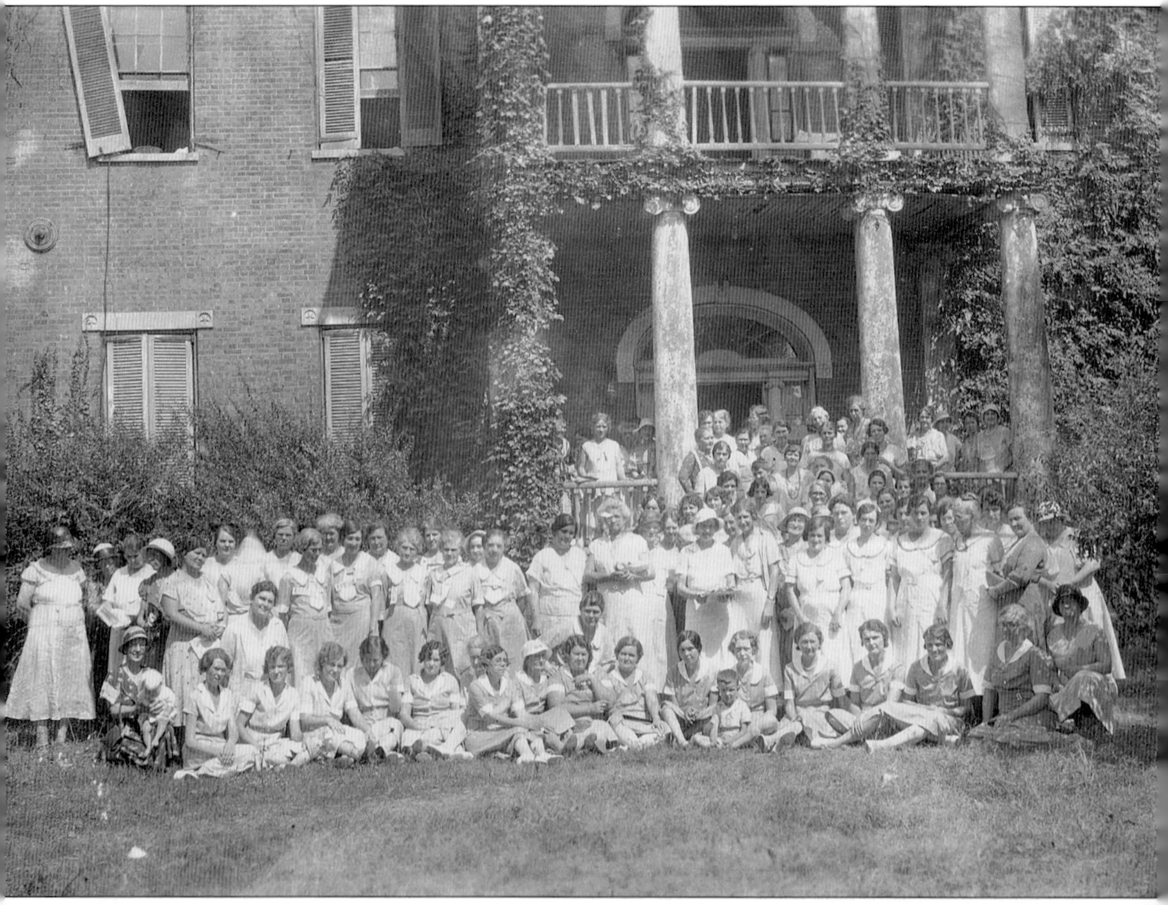

Built in 1832 as the grand plantation home of Isaac Franklin, Fairvue had fallen into disrepair when this photograph of the Sumner County Home Demonstration Club was made in the 1920s. The home was rescued and restored by William Hatch Wemyss and Ellen Stokes Wemyss just prior to their 1939 wedding. Compare this view to the photograph on page 20. (Courtesy of Kenneth C. Thomson Jr.)

Three

CARTOONS

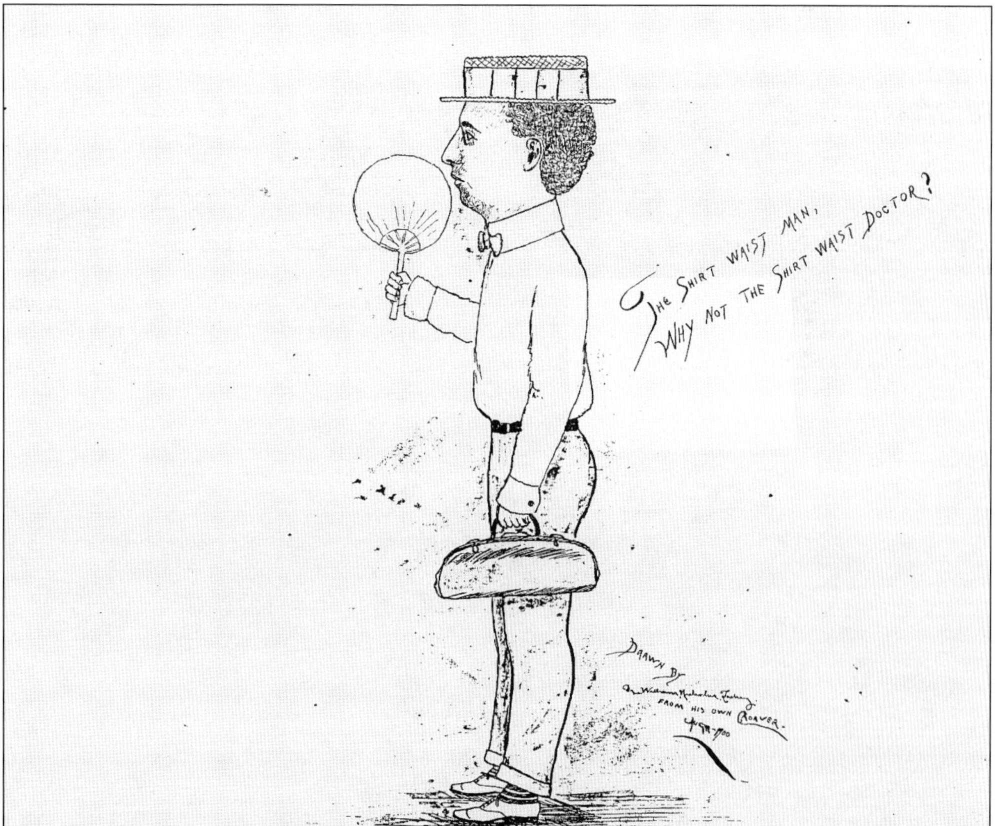

This self-portrait of Dr. William Nicholas Lackey was made in 1900. (Courtesy of Kenneth C. Thomson Jr.)

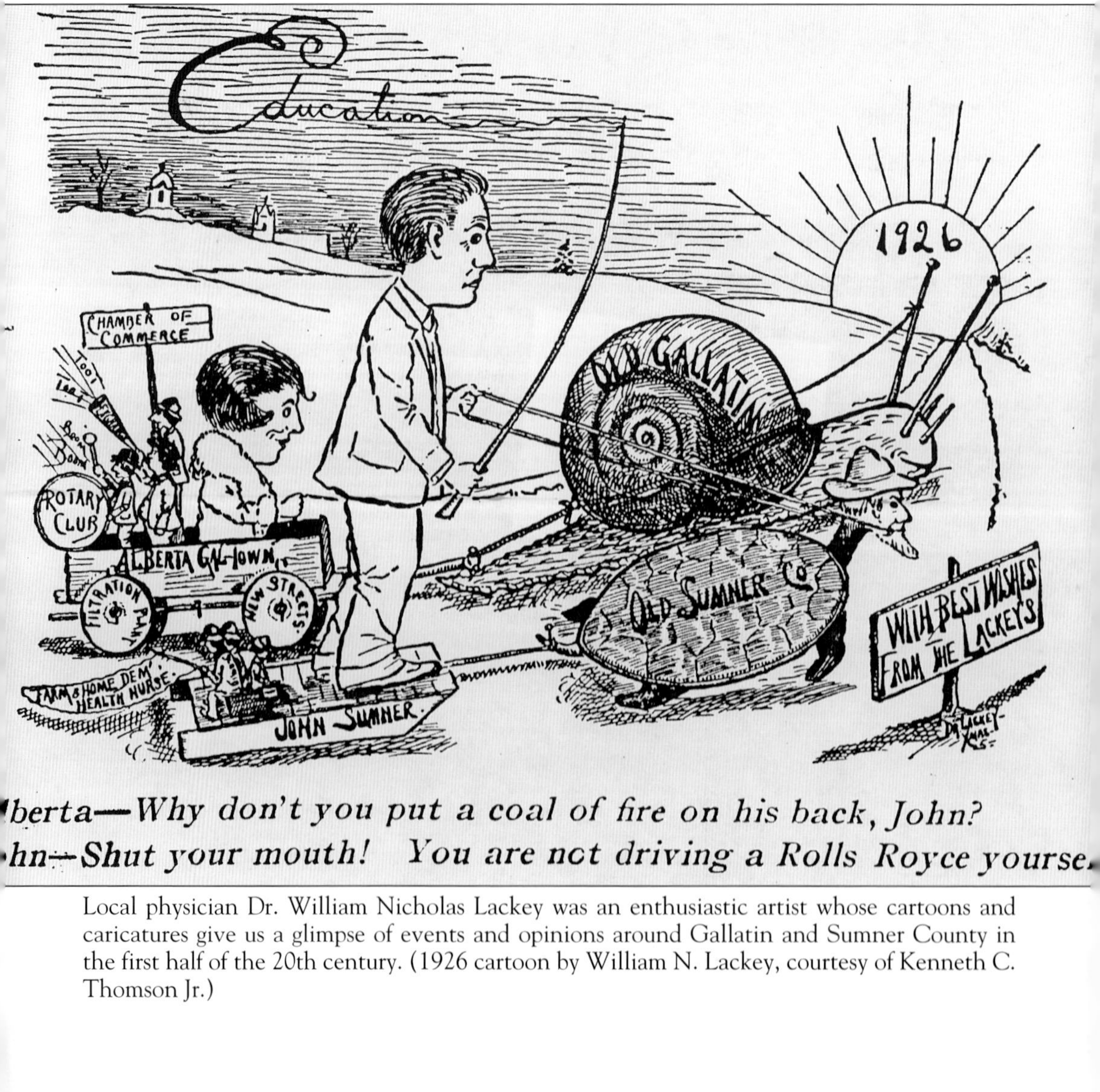

Local physician Dr. William Nicholas Lackey was an enthusiastic artist whose cartoons and caricatures give us a glimpse of events and opinions around Gallatin and Sumner County in the first half of the 20th century. (1926 cartoon by William N. Lackey, courtesy of Kenneth C. Thomson Jr.)

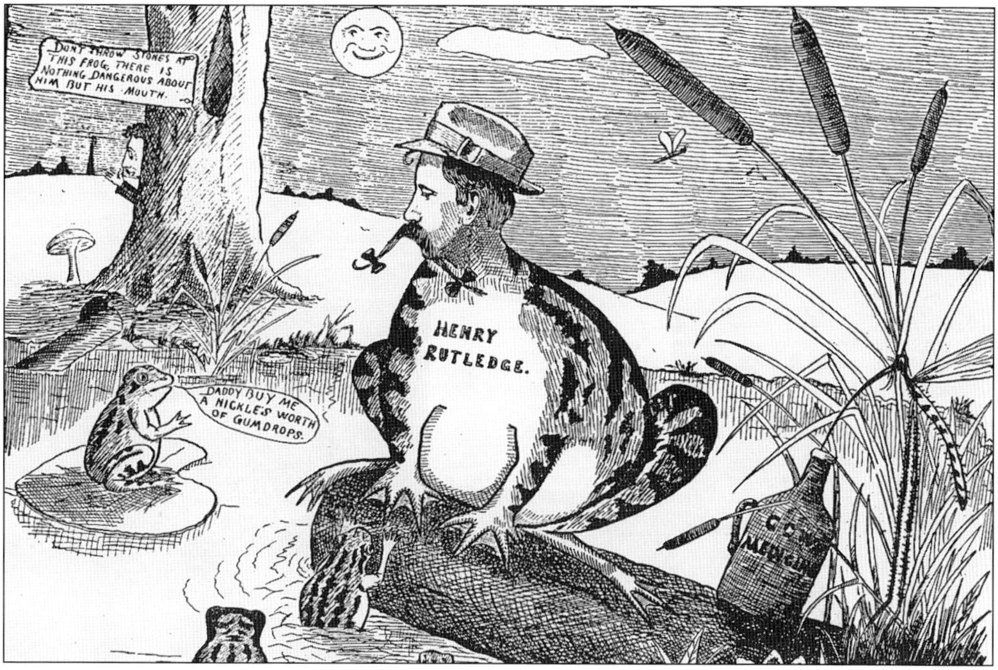

Many of Dr. Lackey's cartoons were framed and displayed on the walls of the Hotel Sumner in Gallatin. (Cartoon by William N. Lackey, courtesy of Kenneth C. Thomson Jr.)

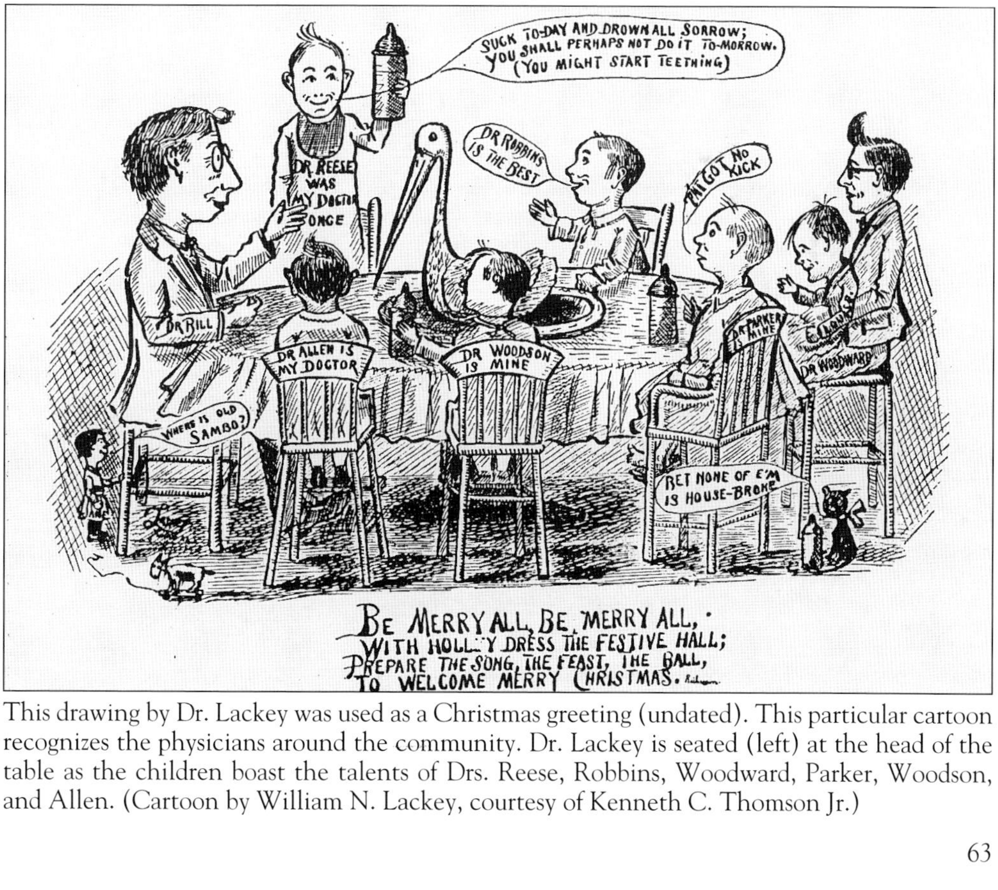

This drawing by Dr. Lackey was used as a Christmas greeting (undated). This particular cartoon recognizes the physicians around the community. Dr. Lackey is seated (left) at the head of the table as the children boast the talents of Drs. Reese, Robbins, Woodward, Parker, Woodson, and Allen. (Cartoon by William N. Lackey, courtesy of Kenneth C. Thomson Jr.)

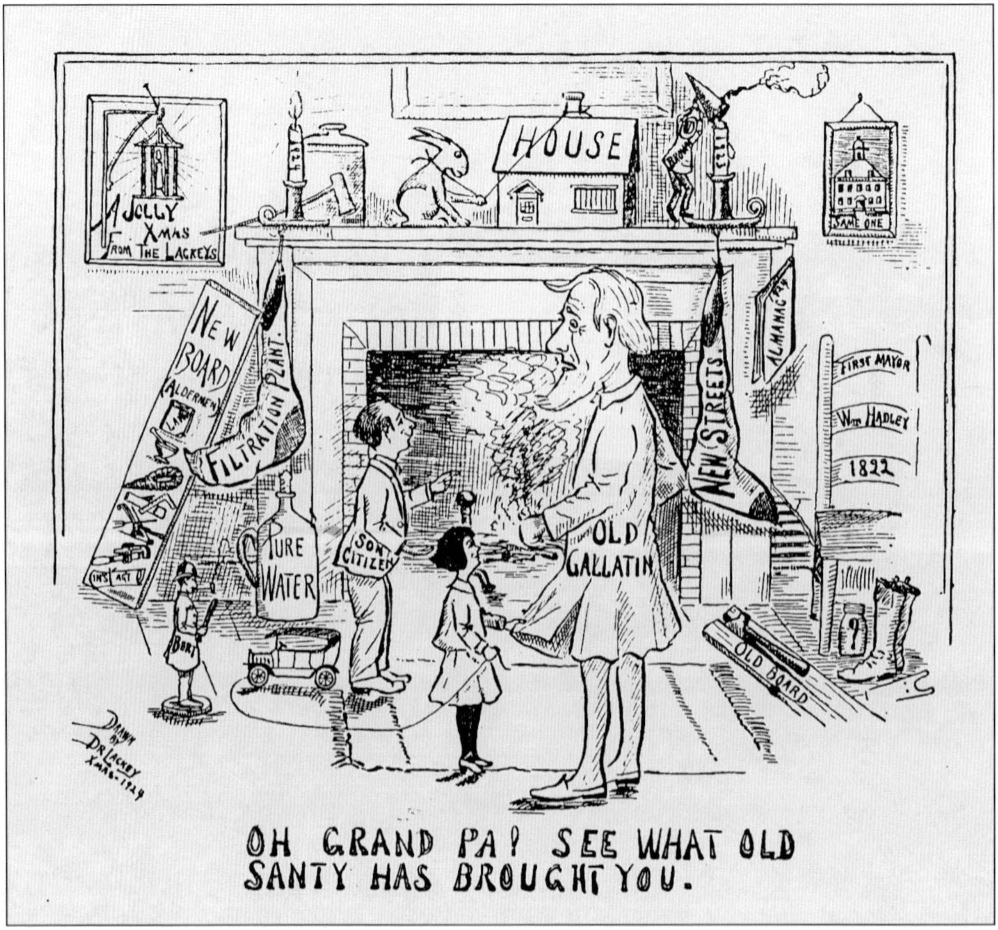

A favorite subject of Dr. Lackey's cartoons were the dramatic changes taking place as Old Gallatin gave way to notions of modern community services. As 1923 gives way to 1924, this Christmas card recognizes the old court house (framed upper right), Gallatin's first mayor, and the old board, while Old Gallatin's children look forward to the newest toys—a new board of aldermen, new streets, a new filtration plant, and the promise of pure water. (1924 cartoon by William N. Lackey, courtesy of Kenneth C. Thomson Jr.)

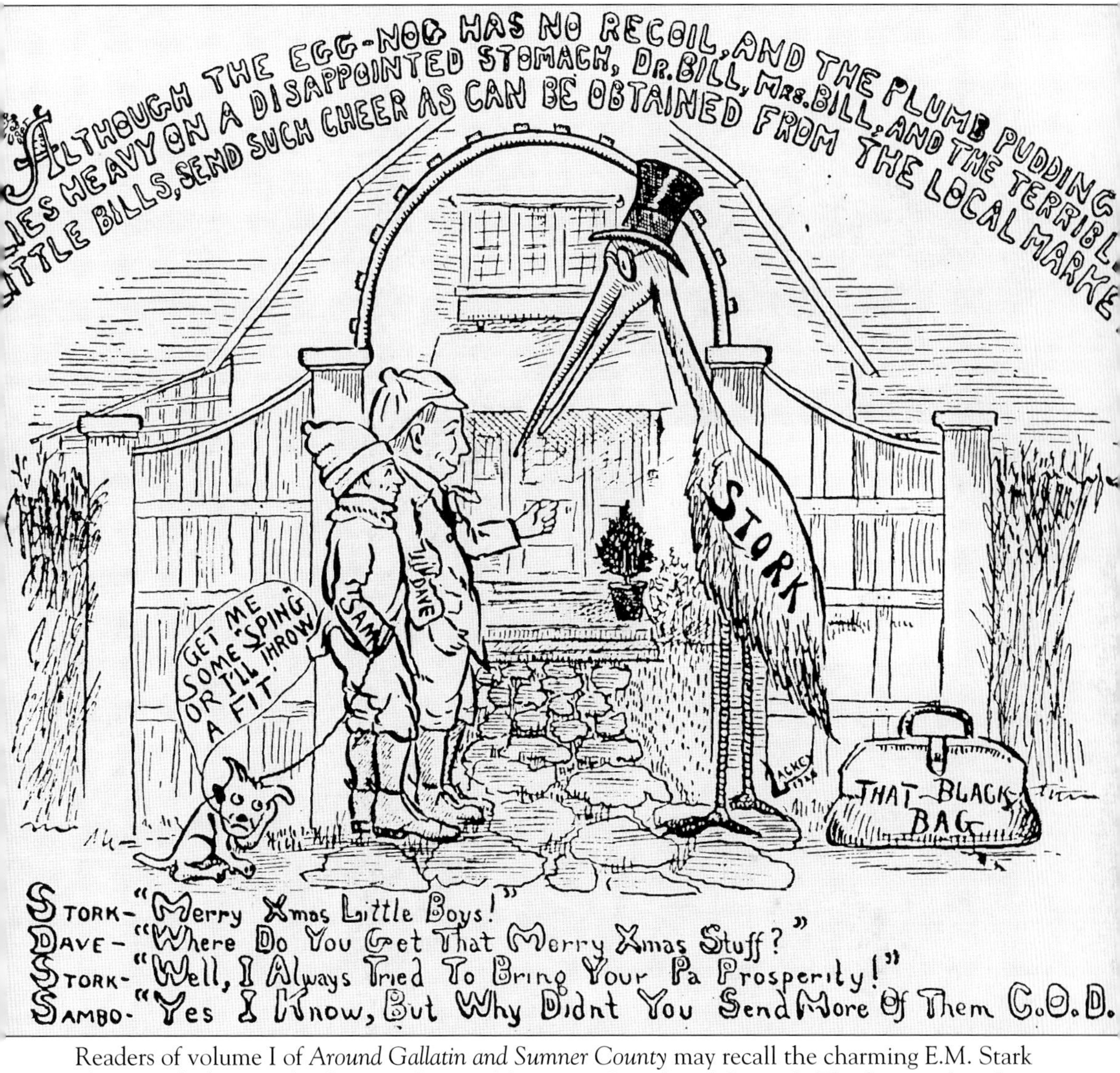

Readers of volume I of *Around Gallatin and Sumner County* may recall the charming E.M. Stark photograph (page 48) of Dr. Lackey and his sons, David and Samuel. The boys, referred to in this greeting as "the terrible little bills," appear in a 1926 Christmas drawing. (Cartoon by William N. Lackey, courtesy of Kenneth C. Thomson Jr.)

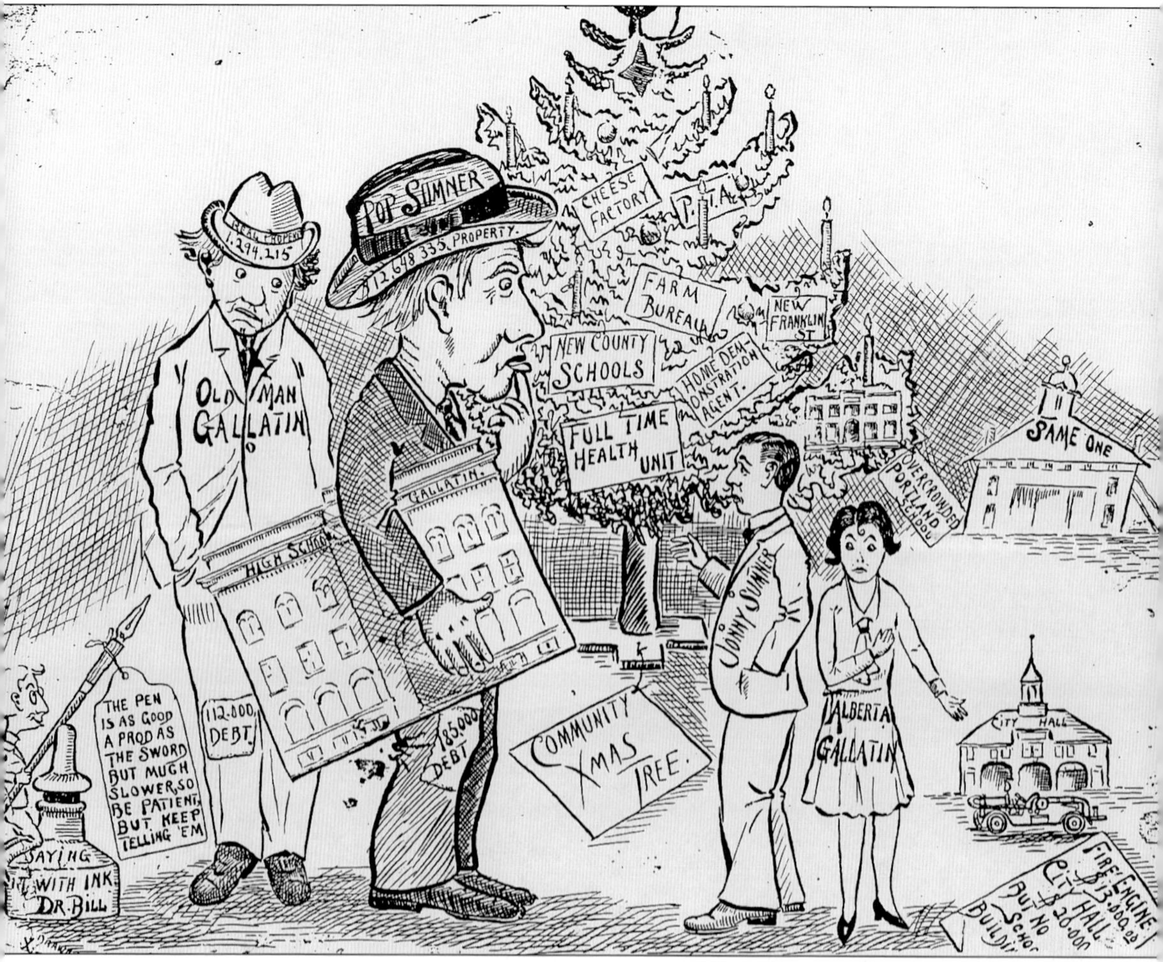

Dr. Bill was still after Old Man Gallatin and Pop Sumner in this greeting, reminding us that "the pen is as good a prod as the sword, but slower, so be patient, but keep telling 'em." This cartoon looks to the promise of the future with a full-time health unit, new schools, a farm bureau, new street, a strong PTA, and a home demonstration agent. He admonishes the city and county for mounting debts and a new city hall, while the courthouse and schools fall into disrepair. (Cartoon by William N. Lackey, courtesy of Kenneth C. Thomson Jr.)

Four

Business

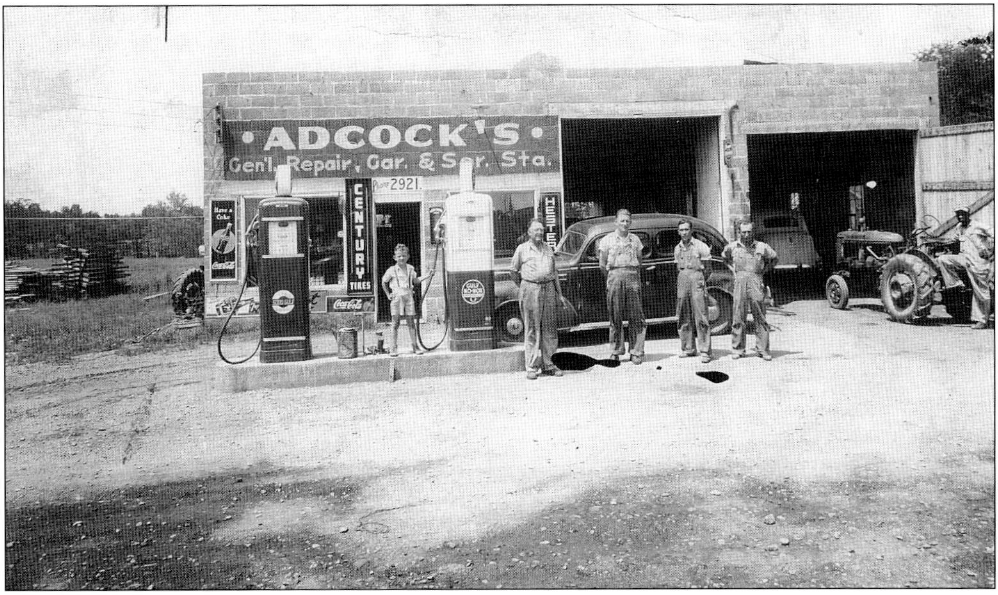

Established in 1945, Adcock's Garage, owned by George Perkins Adcock and George Edward Adcock Jr., continues as a mainstay in the Hendersonville business community under the leadership of a third generation of the family. Originally located in a flood plain on the north side of Gallatin Road at Drakes Creek (near the present-day volleyball courts), the building was forced to move to its present location farther west when the lake was created in 1953. Pictured in this 1948 photograph, from left to right, are partners George Edward Adcock Jr., George Perkins Adcock, and Jessie Gilbert Adcock; local handymen Lewis and Ander Jackson; and Roy Gleaves (beside the tractor), the chauffeur of Miss Sarah Berry. (Courtesy of Adcock Garage.)

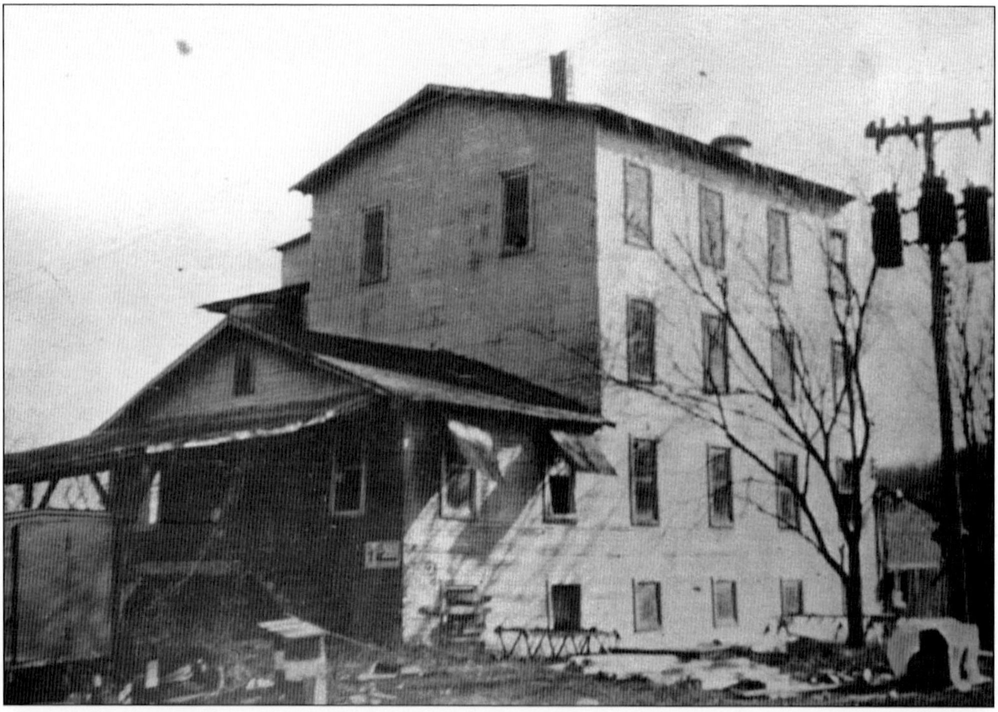

The Old Dorris Mill was a major employer in the New Shackle Island Community. Although the mill burned several times, it always recovered. It was managed by Will Dorris and his wife for 35 years. (Courtesy of the Bob Perry Collection, Sumner County Archives.)

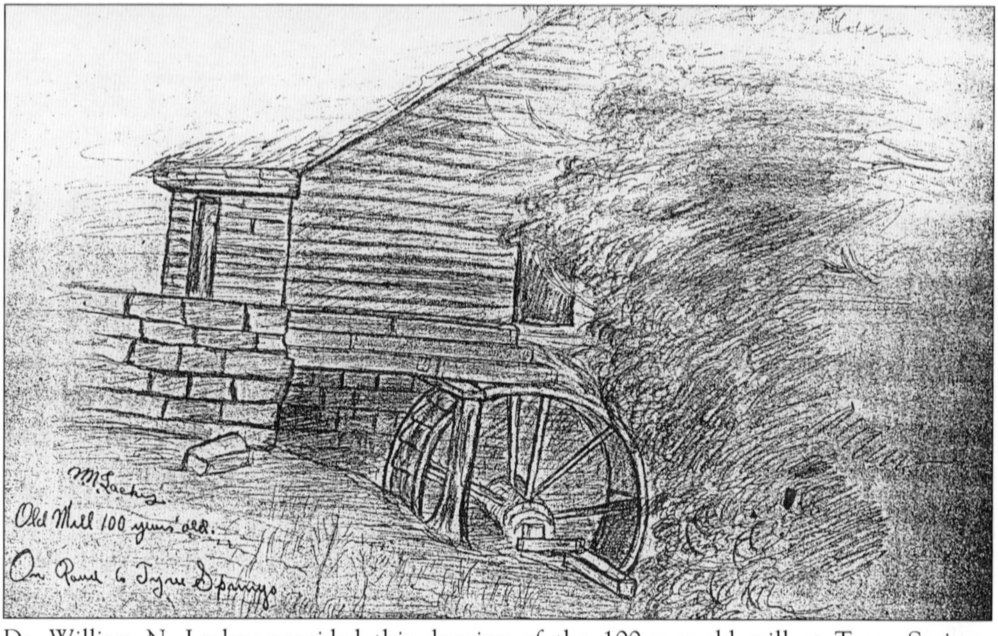

Dr. William N. Lackey provided this drawing of the 100-year-old mill at Tyree Springs. The Tyree Springs area included a popular resort. Part of the appeal of the springs was the combination of a peaceful rural setting and picturesque structures such as the mill. (Drawing by Dr. William N. Lackey, courtesy of Kenneth C. Thomson Jr.)

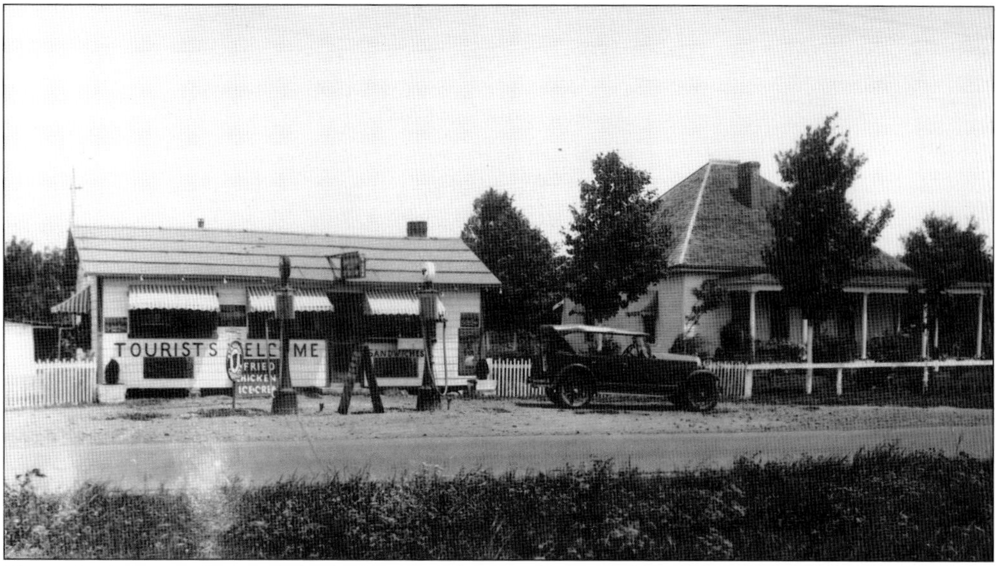

Times had changed since Dr. William Lackey accompanied Nashville's Leland Hume on the first automobile drive from Gallatin to Nashville in 1902 (see volume I of *Around Gallatin and Sumner County*, page 83). By the 1930s, the widespread use of automobiles led to the creation of motels and popular tourist camps, such as this one. (Courtesy of Allen Haynes.)

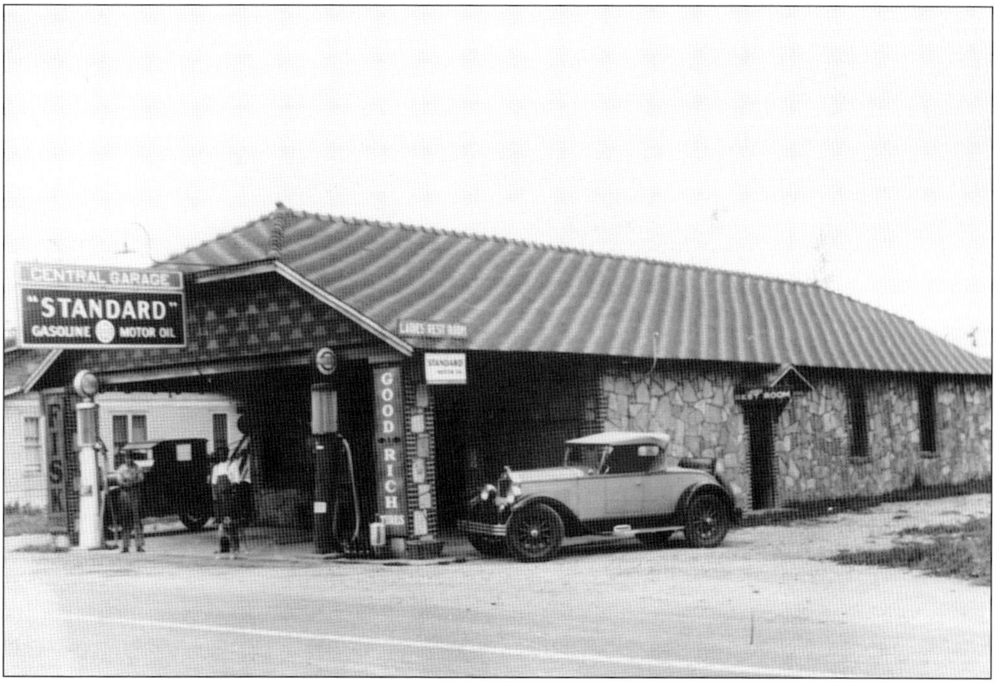

Appealing roadside architecture attracted customers as they rushed along the modern highways in their new automobiles. The stone exterior and handsome tile roof of the Central Garage at Bethpage is an excellent example of business owners' attention to detail. Large signs advertising quality products such as Standard gasoline and Goodrich tires were additional lures for the traveling public. (Courtesy of Allen Haynes.)

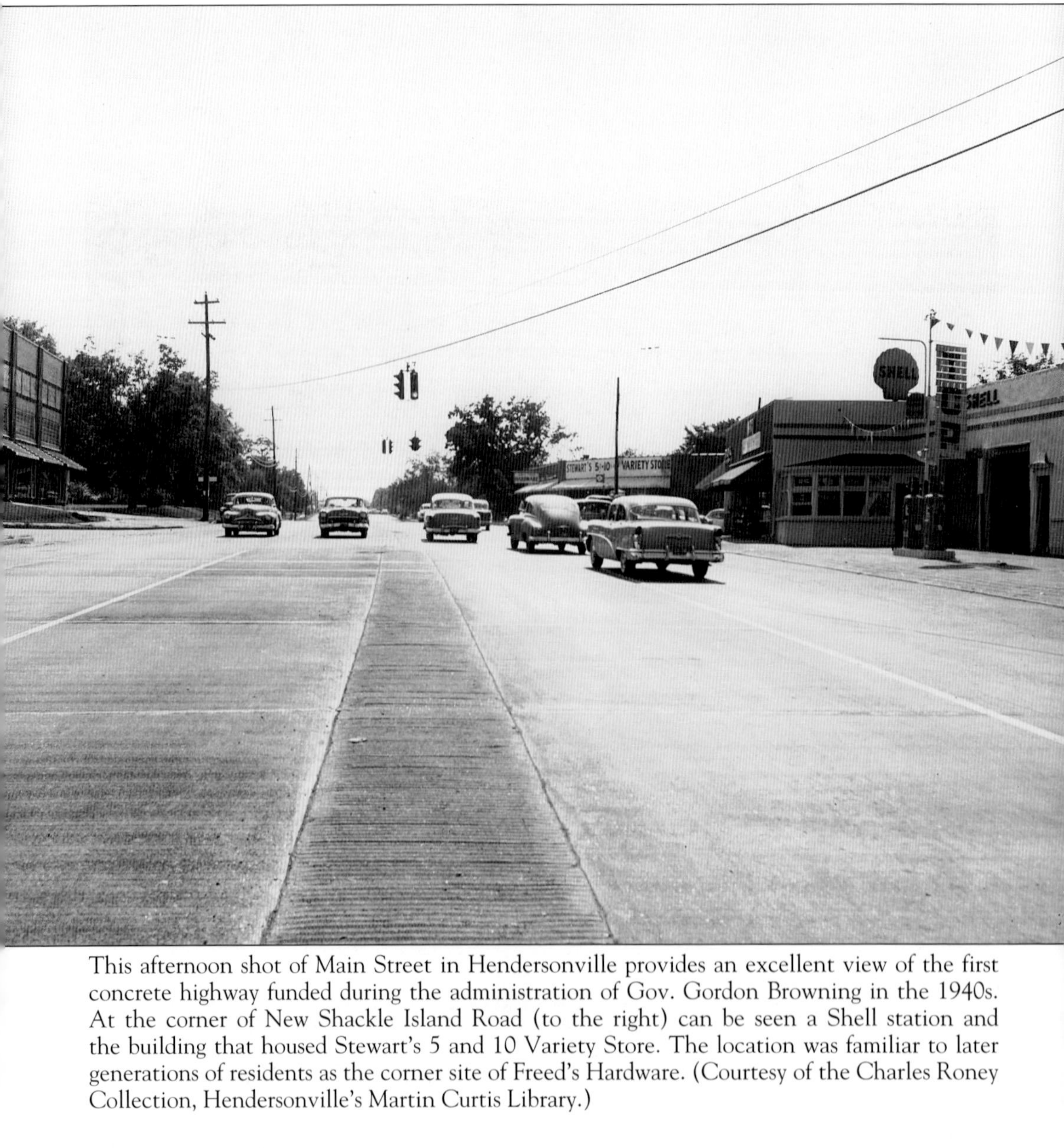

This afternoon shot of Main Street in Hendersonville provides an excellent view of the first concrete highway funded during the administration of Gov. Gordon Browning in the 1940s. At the corner of New Shackle Island Road (to the right) can be seen a Shell station and the building that housed Stewart's 5 and 10 Variety Store. The location was familiar to later generations of residents as the corner site of Freed's Hardware. (Courtesy of the Charles Roney Collection, Hendersonville's Martin Curtis Library.)

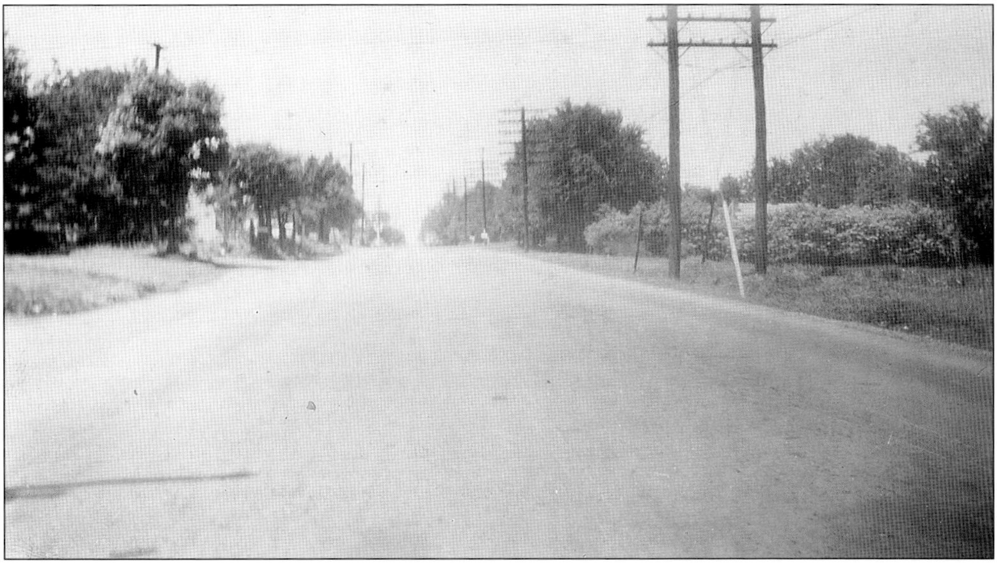

Accustomed to the endless lines of traffic and rows of street-side businesses, today's Hendersonville resident may barely recognize this earlier rural view of Main Street before the widening of the street. (Courtesy of Quinton Coppage.)

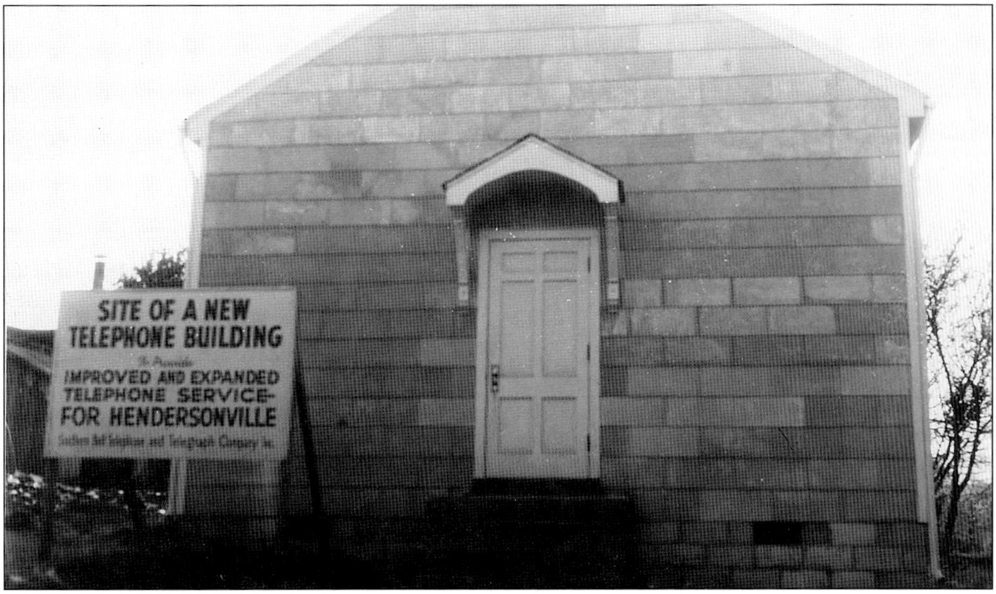

Among the earliest signs of progress for the unincorporated town of Hendersonville was this sign announcing the construction of a new telephone company and the promise of improved service. (Courtesy of the Charles Roney Collection, Hendersonville's Martin Curtis Library.)

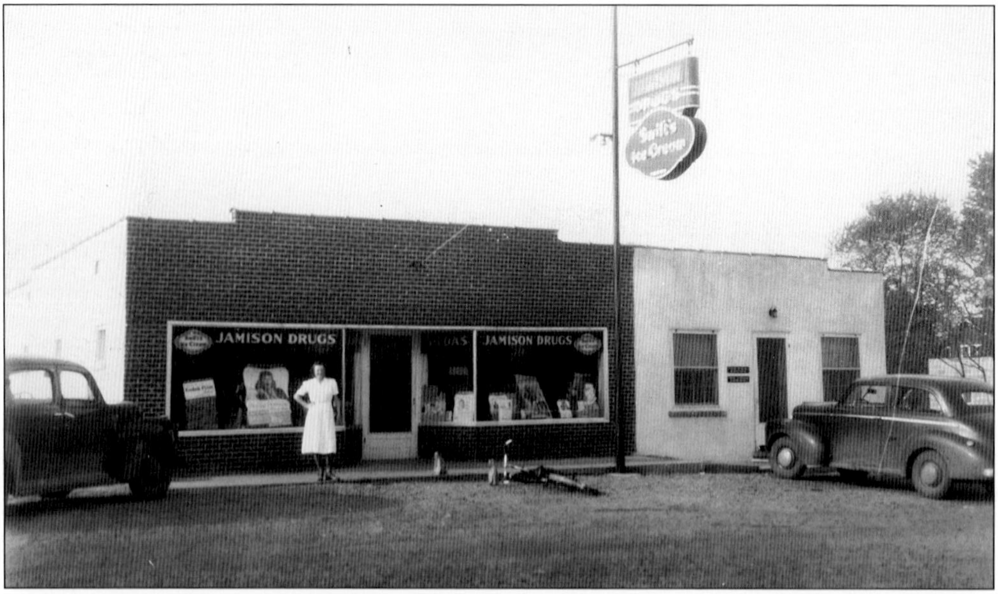

Jamison Drugs (left) was Hendersonville's first drugstore and was conveniently located next door to Dr. Osborne's office (white front building). Today, the U-Haul company is located on this site. (Courtesy of the Charles Roney Collection, Hendersonville's Martin Curtis Library.)

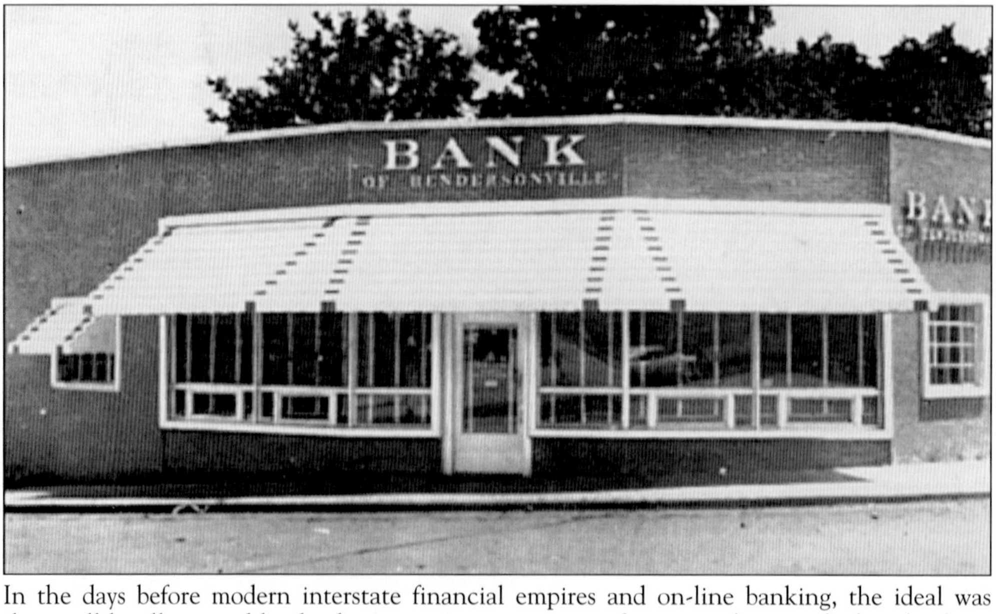

In the days before modern interstate financial empires and on-line banking, the ideal was the small locally owned bank where customers were on a first-name basis with their bankers. This building was home to the Bank of Hendersonville. Later changed to the Volunteer State Bank, it continues as a local financial institution. (Courtesy of the Charles Roney Collection, Hendersonville's Martin Curits Library.)

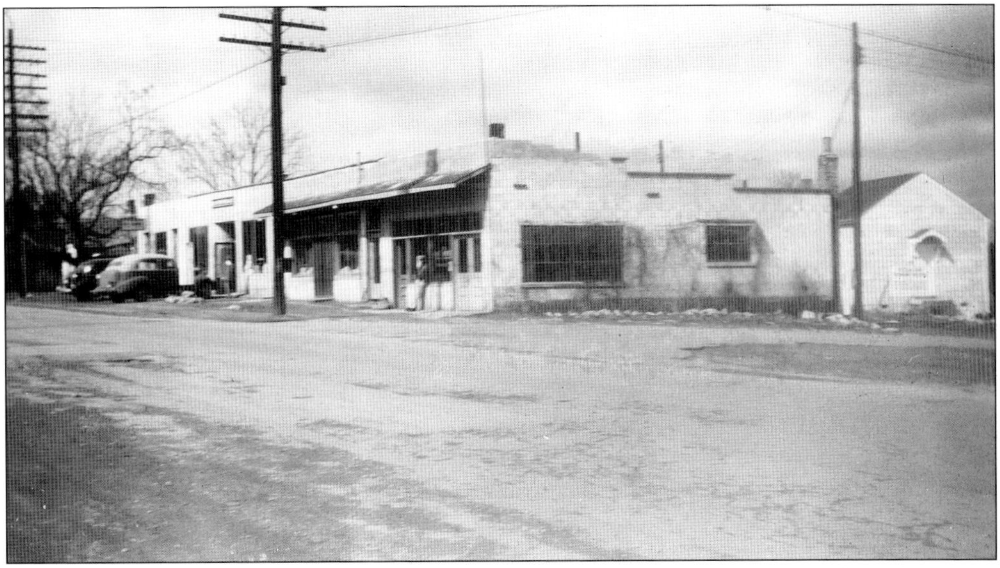

This group of buildings on Hendersonville's Main Street housed the post office, the office of Dr. J.H. Stevens, and General Merchandise. Located at the corner of Shackle Island Road, these businesses were replaced by Stewart's 5 and 10 Variety Store and, later, by Freed's Hardware. (Courtesy of Quinton Coppage.)

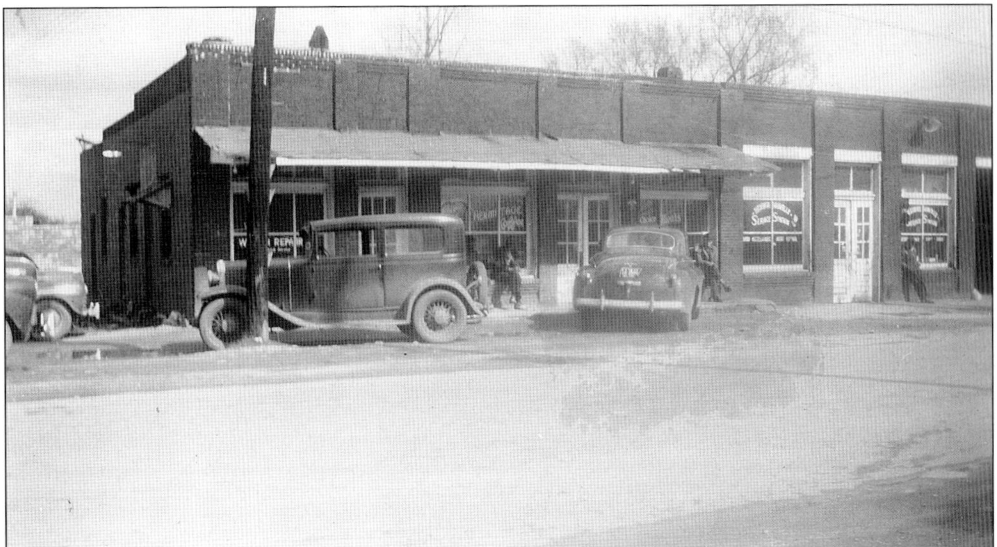

Hurt's Market was a familiar Hendersonville business well into the 1980s. This building, Hurt's first store, was adjacent to a business where locals purchased cream (left corner). (Courtesy of Quinton Coppage.)

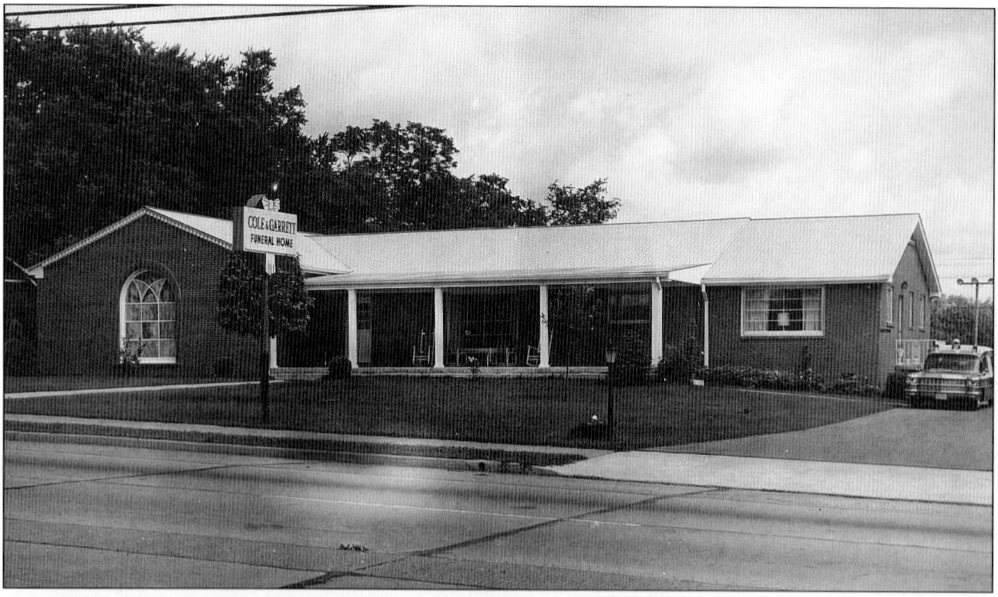

Expanded from its Goodlettsville base and housed in a modern building on Main Street, Hendersonville's Cole and Garrett Funeral Home was the first to feature the luxury of air-conditioned hearses. (Courtesy of Cole and Garrett.)

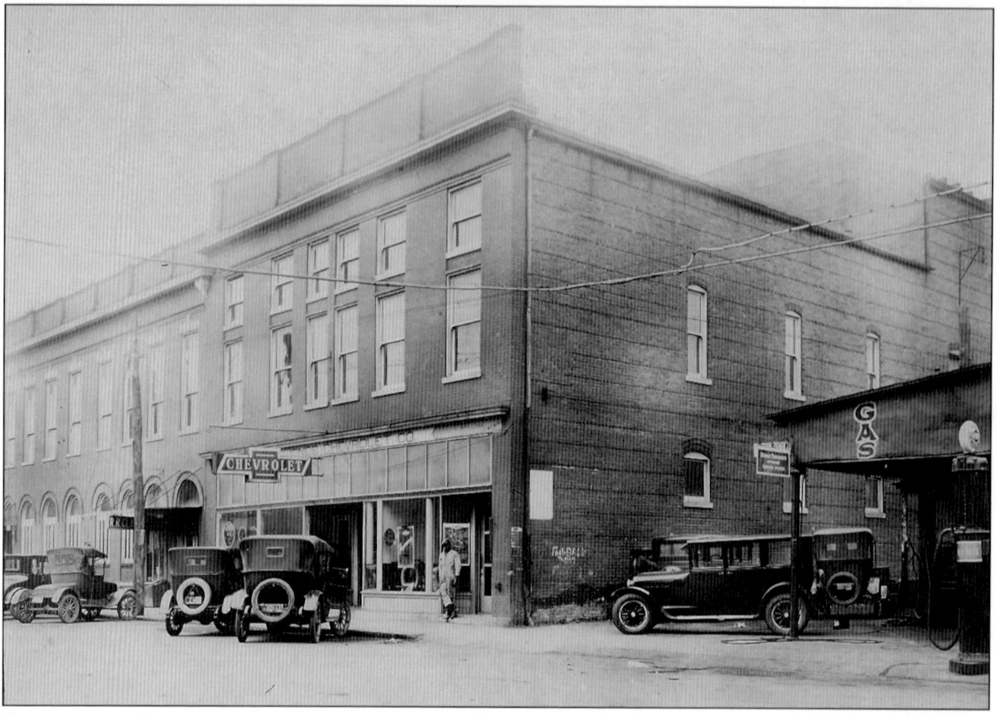

Securing modern transportation was a significant part of the "American Dream," and auto dealerships sprang up to meet the growing consumer demand. The convenience of purchase, financing, and service were readily available on Gallatin's East Main with the aligning of (from left to right) Sumner County Bank, Jones Chevrolet, and a gas/ full-service station. (Courtesy of Kenneth C. Thomson Jr.)

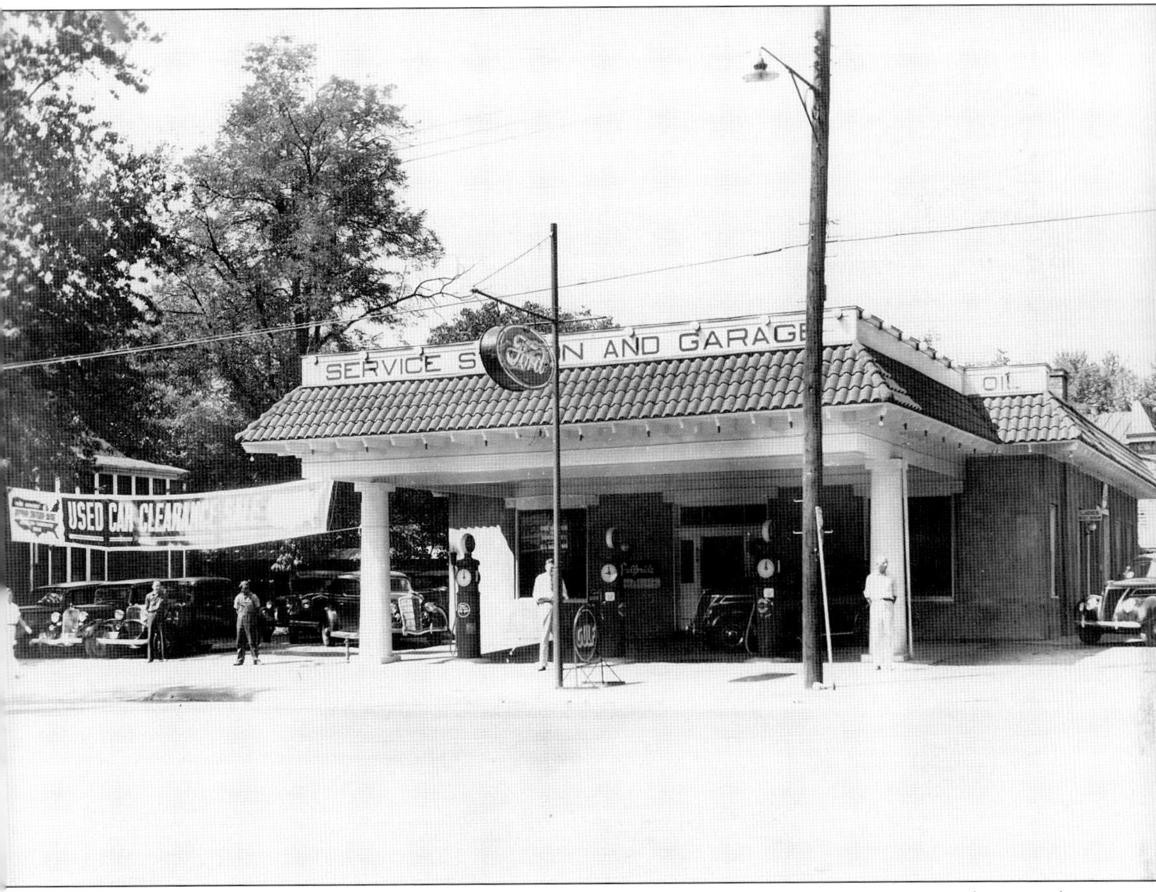

For many years, automobile agencies were exclusive franchises, under contract with a single automobile manufacturing company. The Gallatin Motor Company on East Main Street was the Ford Agency. Here, Nathan Bedford Franklin stands beside a gas pump under the Ford sign, while to the left, giant banners advertise a used car clearance. (Courtesy of Kenneth C. Thomson Jr.)

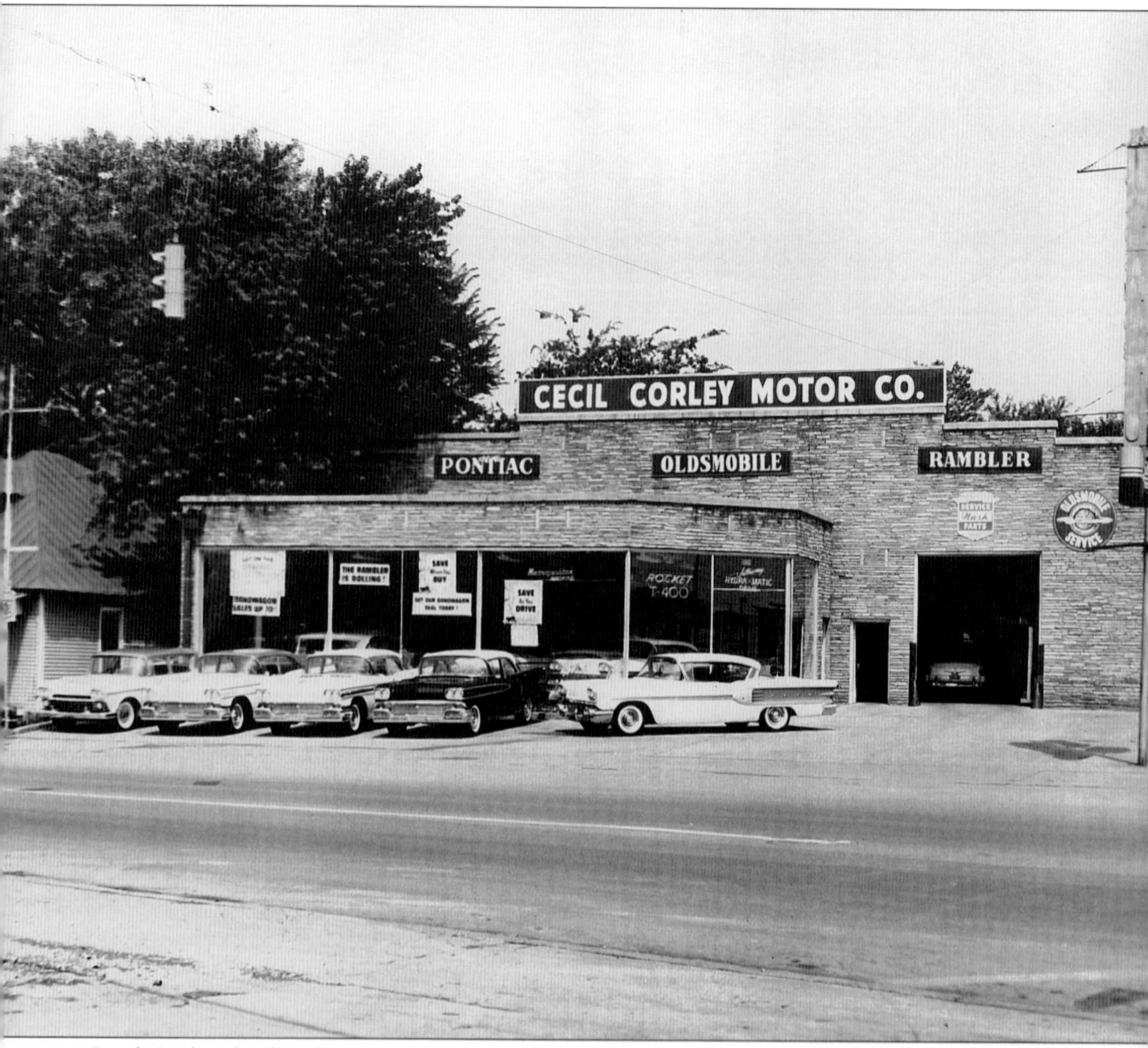

Cecil Corley displayed many of the fine Pontiacs, Oldsmobiles, and Ramblers in front of his Gallatin dealership on Nashville Pike. Automobiles reflected America's growing obsession with the space age and rocketry in design elements, such as fins, and in names such as the Rocket T 400. (Courtesy of the Bob Perry Collection, Sumner County Archives.)

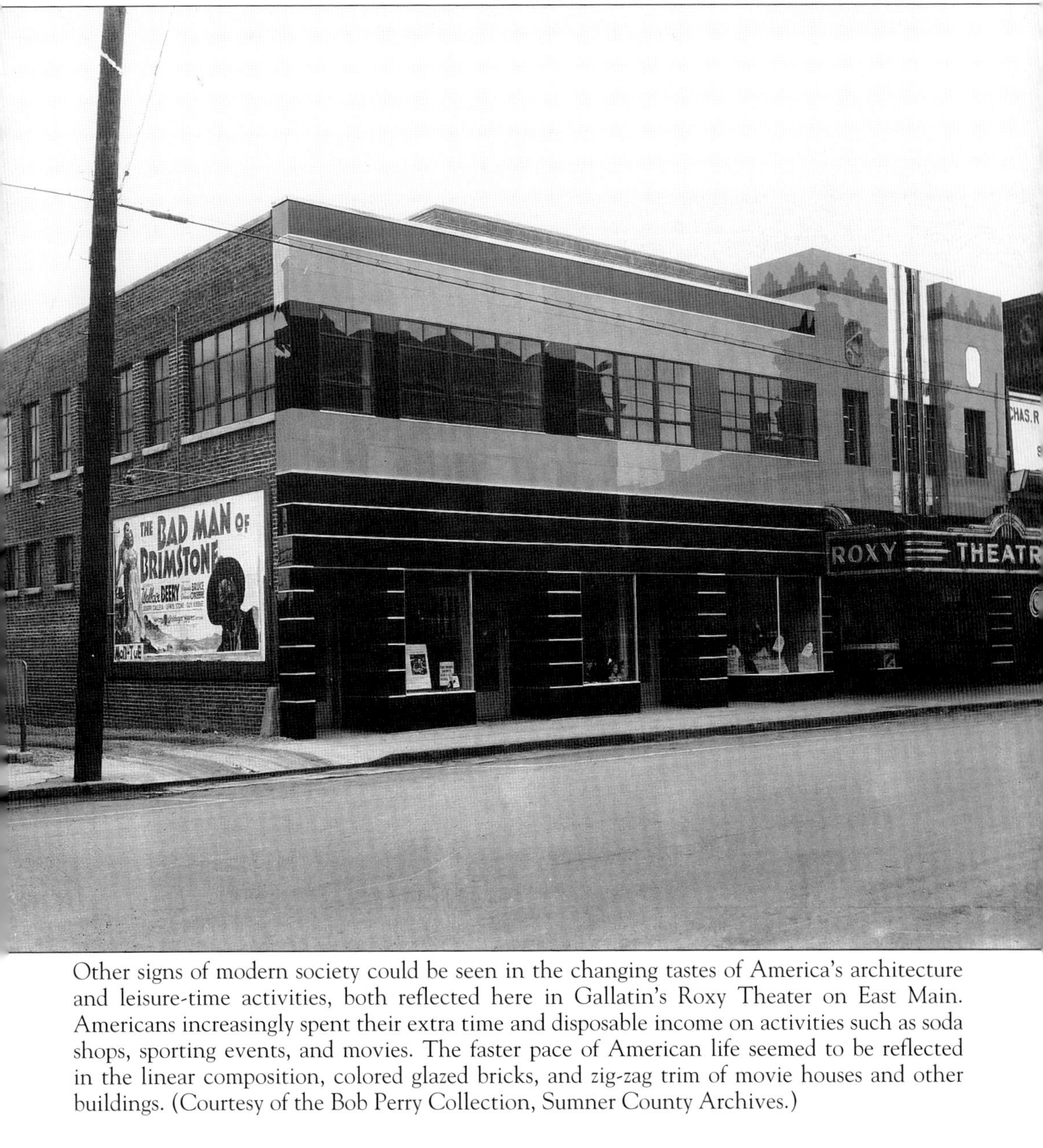

Other signs of modern society could be seen in the changing tastes of America's architecture and leisure-time activities, both reflected here in Gallatin's Roxy Theater on East Main. Americans increasingly spent their extra time and disposable income on activities such as soda shops, sporting events, and movies. The faster pace of American life seemed to be reflected in the linear composition, colored glazed bricks, and zig-zag trim of movie houses and other buildings. (Courtesy of the Bob Perry Collection, Sumner County Archives.)

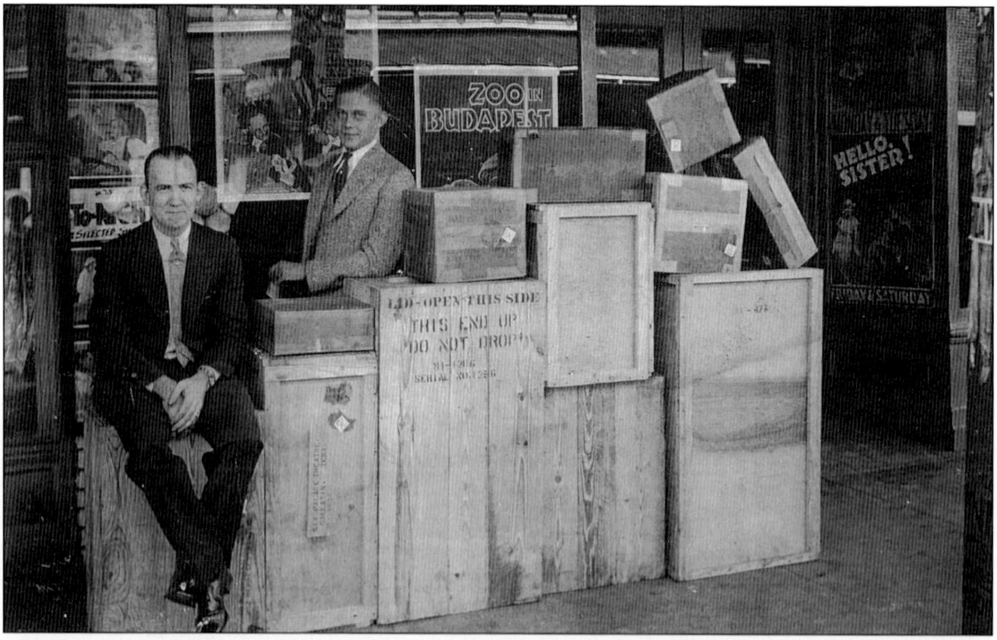

The dramatic shift from silent films to sound brought a new excitement to theater audiences. Here, William Frederick Roth Jr. and Dave Kennedy unload the new sound equipment for installation in Gallatin's New Palace Theater in 1927. We can only imagine the thrill of audiences that flocked to the Palace to view the new "talkies." (Courtesy of Allen Haynes.)

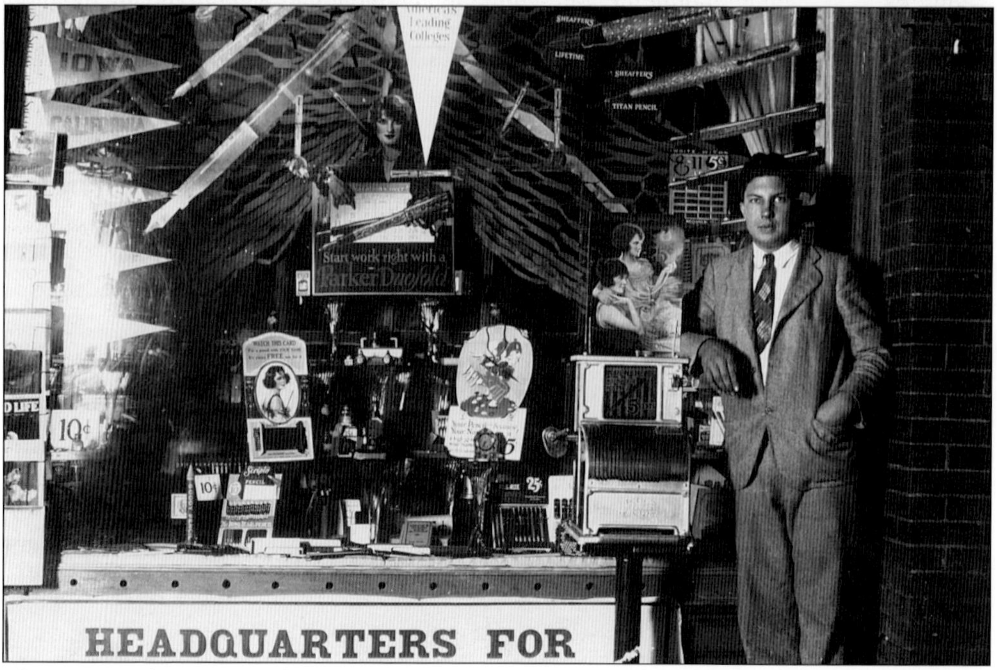

The new emphasis on modern youth is reflected in the window display of one Public Square store in Gallatin that touts itself as the "headquarters for school supplies" (c. 1930s). The man posing beside the attractive display is Edward L. McDonald, later mayor of Gallatin. (Courtesy of the Bob Perry Collection, Sumner County Archives.)

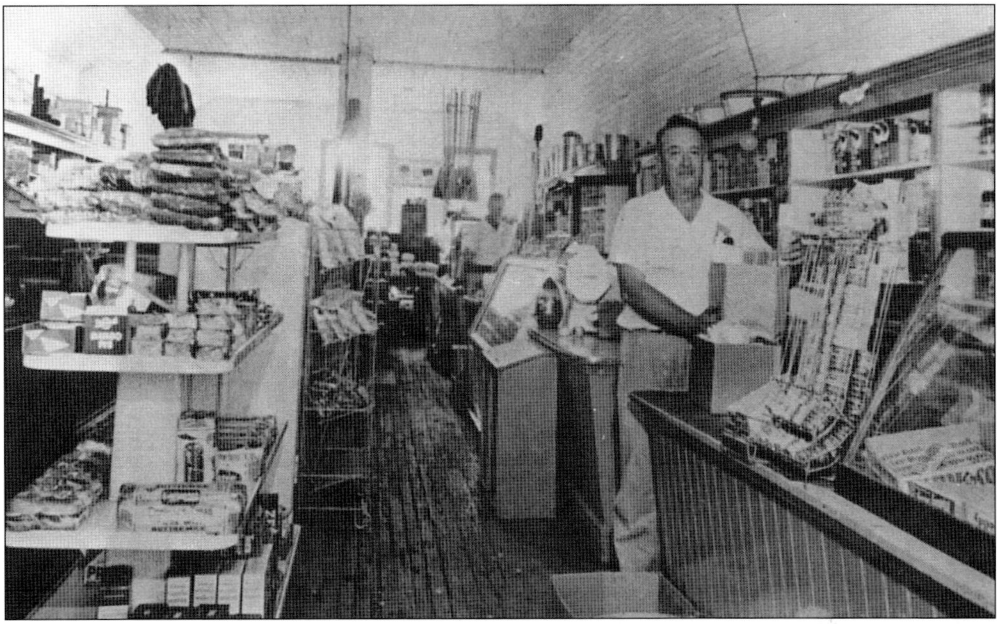

Changes in retail were neither speedy nor widespread, and many small markets such as this one continued operation well into the 1960s before the mom and pop stores gave way to chain stores. (Courtesy of the Bob Perry Collection, Sumner County Archives.)

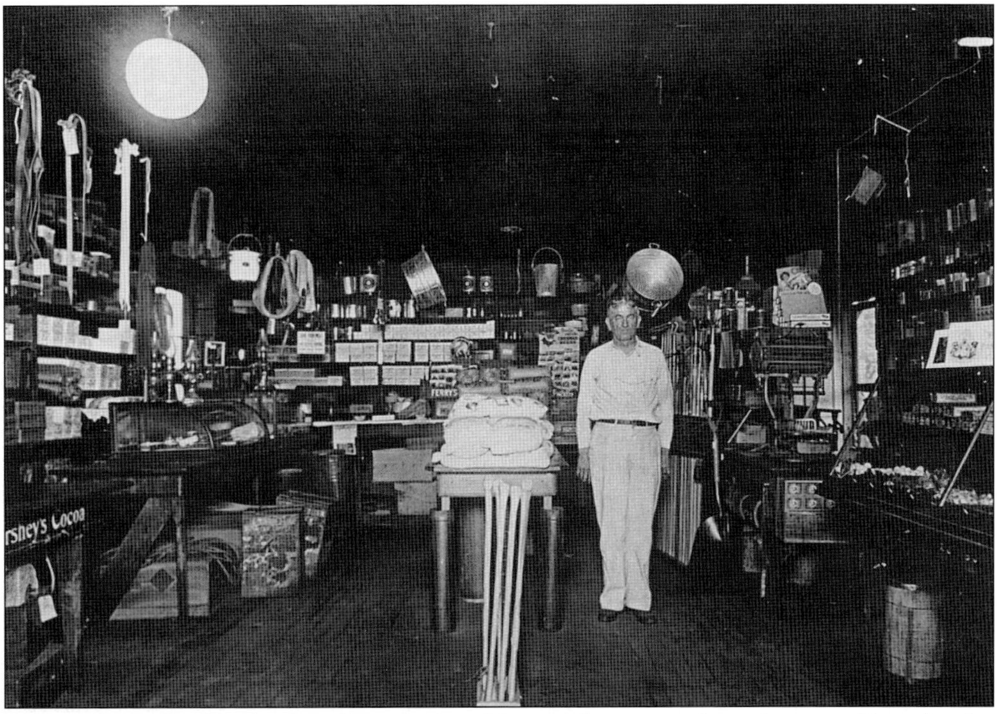

Rarer still, as the decades passed, were the old general stores such as this one. Considered a fixture in retail through the 1930s, by the 1940s and 1950s, these stores were being supplanted as department stores refined the shopping experience. (Courtesy of the Bob Perry Collection, Sumner County Archives.)

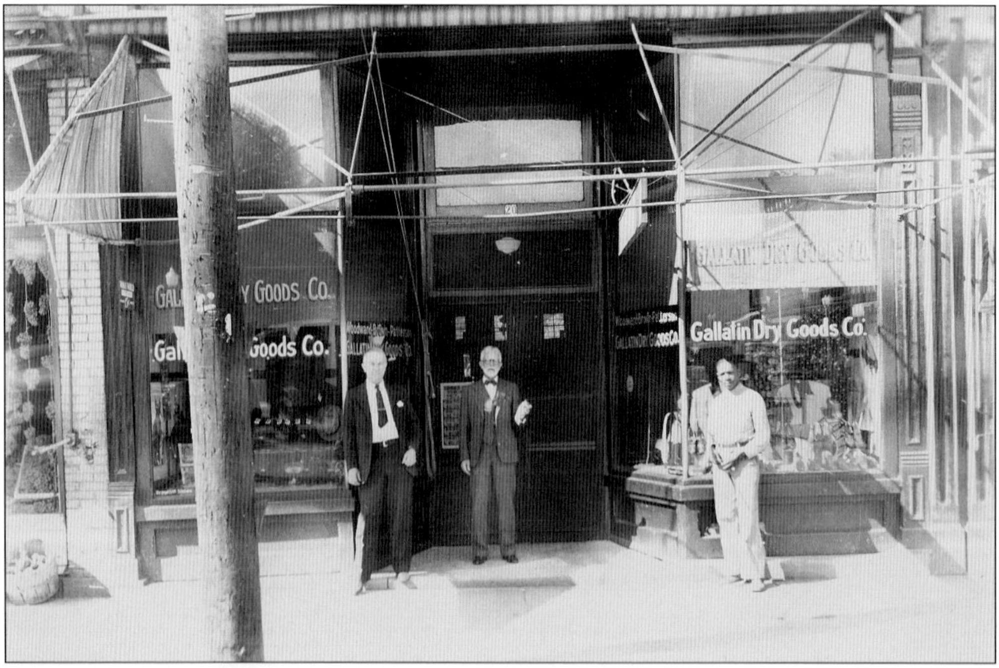

In this E.M. Stark photograph, the awning has been rolled back to reveal the store front of Gallatin Dry Goods Company on the Public Square. Pictured from left to right are: George Thompson Brown, Frederick Augustine Woodward, and an unidentified man. (Courtesy of Kenneth C. Thomson Jr.)

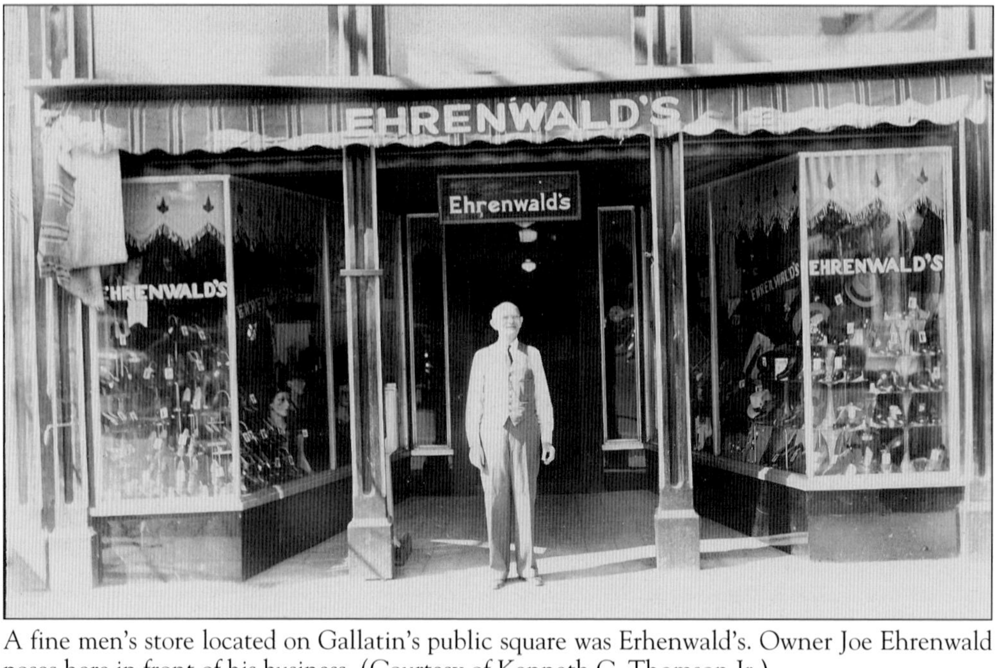

A fine men's store located on Gallatin's public square was Erhenwald's. Owner Joe Ehrenwald poses here in front of his business. (Courtesy of Kenneth C. Thomson Jr.)

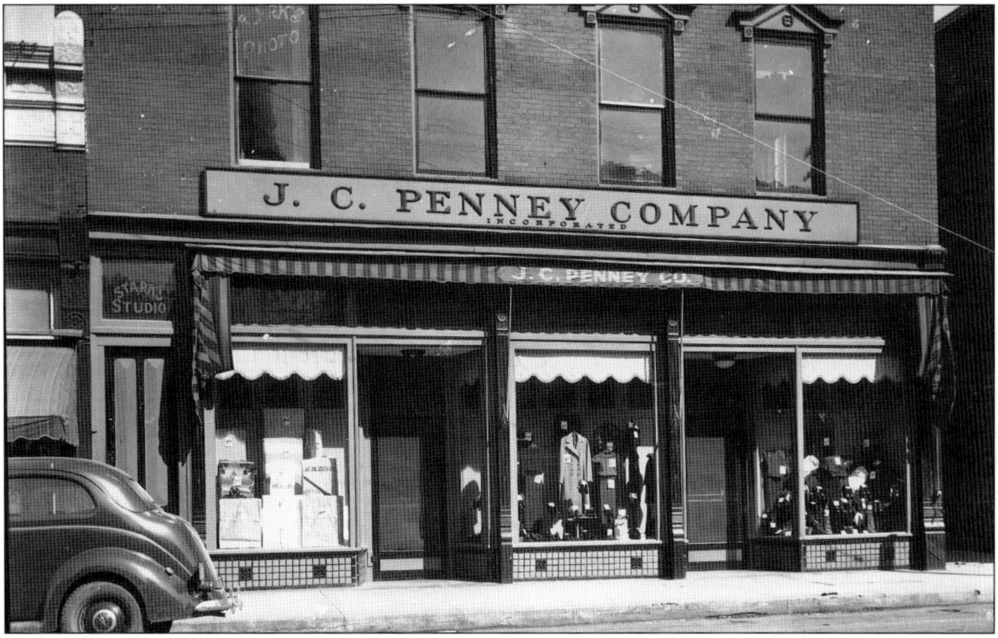

The arrival of J.C. Penney Company to North Water Street in Gallatin (1937) signaled the first appearance of a major retail chain to the city. H.B. Simmons was the manager and Arthur Rutledge Jr. was the store's assistant manager. The studio of photographer E.M. Stark was located on the second floor of the building. (Courtesy of Kenneth C. Thomson Jr.)

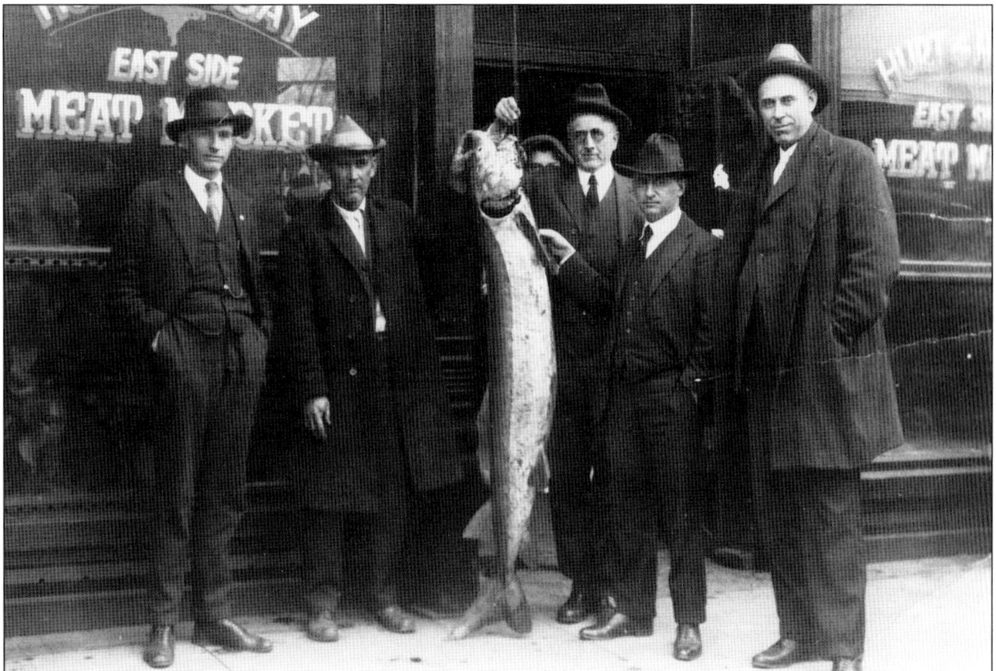

Pictured here, from left to right, Judge Tim Walker, an unidentified man, Dr. Asburn, Judge William Henry Brown, and Brode Rippy gather before Hurt and Hosay's East Side Meat Market in Gallatin to show off their fine catch. (Courtesy of Kenneth C. Thomson Jr.)

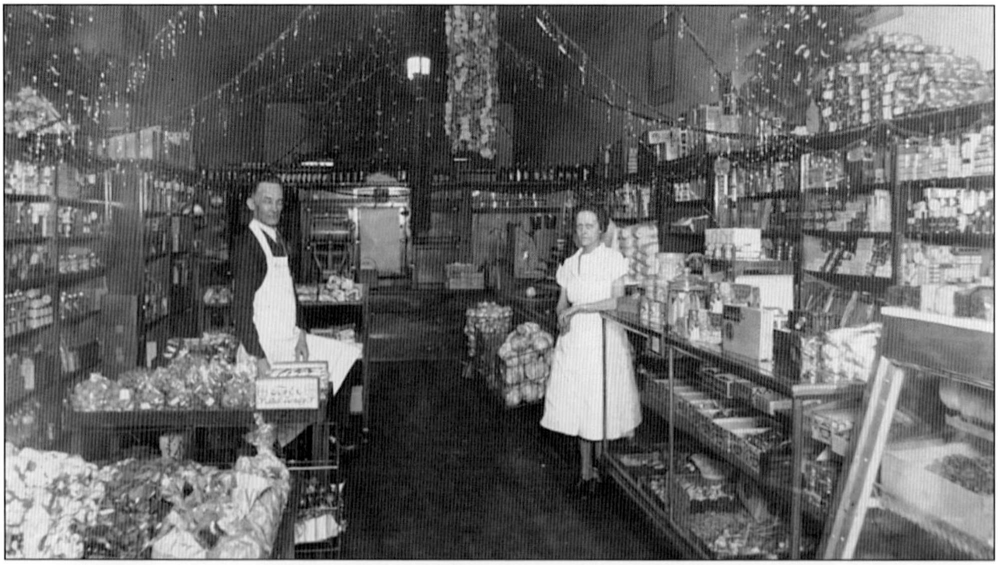

Mr. and Mrs. Robert Crowder pose inside their grocery store in Gallatin. Apparently decorated for the Christmas holidays, the grocery shelves and display cases and tables maintain much of the look of the old general store. (Courtesy of Kenneth C. Thomson Jr.)

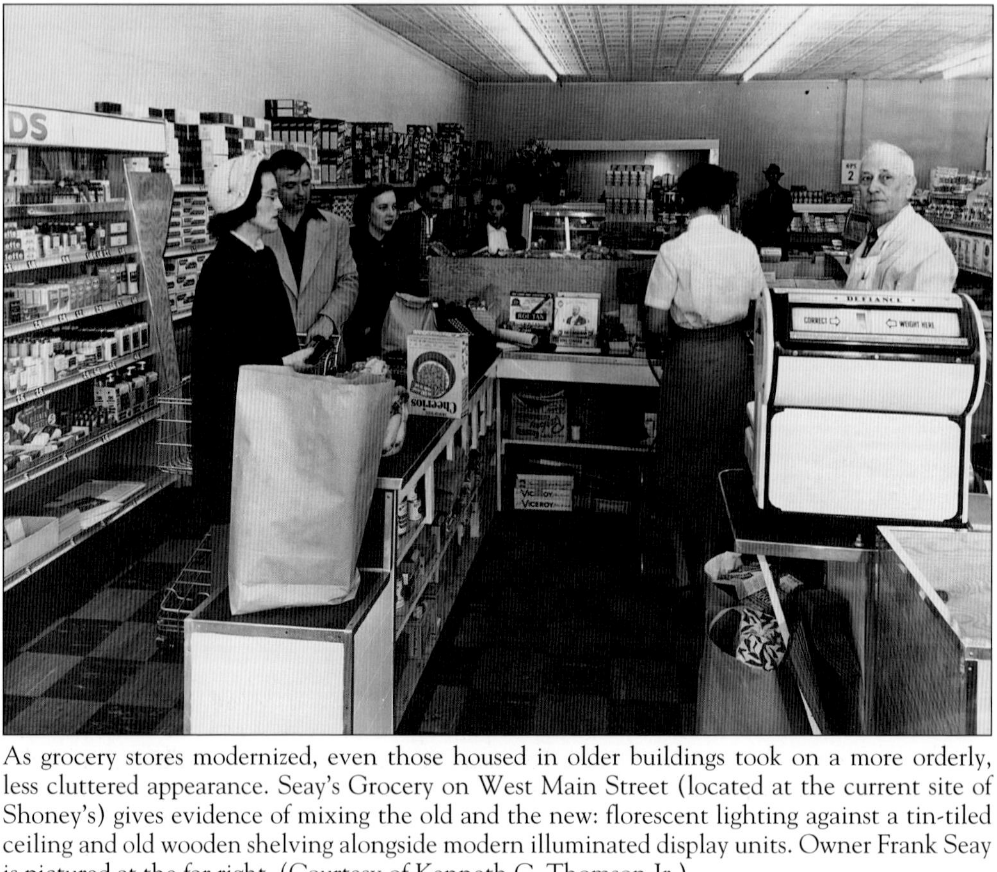

As grocery stores modernized, even those housed in older buildings took on a more orderly, less cluttered appearance. Seay's Grocery on West Main Street (located at the current site of Shoney's) gives evidence of mixing the old and the new: florescent lighting against a tin-tiled ceiling and old wooden shelving alongside modern illuminated display units. Owner Frank Seay is pictured at the far right. (Courtesy of Kenneth C. Thomson Jr.)

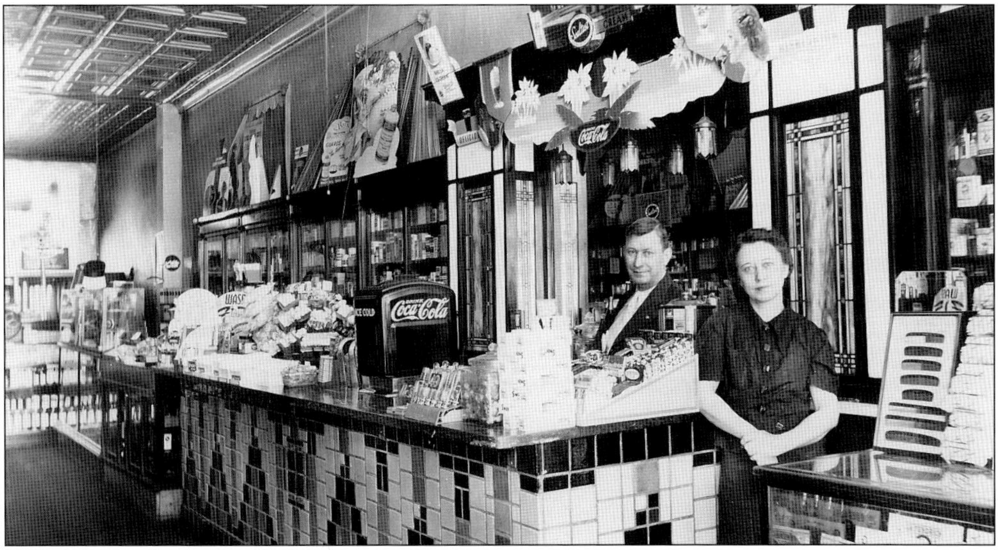

Art Deco tile along the counter and bordering the glass panels behind the counter gave a modern look to Smith's Drug Store in Gallatin, *c.* 1937. Owners Herschel and Naomi (Dowell) Smith opened the drug store/soda fountain on January 1, 1935. Before moving to Gallatin, Herschel Smith owned a store in Scottsville, Kentucky for 21 years. (Courtesy of Kenneth C. Thomson Jr.)

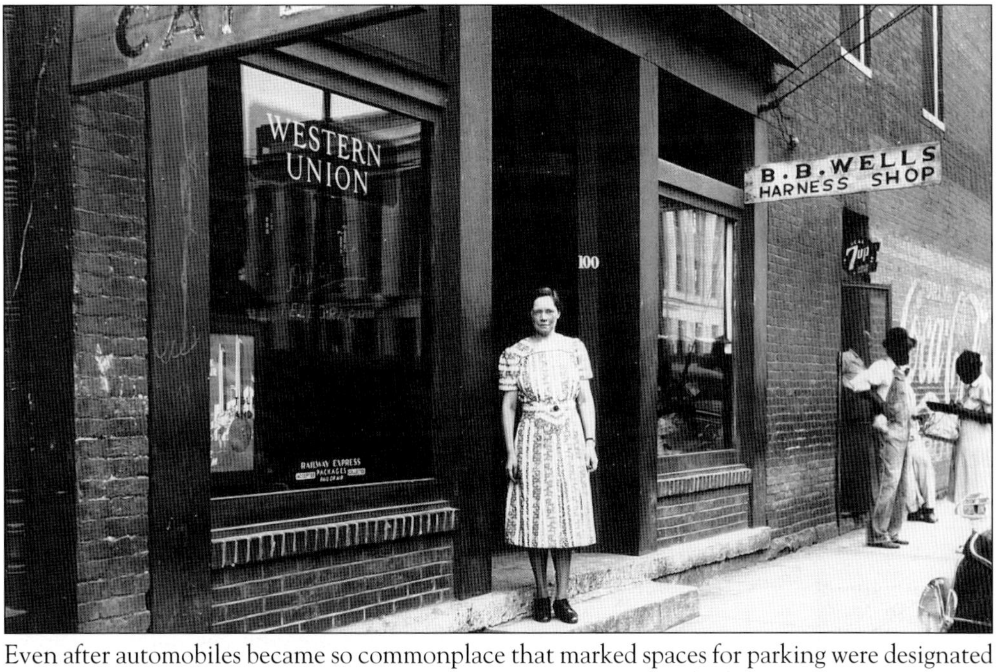

Even after automobiles became so commonplace that marked spaces for parking were designated along the streets (as evidenced by the angled parking of the vehicle at bottom right of this photograph), many old ways continued. For example, B.B. Wells Harness Shop remained a fixture on the public square. This photograph was made sometime after 1940 because the new Sumner County Court House is clearly visible in the windows of Wells Harness and Western Union. Mrs. Ivy Dalton poses on the front steps of Western Union. (Courtesy of the Bob Perry Collection, Sumner County Archives.)

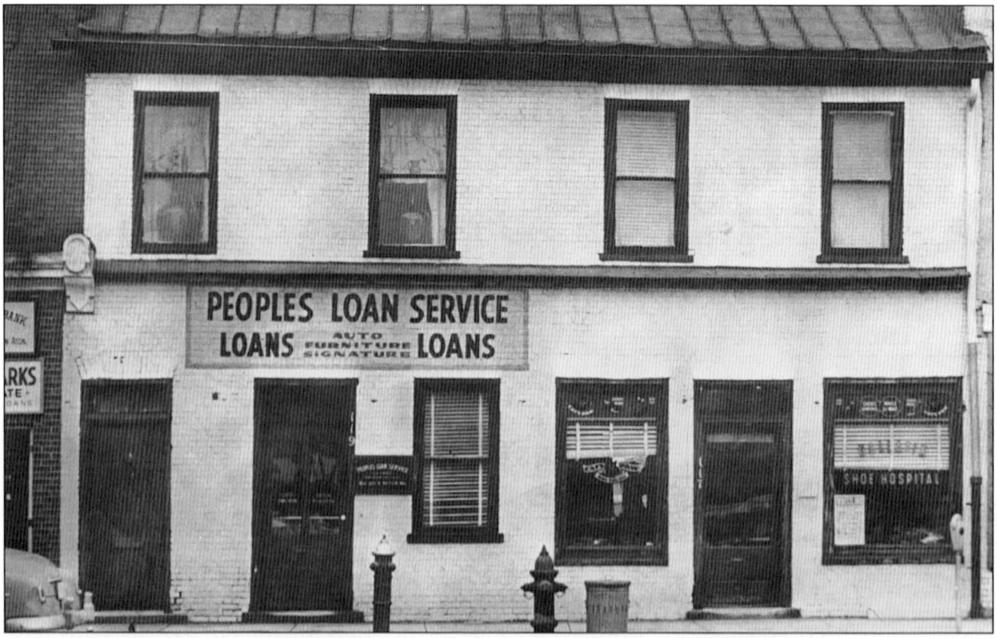

This nondescript building on the east side of the Public Square in Gallatin had a colorful history before it was finally torn down. In the early 1800s, Andrew Jackson practiced law here. In the 1930s, a local eccentric and former Texas Ranger named Jesse Moore lived in rooms on the upper floor. Perhaps most famous among Jesse's many exploits was the time he skated the frozen Cumberland River from Cairo to Nashville. (Courtesy of the Bob Perry Collection, Sumner County Archives.)

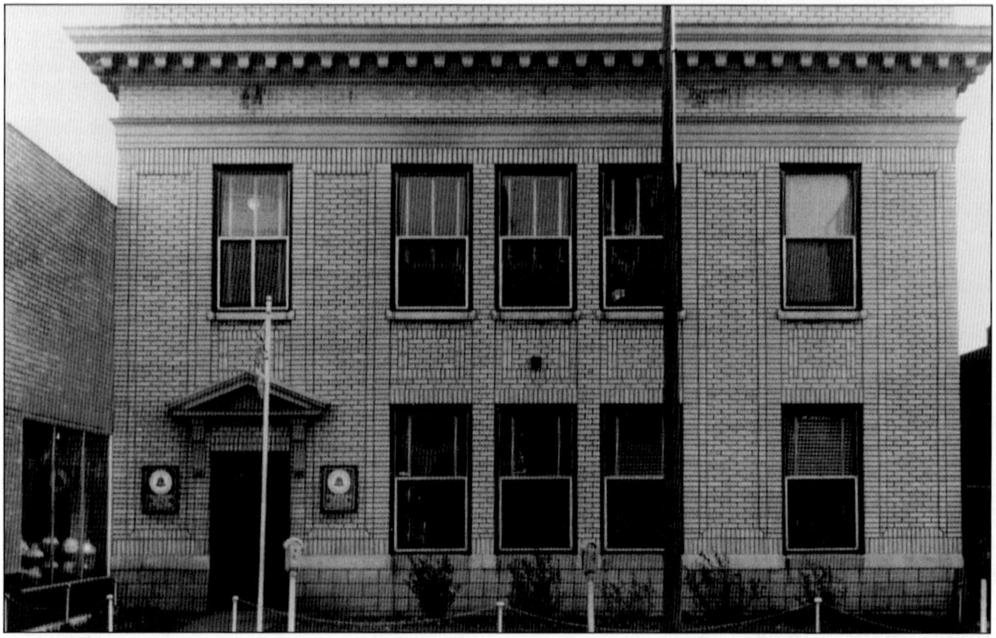

Complicated decorative brick work adds interest to the Gallatin Telephone Company building completed in 1917. The company served the community until 1960. (Courtesy of Allen Haynes.)

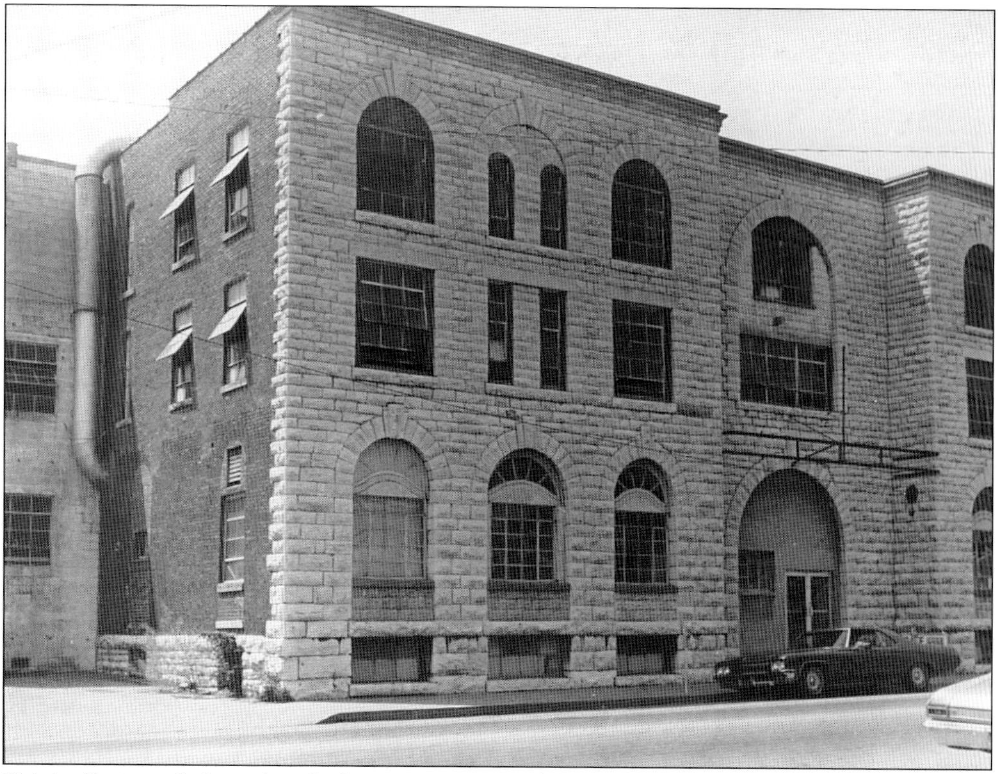

Originally intended as a hotel, this structure served for a number of years as the Central High School before its conversion into a manufacturing plant for General Shoe (later Genesco). The stone facade of the building, with its rounded arches and deep-set windows, is reminiscent of Richardson Romanesque architecture. (Courtesy of the Bob Perry Collection, Sumner County Archives.)

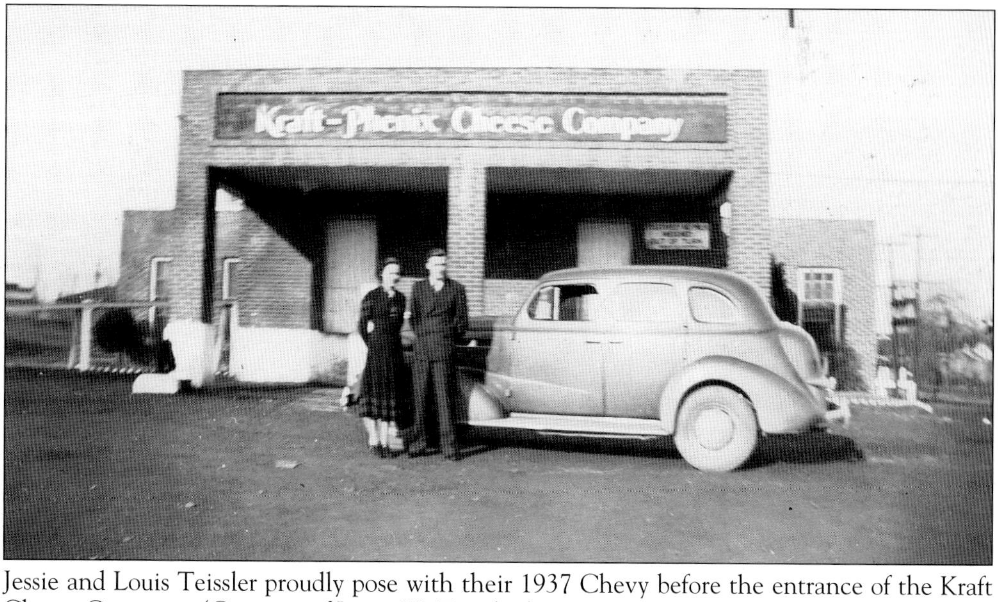

Jessie and Louis Teissler proudly pose with their 1937 Chevy before the entrance of the Kraft Cheese Company. (Courtesy of Louis W. Teissler.)

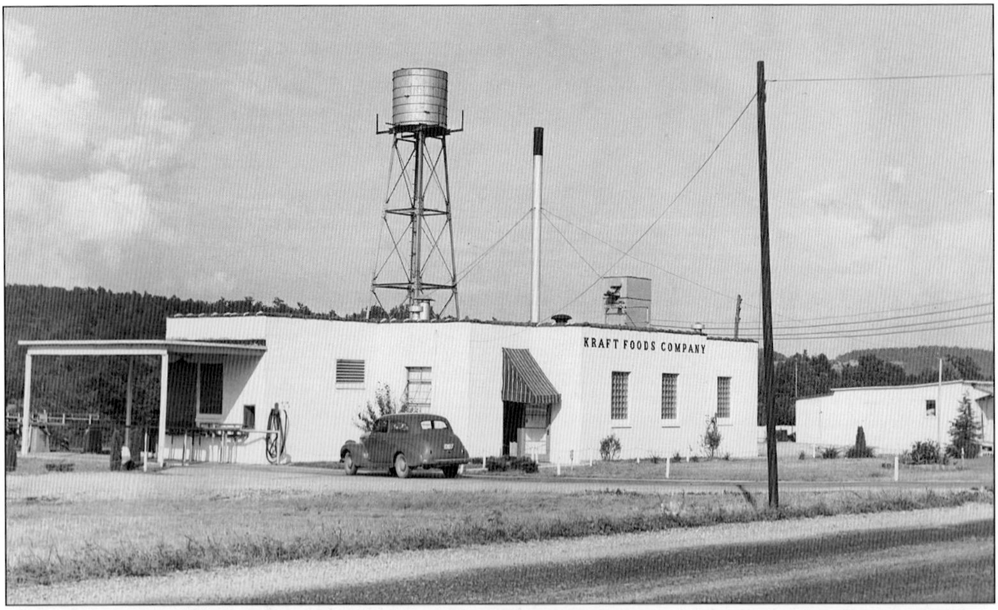

A point of particular civic pride was the successful recruitment of the Kraft Cheese Company to Gallatin in the 1920s. The company remained an active partner in the community and a major employer in the area for 50 years. (Courtesy of Kenneth C. Thomson Jr.)

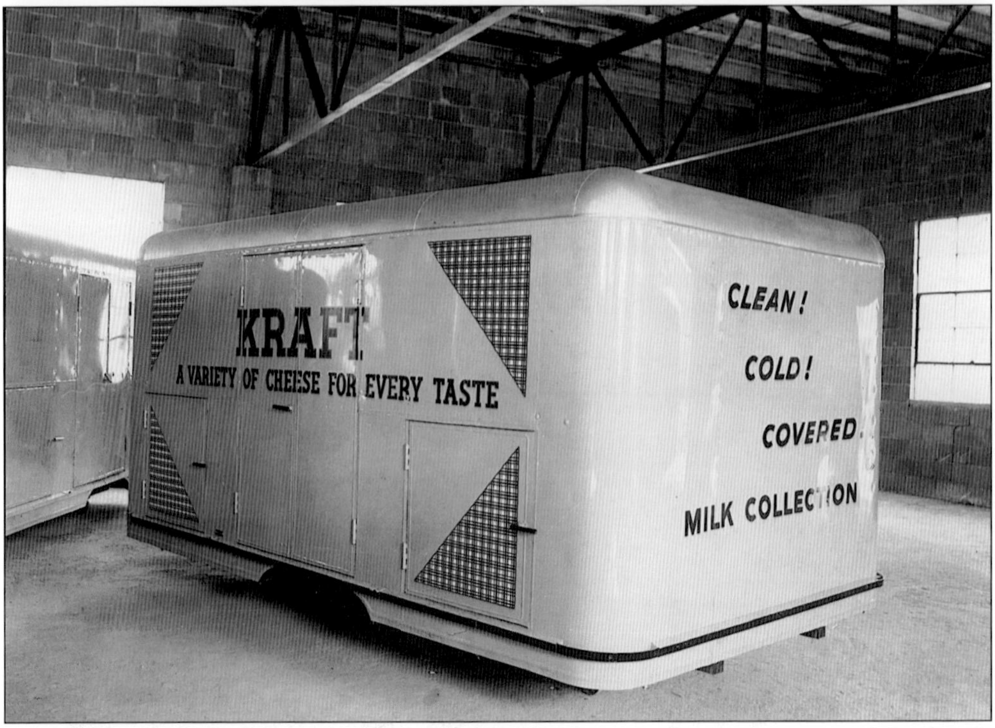

A major local innovation for the Kraft Cheese Company was the construction of these milk collection containers built by Horace E. Franklin and Sons of Franklin Street in Gallatin. The new devices assured customers of freshness with "clean, cold, covered milk collection." (Courtesy of Peggy Franklin Kobe, granddaughter of Horace Franklin.)

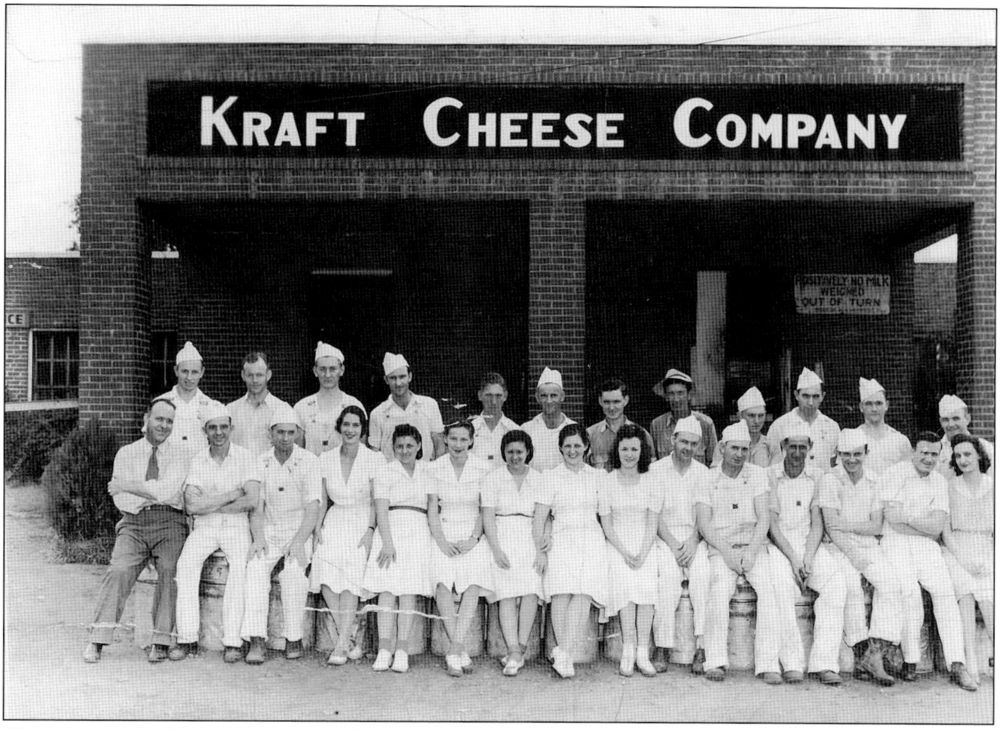

Plant manager Noel Hemmert (front row, far left) joins other Kraft Cheese employees for a company photograph in 1941, just three months before America entered WW II. (Courtesy of Louis W. Teissler.)

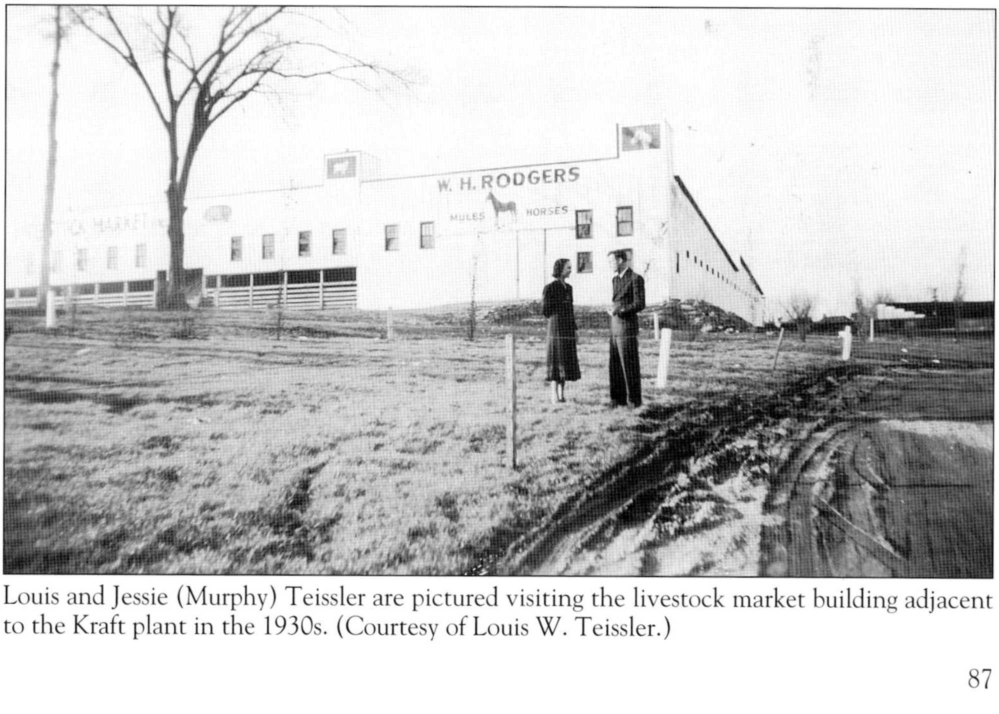

Louis and Jessie (Murphy) Teissler are pictured visiting the livestock market building adjacent to the Kraft plant in the 1930s. (Courtesy of Louis W. Teissler.)

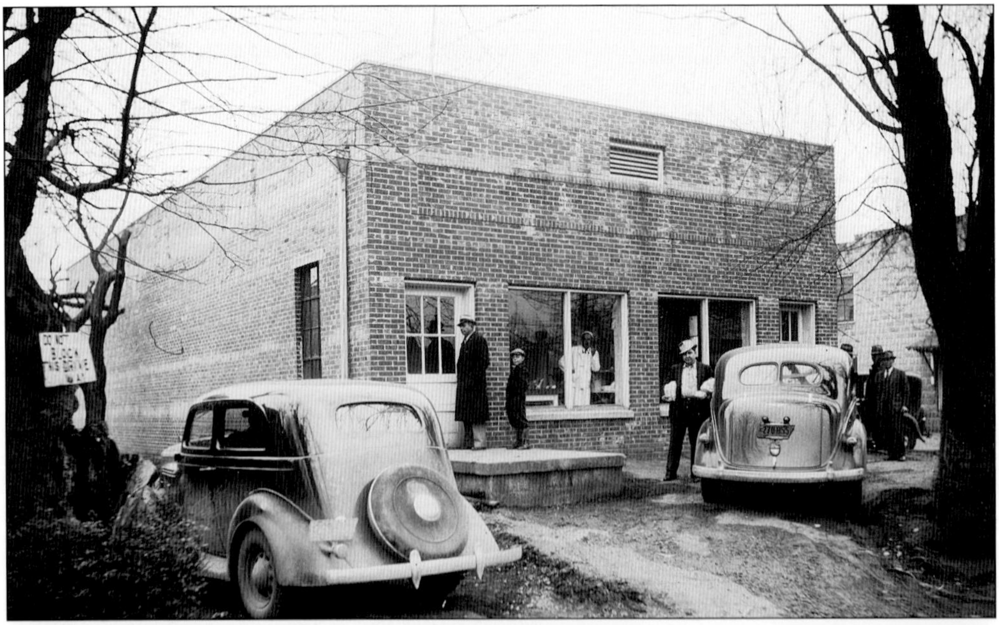

As the technology for supplying frozen meats surged ahead of consumer refrigeration products capable of storing the meat, many communities developed locker plants, such as this one on Depot Avenue in Gallatin. (From the album of Junius Gleaves Turner Jr., courtesy of Kenneth C. Thomson Jr.)

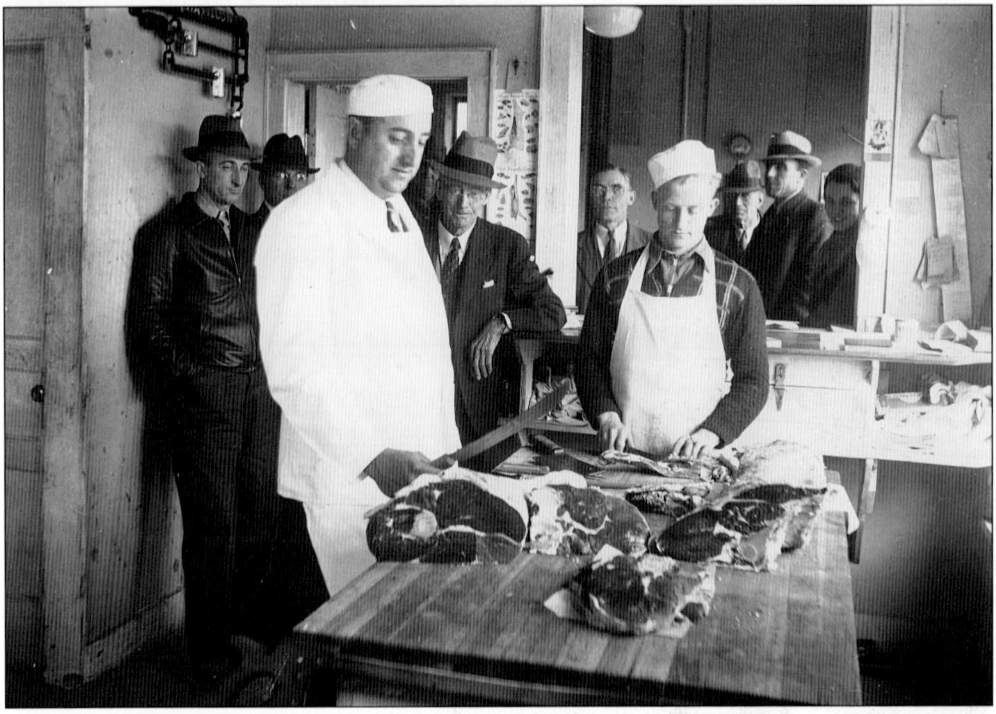

Butchers at Gallatin's Locker Plant cut up, packaged, and stored meat for customers. Here, Junius Gleaves Turner Jr. (far left) and other local men watch the butchers working on a side of beef. (From the album of Junius Gleaves Turner Jr., courtesy of Kenneth C. Thomson Jr.)

Local residents, such as these ladies, could rent refrigerated storage space in the Locker Plant, assuring their families of a good supply of top quality meat. (From the album of Junius Gleaves Turner Jr., courtesy of Kenneth C. Thomson Jr.)

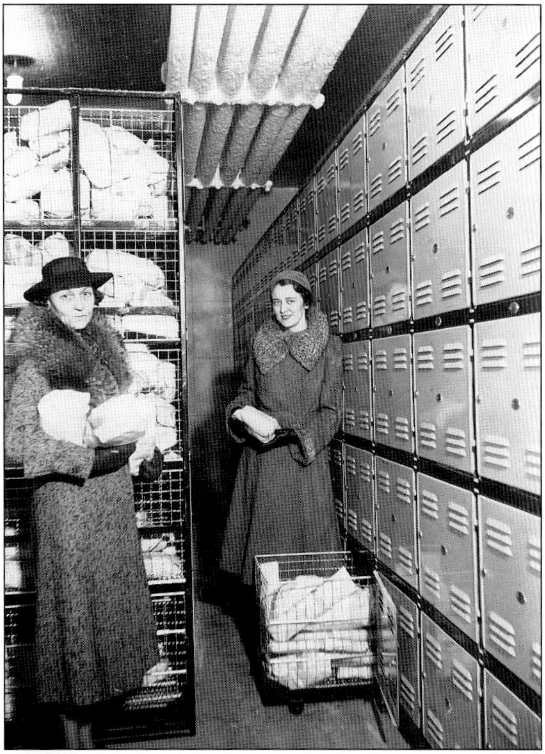

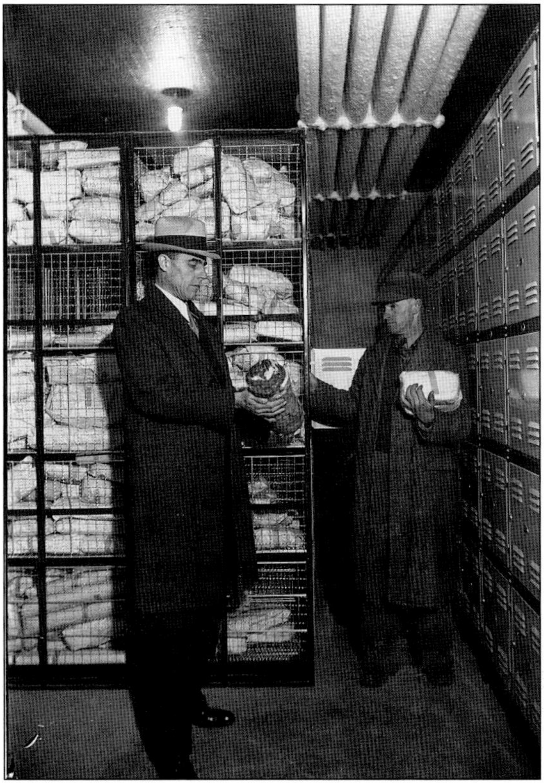

Notice the ice particles on the overhead pipes in the locker room. Whether residents rented locker space or made a selection from the packaged meat in the cages to the left, the Locker Plant offered convenience and the security of purchasing meat "from folks you know." Later, the improvements in capacity and cooling systems of home refrigerators removed the necessity for Locker Plants. C.W. Robison stands center. (From the album of Junius Gleaves Turner Jr., courtesy of Kenneth C. Thomson Jr.)

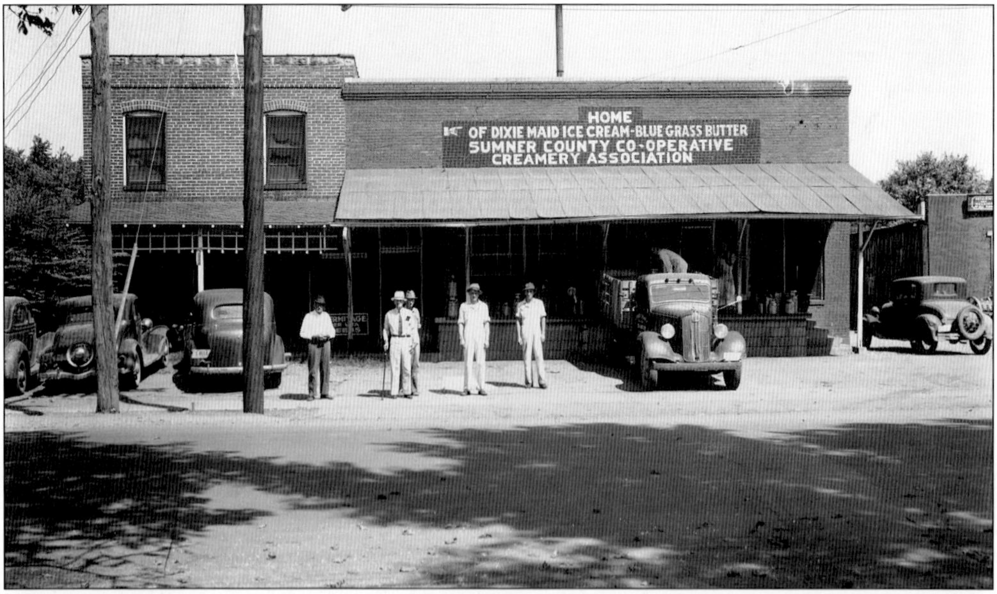

Junius Gleaves Turner Jr. (third from left) served for 35 years as the president of Sumner County Cooperative Creamery Association. The creamery was established in the 1920s as an outlet for products of local dairymen, including Dixie Maid Ice Cream and Blue Grass Butter. (Courtesy of Kenneth C. Thomson Jr.)

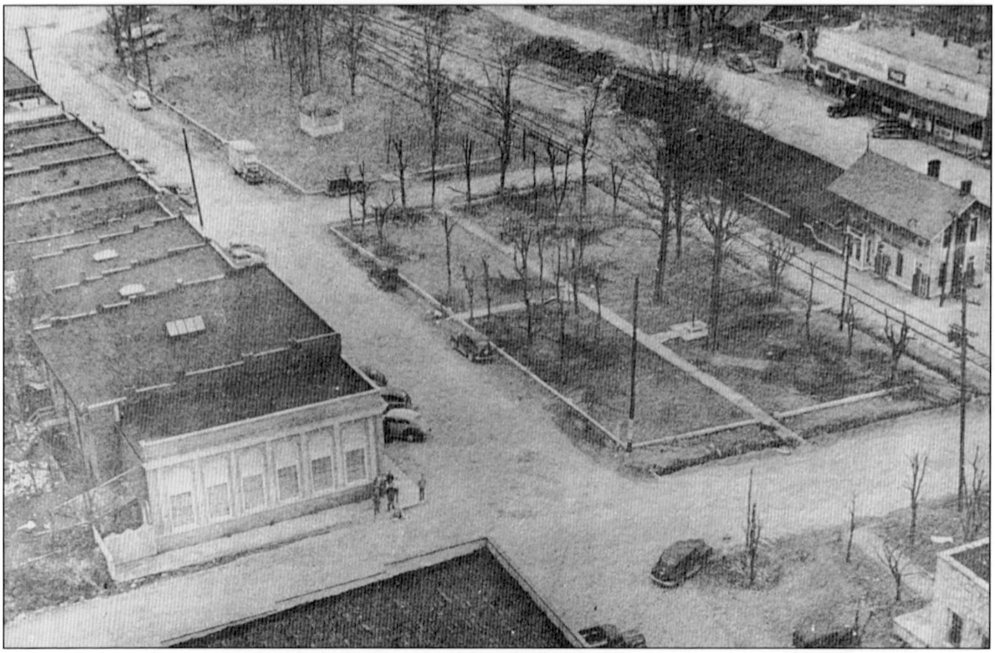

This 1948 aerial view of Westmoreland is reminiscent of scenes from the movie *It's a Wonderful Life*, with the business district intersected by a park. The row of buildings on the east side burned in the late 1950s, and the depot (*c.* 1886) was destroyed in the late 1960s. The park was converted into a parking area in 1973, and the last train through the town ran in December 1976. (1948 photograph by H.G. Kirby and owned by John F. Creasy.)

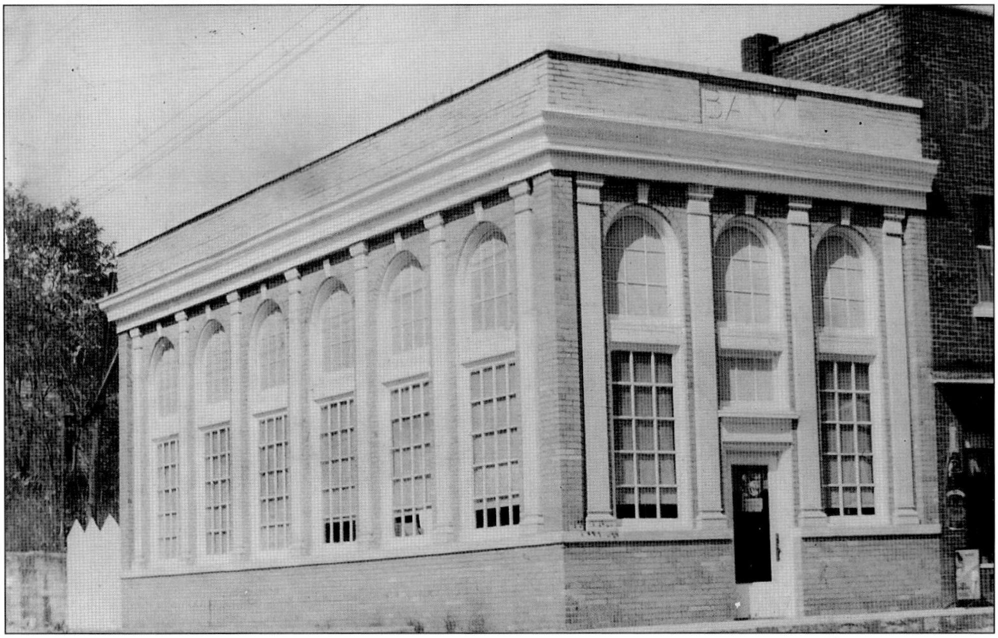

The Farmers and Merchants Bank of Westmoreland, located on the corner of Park Street and Highway 52, was constructed in 1925, and the vault was built by Earl Brown. Purchased by Dominion Bank, the building was donated to the city in the early 1980s and now serves as the city hall. (Photograph by Floyd Rhodes, courtesy of John F. Creasy.)

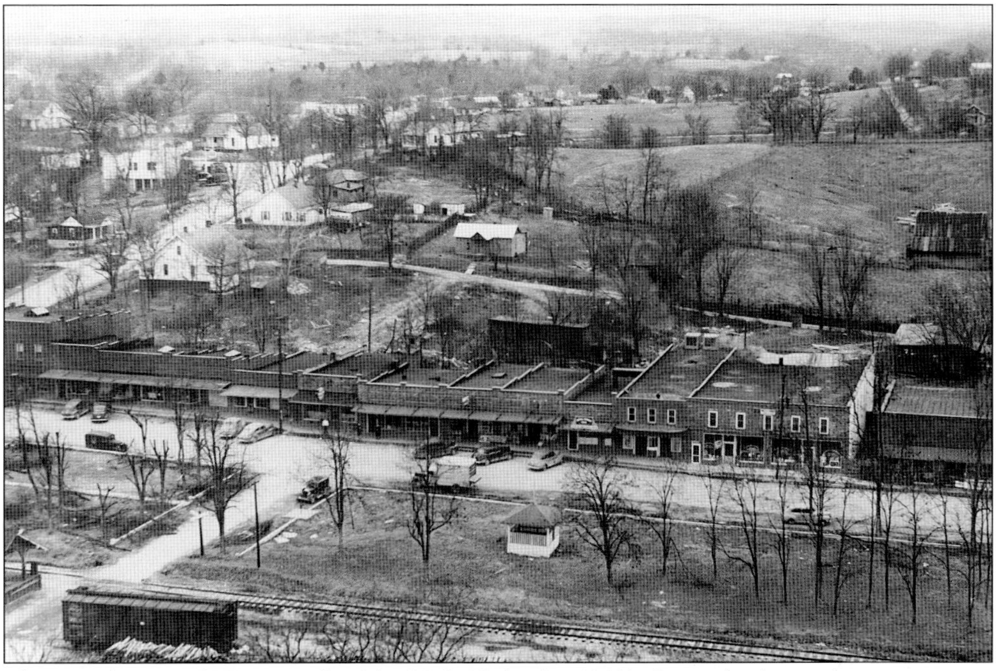

This aerial view of Westmoreland by H.G. Kirby (*c.* 1948) shows the lower downtown area, including the gazebo in the park. In the foreground is a stack of cordwood awaiting shipment by railroad to points east. The timber industry was extremely vital to the town's early economy. (Courtesy of John. F. Creasy.)

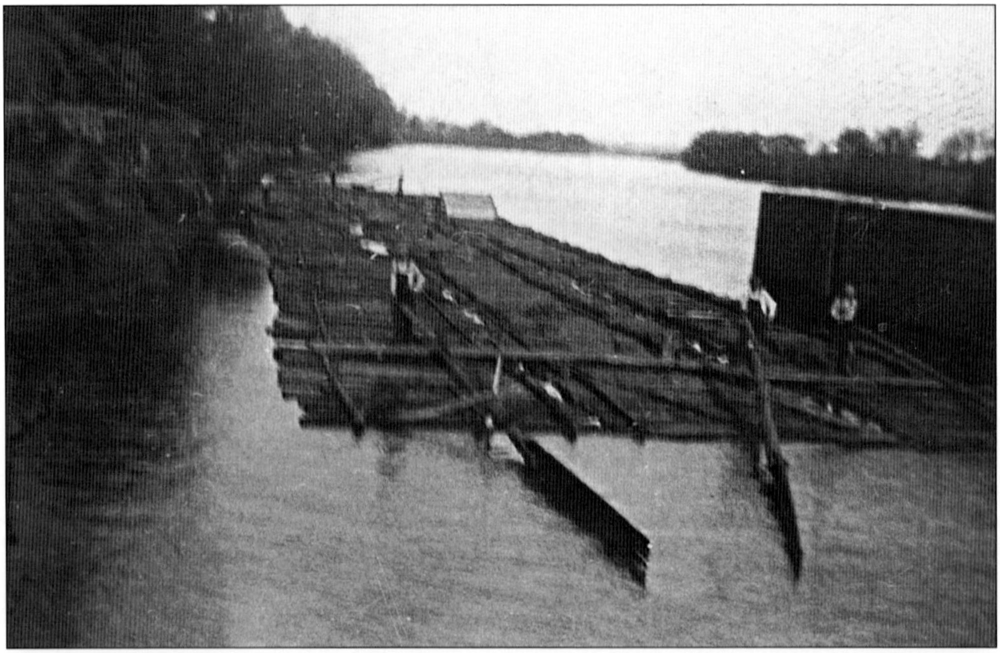

The Cumberland River was a vital element in the economic development of the county from the earliest settlers into the middle of the 20th century. The importance of the river, with its barge and ferry traffic, can still be seen in the names of local roads such as Walton Ferry and Sanders Ferry. The building of the dam in 1953 and the creation of Old Hickory Lake as a recreational facility ended barge traffic such as this example near Cairo. (Courtesy of Joseph C. Denny.)

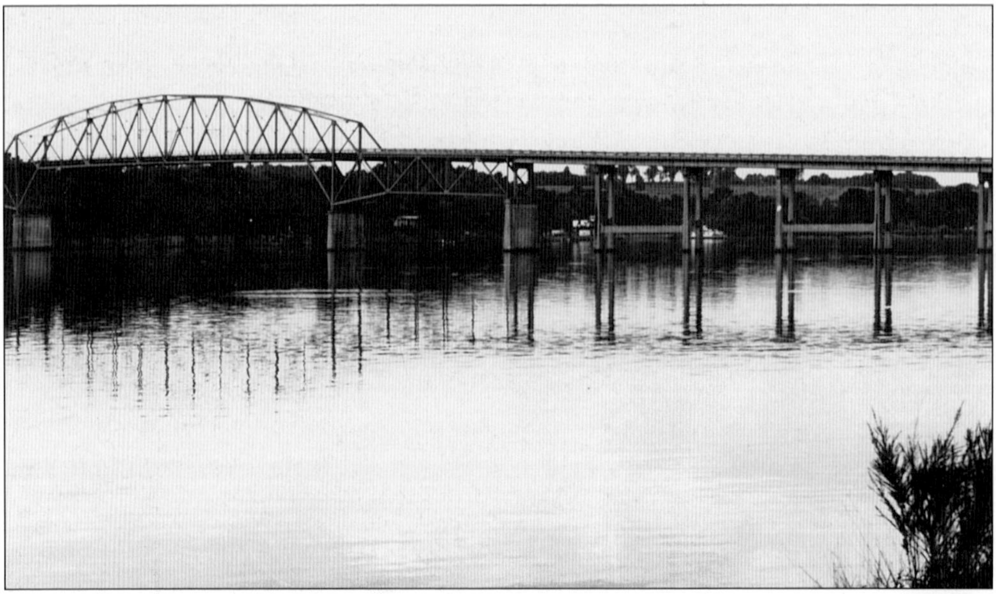

Following the creation of Old Hickory Lake, the construction of this bridge over the Cumberland River on Highway 109 brought an end to the last of the ferry traffic and provided the county with a vital link to Interstate 40 to the south. (Courtesy of the Bob Perry Collection, Sumner County Archives.)

Five

Community Life

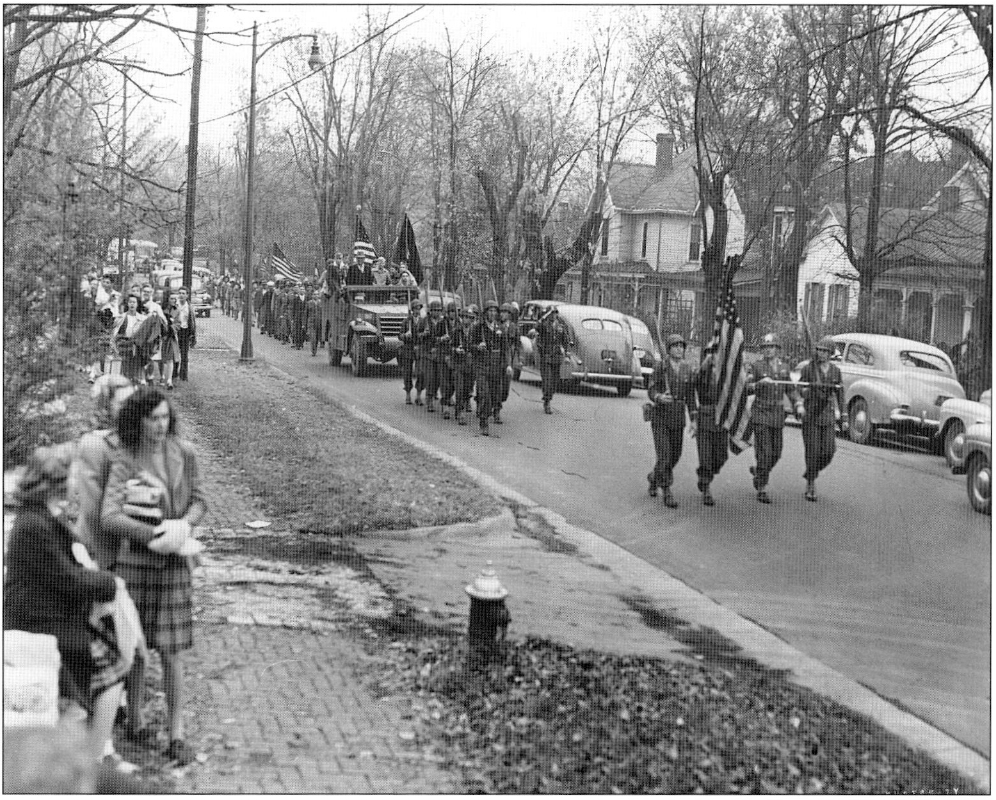

The unity suggested in the word "community" is demonstrated here in a WW II-era parade along East Main Street in Gallatin. (Photograph by W.C. Hackett, courtesy of Evelyn Hackett Tuttle.)

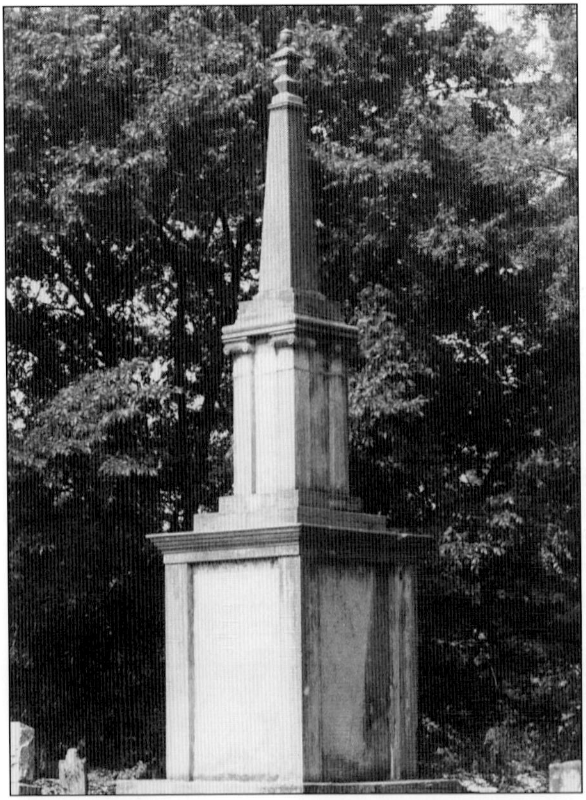

Erected in honor of Sumner County sons who served in the Mexican War, this monument stands in the old city cemetery. As a result of the enthusiastic response to the call for troops during the War of 1812, Sumner County attained the nickname "The Volunteer County" in the Volunteer State. The response of Sumner men to subsequent wars, including the war for which this monument was erected, kept alive that tradition of honor and service to country. (Courtesy of the Bob Perry Collection, Sumner County Archives.)

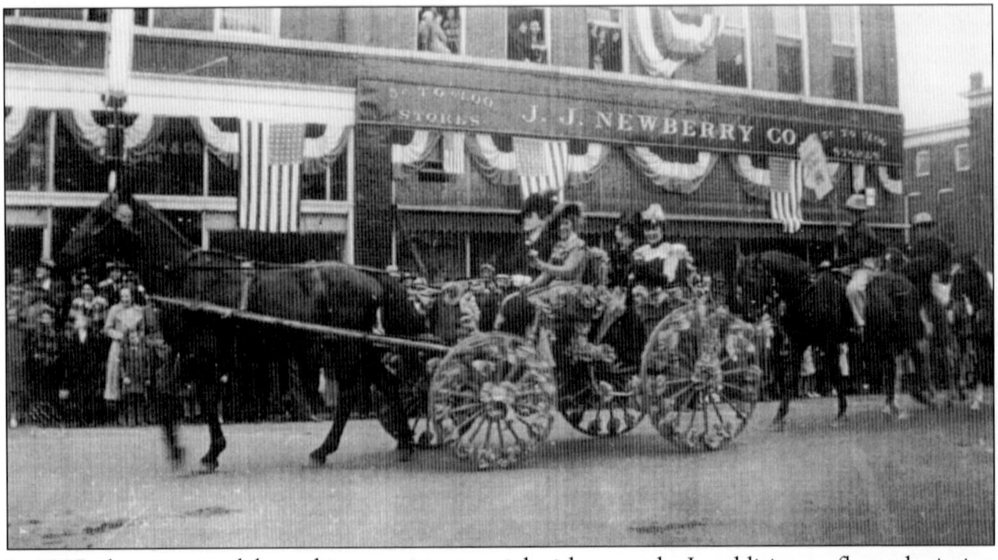

In 1937, the county celebrated its sesquicentennial with a parade. In addition to floats depicting Sumner County events, people, and buildings, flower-bedecked carriages such as this one delighted crowds that lined the streets and windows of buildings. (Courtesy of Kenneth C. Thomson Jr.)

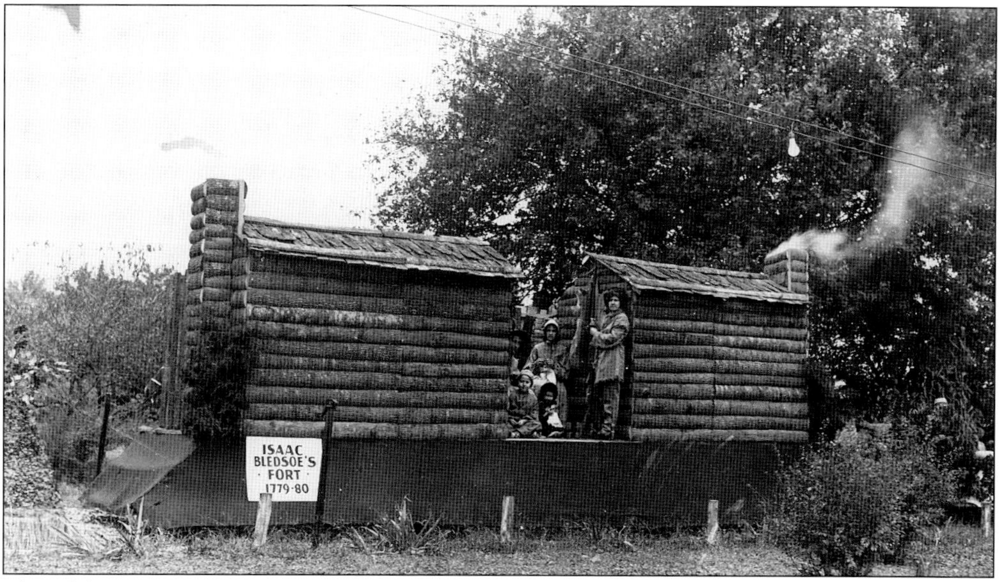

This elaborate sesquicentennial float honored Sumner County's rich history with a recreation of Isaac Bledsoe's Fort at Castalian Springs (1779–1780). (Courtesy of Kenneth C. Thomson Jr.)

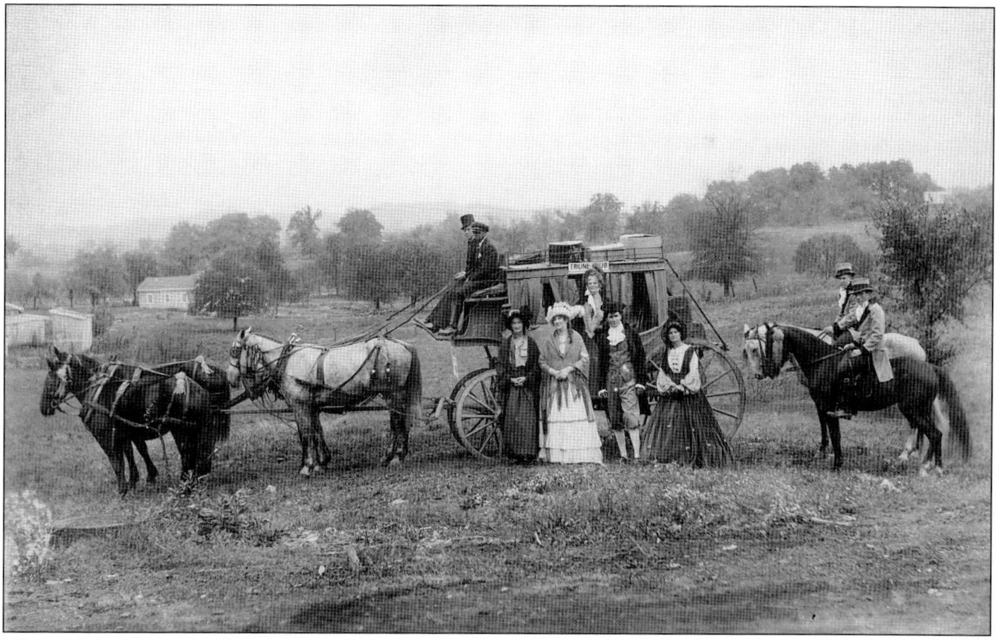
The old stagecoach also appeared in the sesquicentennial parade. Passengers included Rebecca Broderick (standing in doorway) and, from left to right, (front row) Mrs. George Winchester Wynne of Wynnewood, Mrs. Lewis Cass Guild of Rosemont, Judge William Puryear Jr., and Mrs. John M. Branham of Foxland Hall. (Courtesy of Kenneth C. Thomson Jr.)

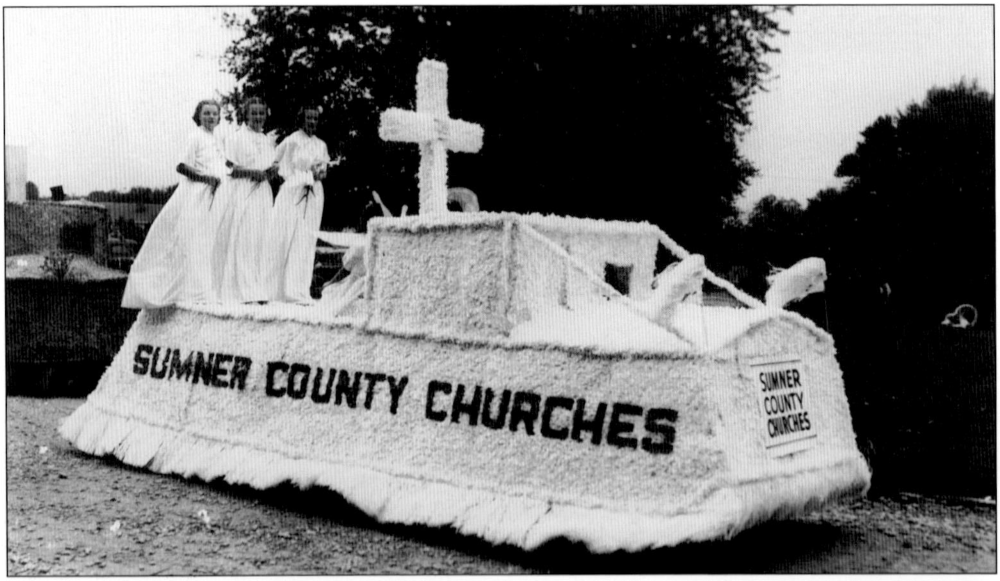

Pictured from left to right, Frances Withers, Martine Chaffin, and Kate Garth Dunklin grace the float representing the various churches of Sumner County in the sesquicentennial parade in 1937. (Courtesy of Kenneth C. Thomson Jr.)

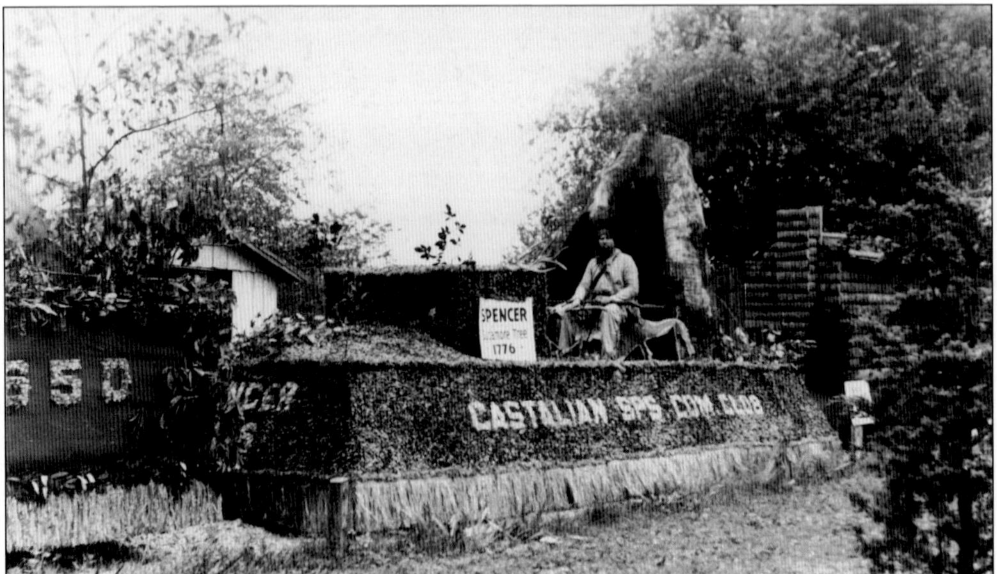

One of Sumner County's most eccentric characters, "Big Foot" Spencer, is depicted roasting a chicken in front of his sycamore tree home on this sesquicentennial float. (Courtesy of Kenneth C. Thomson Jr.)

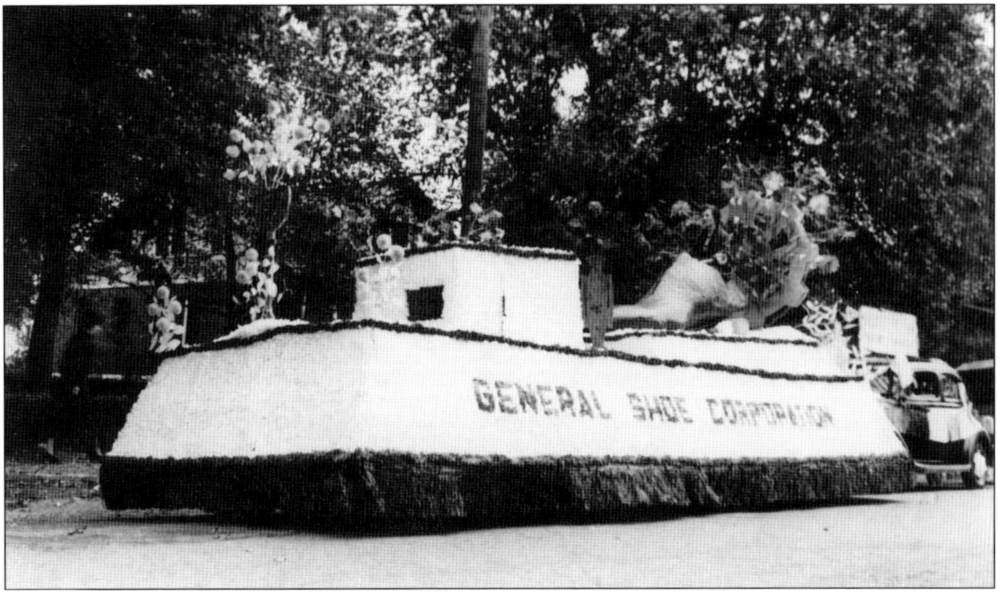

Business and industry was also represented in the parade. Here, Mr. Sam Hassell is seated in a big leather shoe aboard the float representing General Shoe Corporation. (Courtesy of Kenneth C. Thomson Jr.)

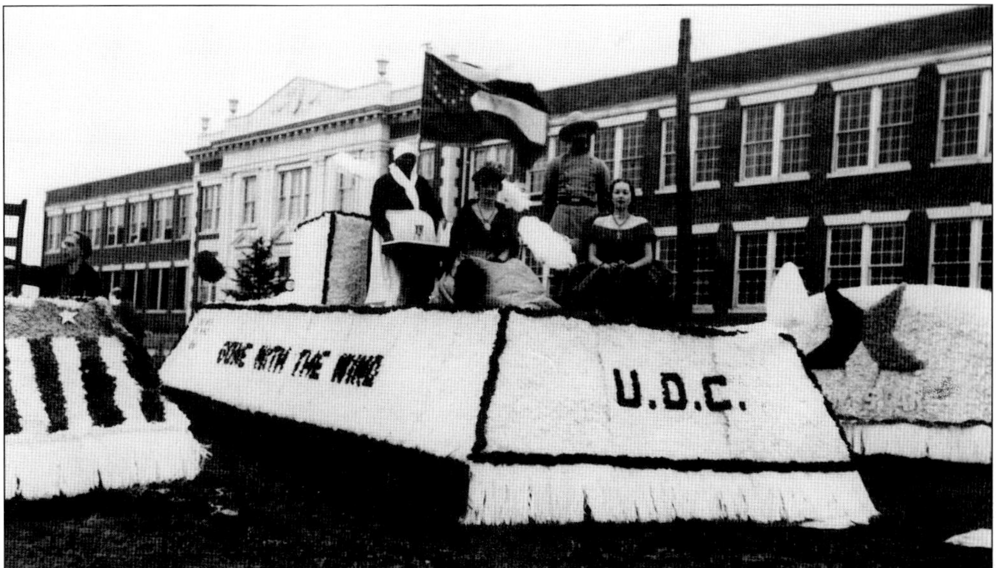

Margaret Mitchell's popular novel, *Gone with the Wind*, was the theme for the float sponsored by the United Daughters of the Confederacy. The float is pictured alongside others in front of Gallatin High School in preparation for the parade. (Courtesy of Kenneth C. Thomson Jr.)

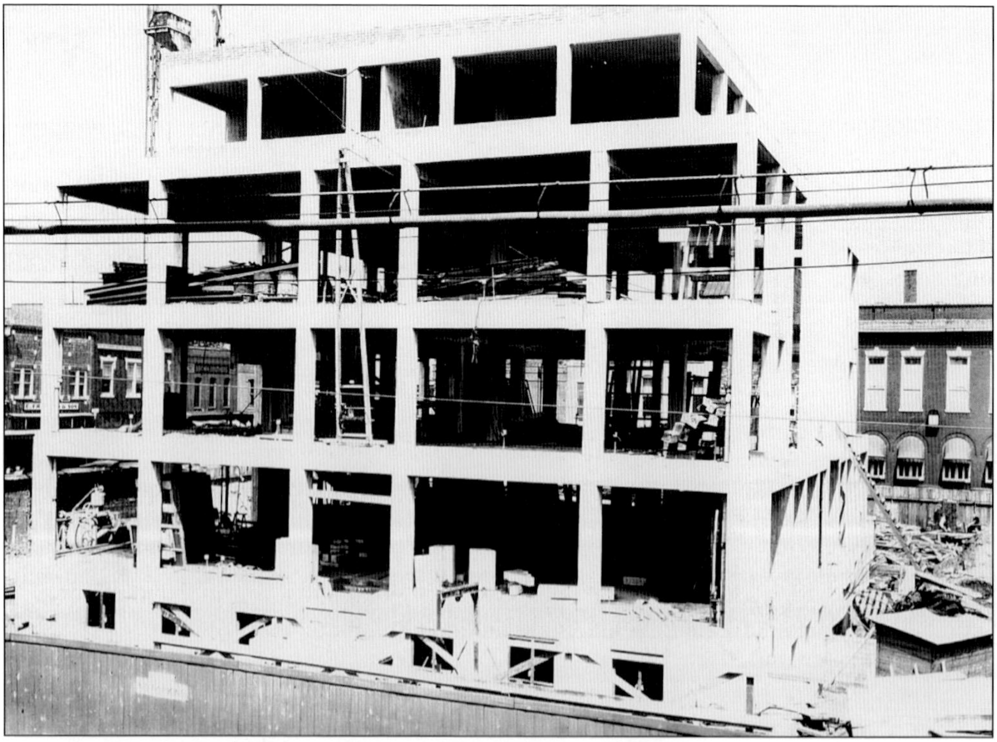

This photograph showing the construction of the new courthouse in the late 1930s reveals the skeleton of the structure. (Courtesy of the Bob Perry Collection, Sumner County Archives.)

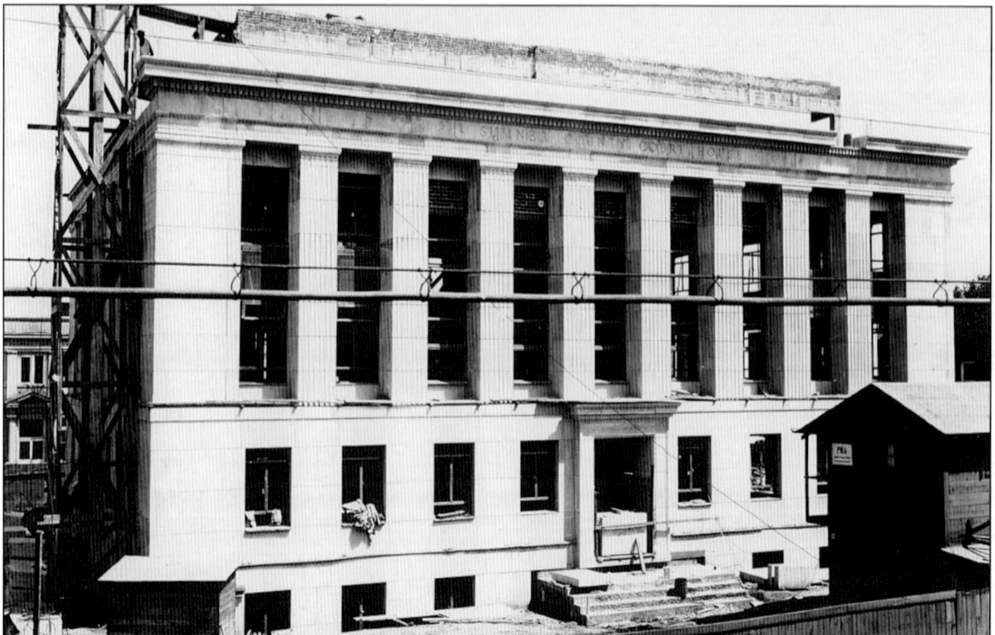

The sign for Mare and Holman Architects (lower left) sits atop the protective fence that surrounded the courthouse during construction. The building replaced the 1837 brick courthouse. (Courtesy of the Bob Perry Collection, Sumner County Archives.)

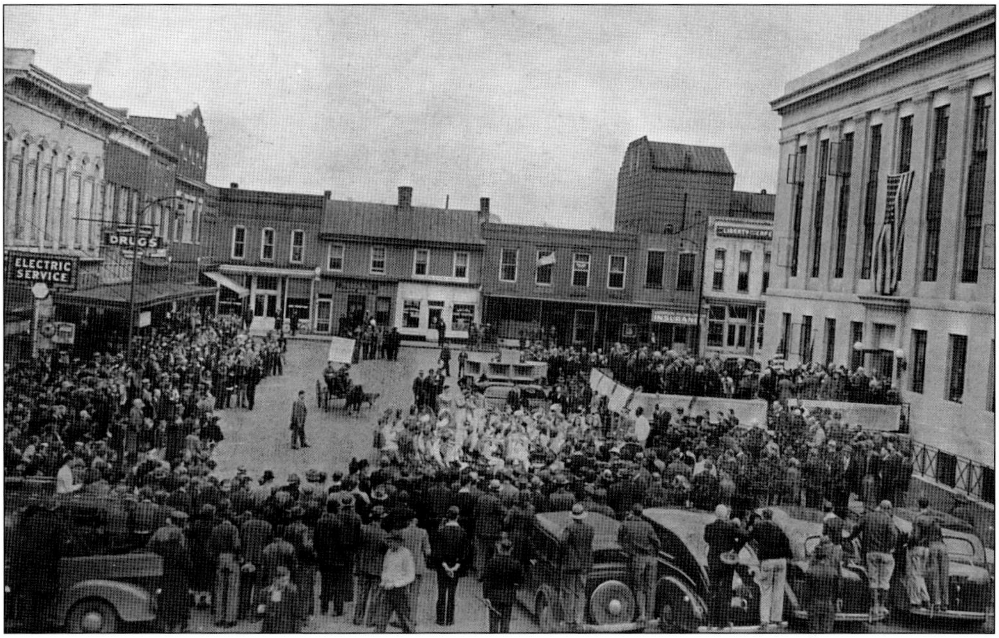

Crowds and automobiles line the Public Square at the dedication ceremonies for the new courthouse on May 1, 1940. The row of amplifiers behind the band in the center of the photograph enabled the crowds to hear the activities coming from the crowded speakers' platform. (Courtesy of the Bob Perry Collection, Sumner County Archives.)

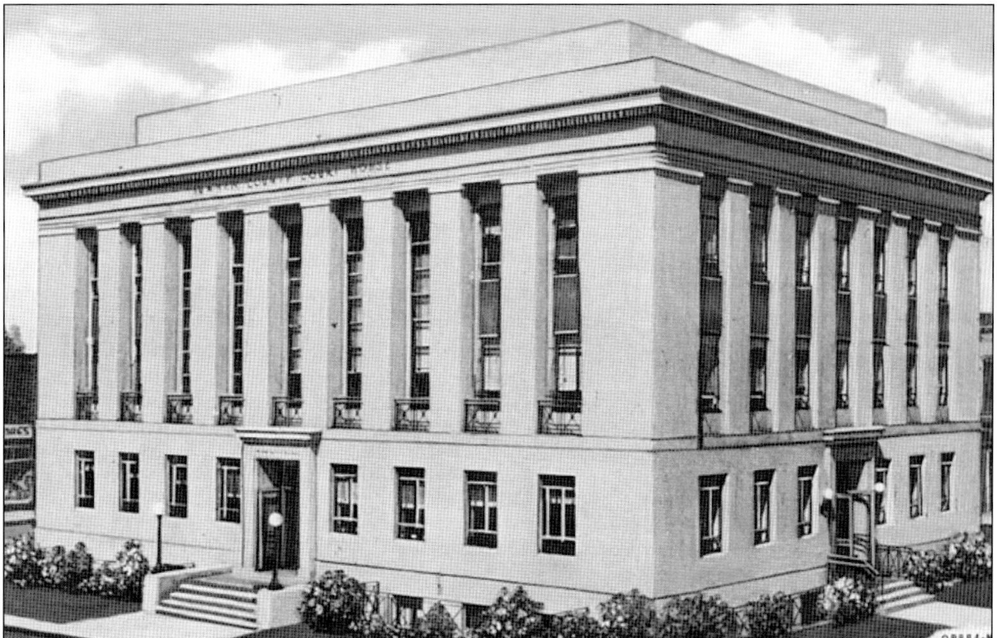

This old postcard shows the completed Sumner County Court House on the Public Square in Gallatin. (Courtesy of Kenneth C. Thomson Jr.)

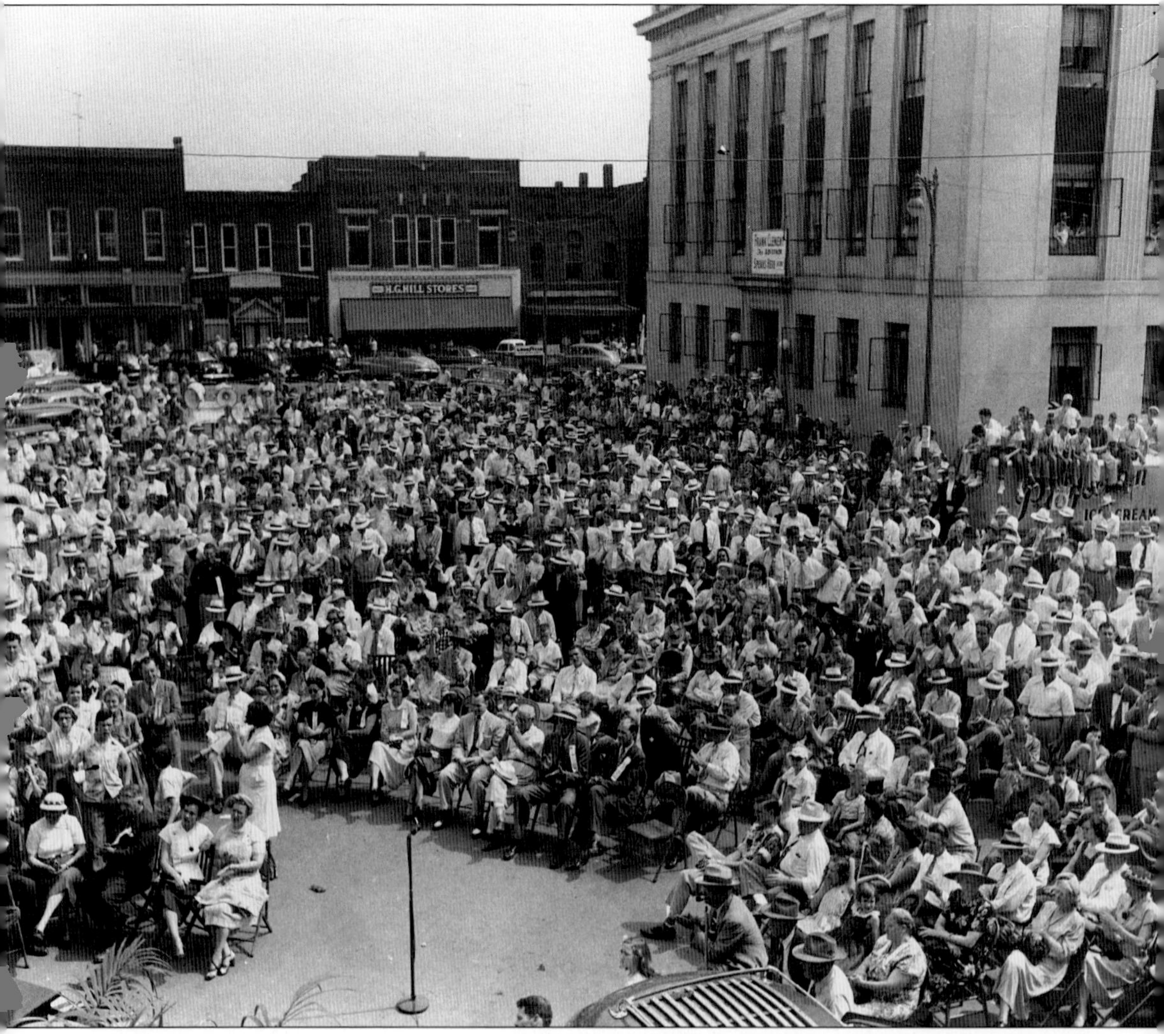

In the days before television began to dominate political campaigns, local rallies were heavily attended as voters gathered to hear candidates. This is part of a large crowd that gathered on the public square in Gallatin in June 1952 to hear Frank Clement during his first bid for governor. Maynard Meguiar introduced the speaker. A Clement banner hangs above the courthouse doorway. In this photograph, the speakers' platform is located to the left just out of the frame. (Courtesy of Pat Meguiar.)

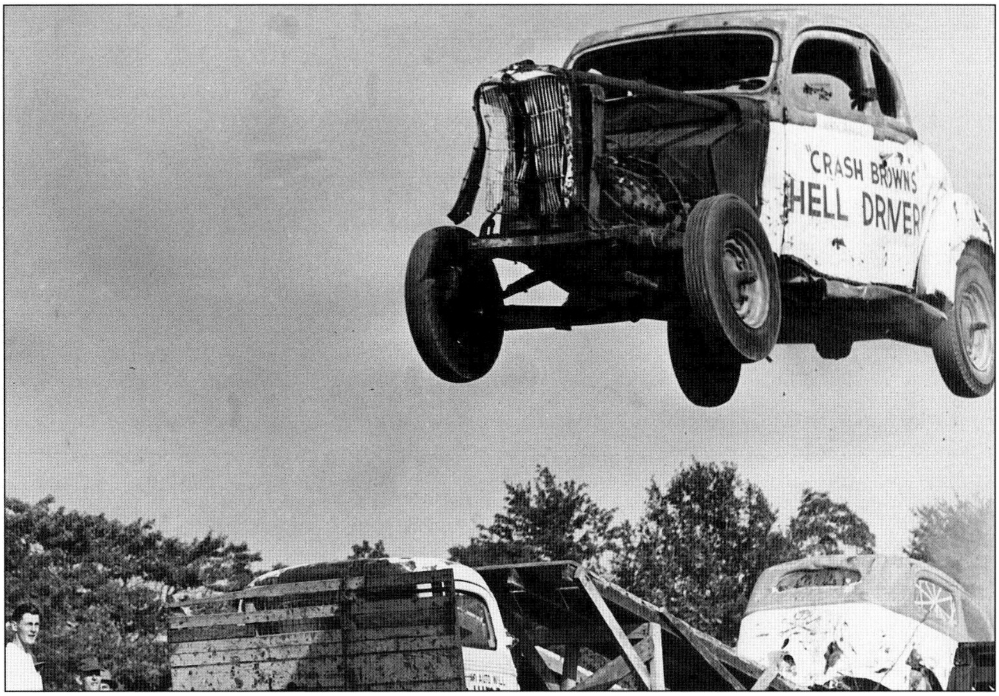

Political speakers were not the only ones capable of drawing huge crowds. Local celebrity and stunt driver "Crash" Brown and his "Hell Drivers" provided audiences with thrills and spills that included jumping automobiles. (Courtesy of Kenneth C. Thomson Jr.)

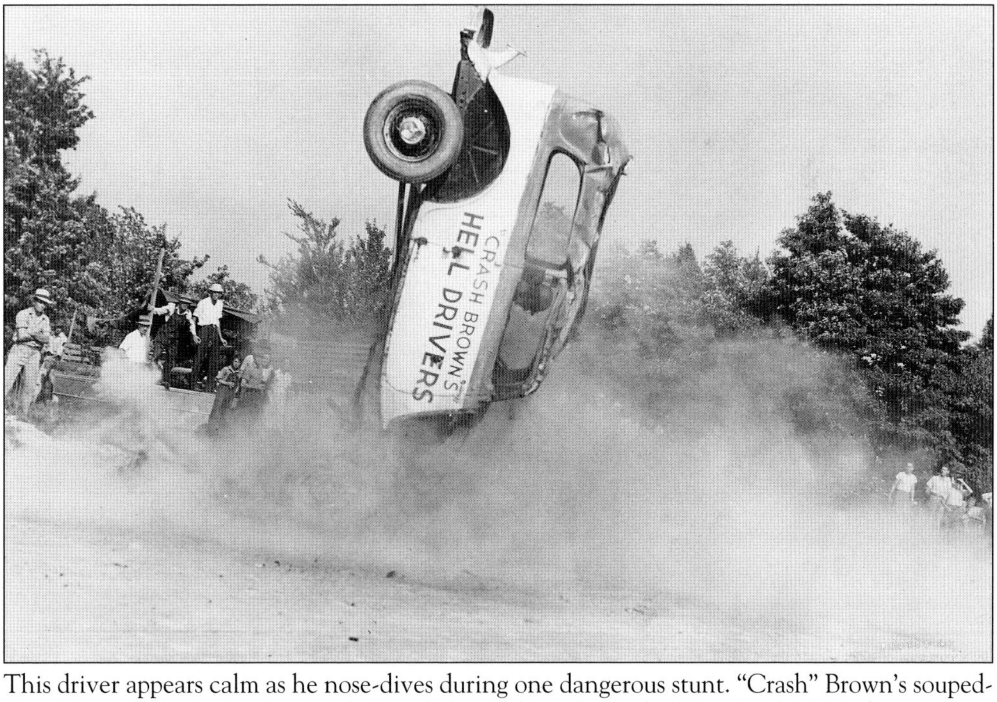

This driver appears calm as he nose-dives during one dangerous stunt. "Crash" Brown's souped-up jalopies performed at fairs and special shows throughout the 1950s and 1960s. (Courtesy of Kenneth C. Thomson Jr.)

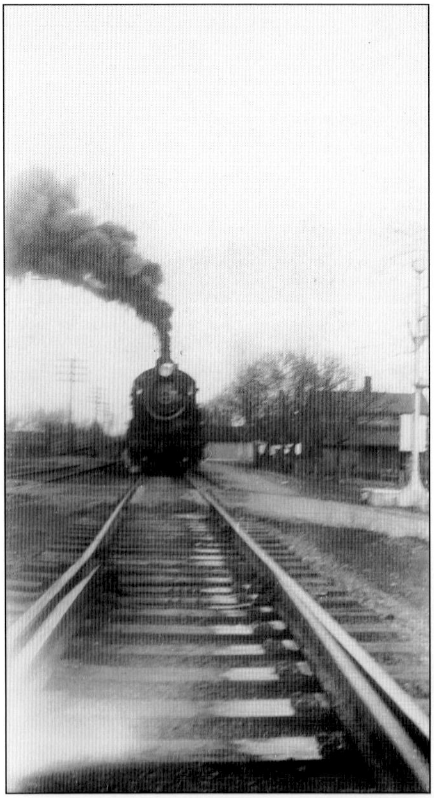

Traveling from Scottsville, Kentucky to Nashville, this steam-engine powered train traveled a regular route through Hendersonville. (Courtesy of Quinton Coppage.)

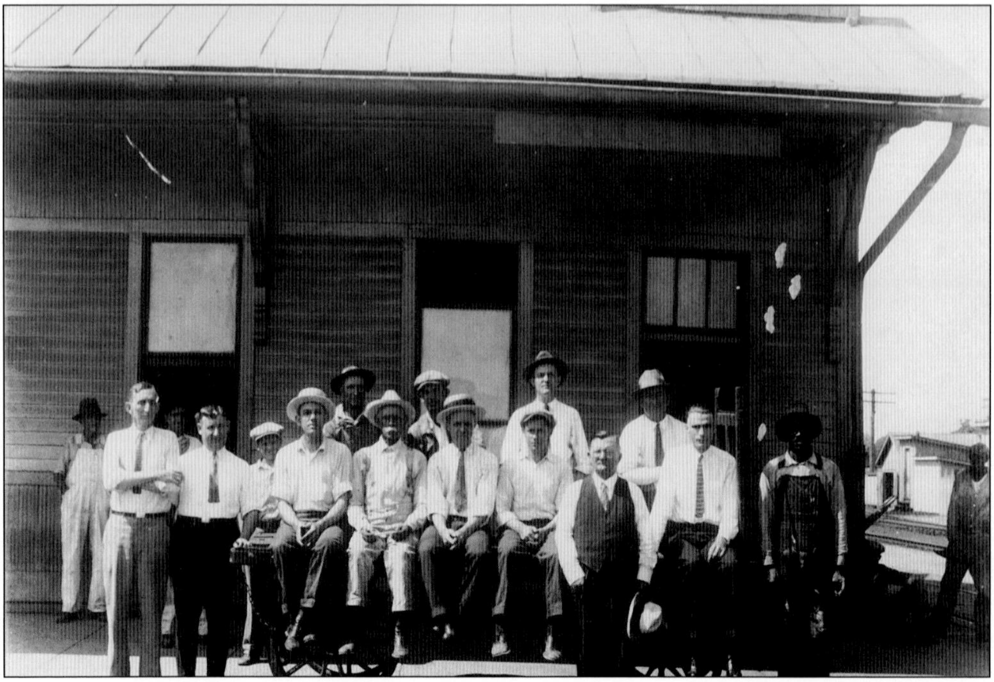

Gallatin Mayor Empsey W. Thompson (seated, center, and wearing tie) joins a number of friends aboard a wagon outside the Gallatin train depot. (Courtesy of Elvera M.G. Neal.)

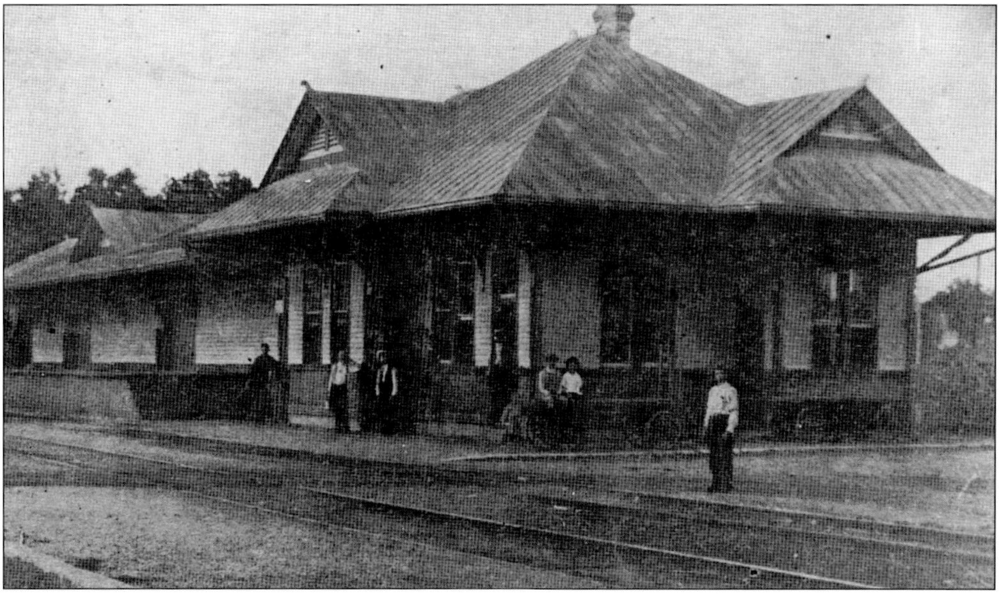

For many years the Portland Depot played a vital role in the life of the community. Lumber, local manufacturing, and a dynamic strawberry industry kept trains rolling in and out of Portland, while passenger trains transported family members, soldiers, and visitors. (Courtesy of Allen Haynes.)

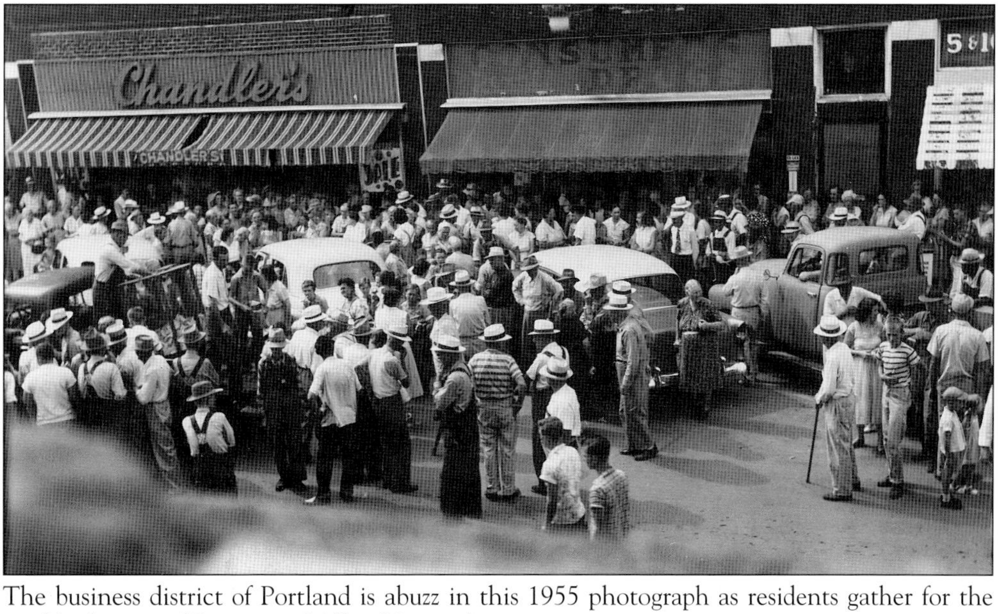

The business district of Portland is abuzz in this 1955 photograph as residents gather for the weekly drawing. (Courtesy of Allen Haynes.)

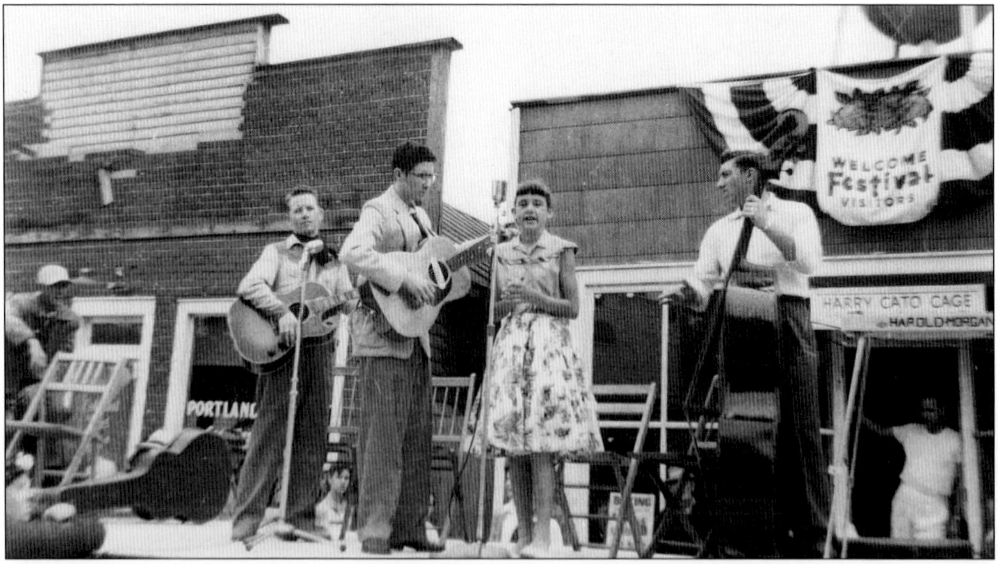

One of Tennessee's premier annual events is the Portland Strawberry Festival. On-stage performances, band competitions, crafts, and parades highlight the festival. Here, young Janet Groves entertains crowds from one of the many temporary stages scattered around the town. (Courtesy of Allen Haynes.)

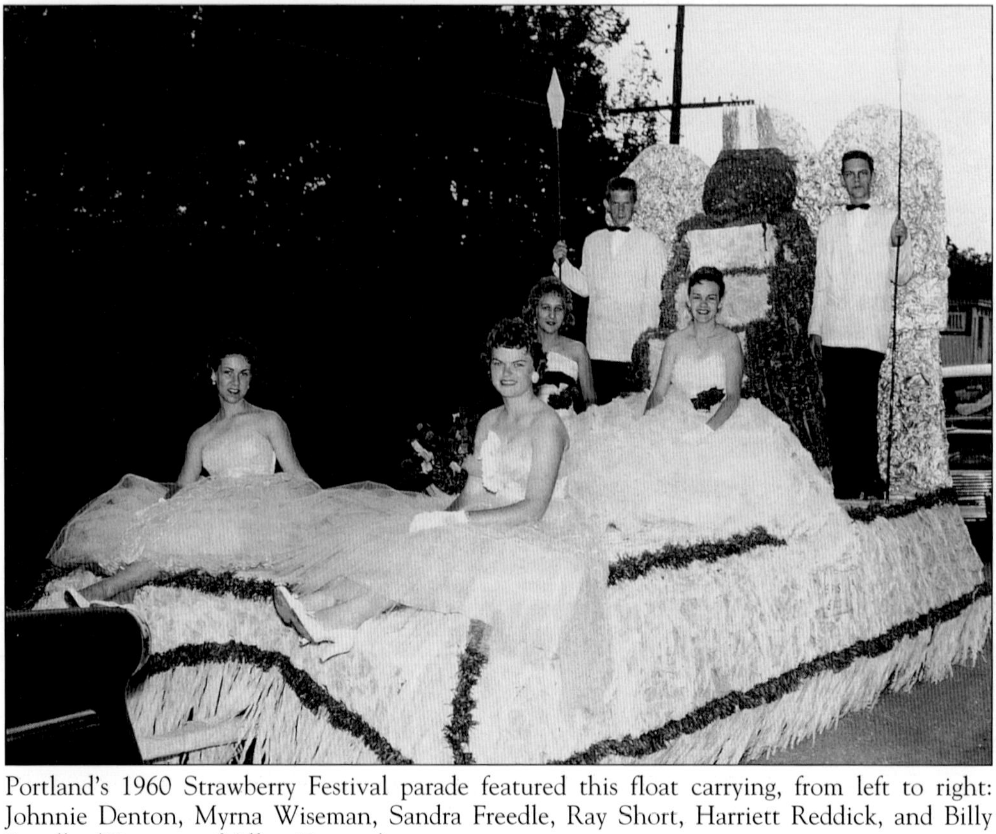

Portland's 1960 Strawberry Festival parade featured this float carrying, from left to right: Johnnie Denton, Myrna Wiseman, Sandra Freedle, Ray Short, Harriett Reddick, and Billy Freedle. (Courtesy of Allen Haynes.)

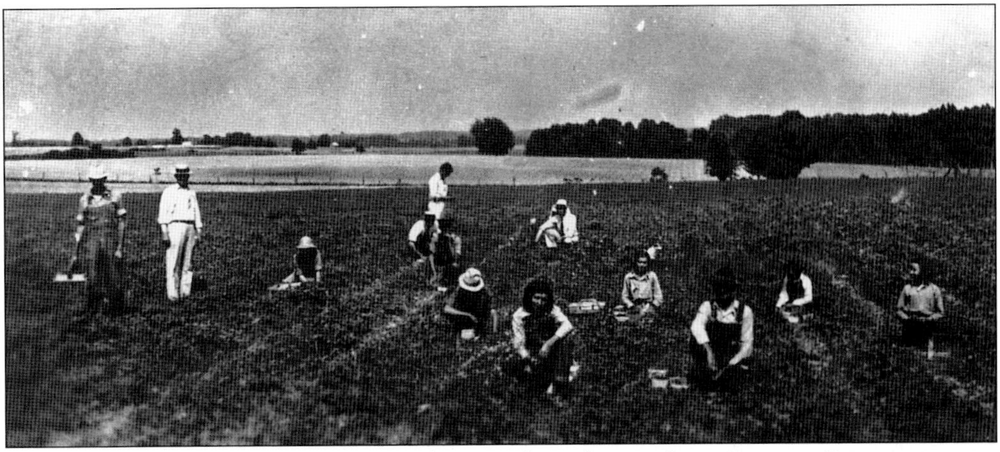

The strawberry industry was a major claim to fame for northern Sumner County since its introduction in the late 1800s. By the 1930s, Portland and surrounding communities furnished an estimated 20 percent of the nation's strawberry crop. That percentage dropped dramatically by the 1980s, but the famed strawberry festival continues to be a major community event. (Courtesy of the Bob Perry Collection, Sumner County Archives.)

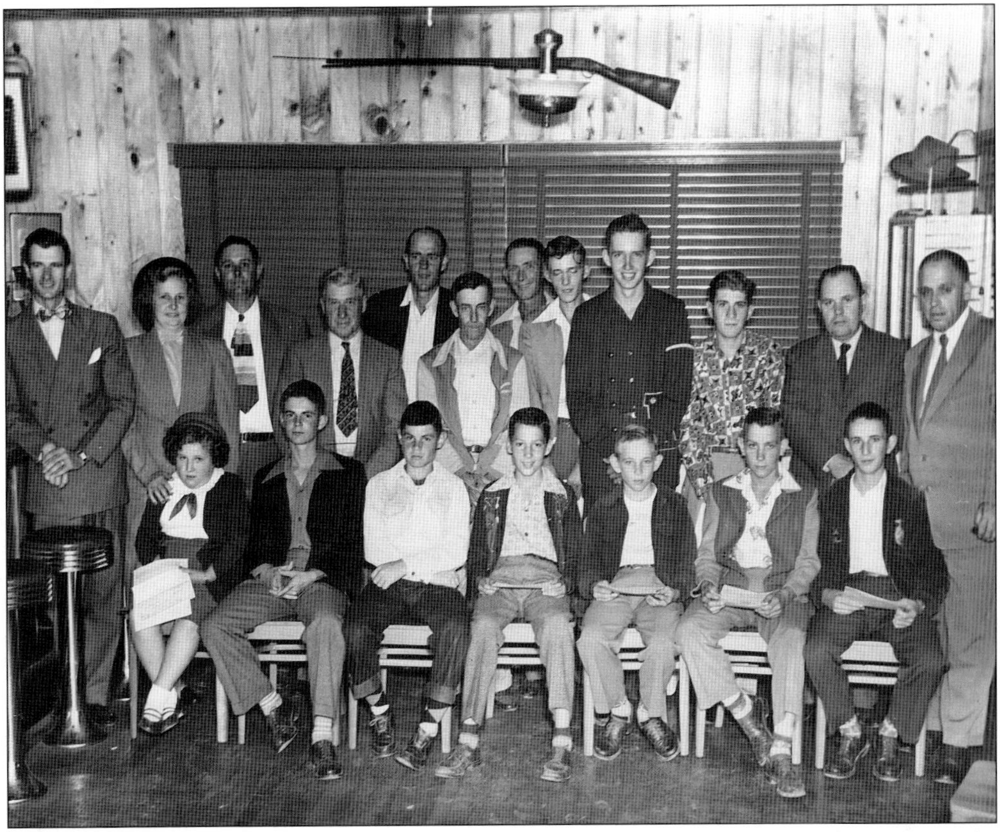

The Future Farmers of America has served generations of young people as they prepare for careers in agriculture. Hugh Love, who contributed a number of photographs to volume I of *Around Gallatin and Sumner County*, is pictured on the far left of the back row. (Courtesy of Kenneth C. Thomson Jr.)

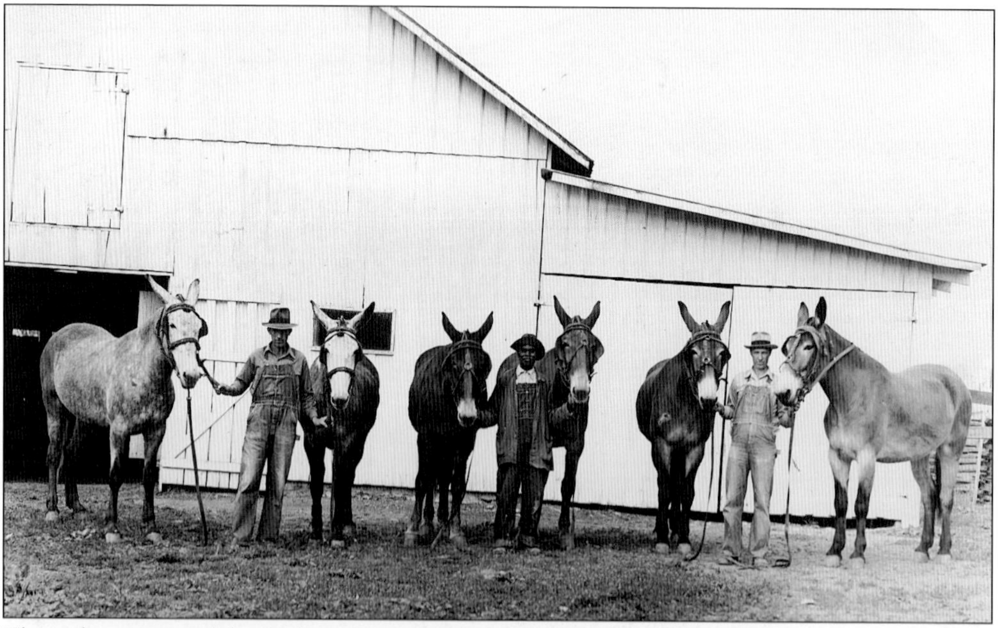

Throughout most of the 20th century, Sumner County remained a largely rural area, with the majority of the population involved in some form of agriculture. Pictured here are six excellent mules from the Reese Mule Farm. The quality of mules raised in Sumner County was recognized throughout the nation. For example, Sumner County has provided many of the mules used for treks down the Grand Canyon. (Courtesy of Evelyn Hackett Tuttle.)

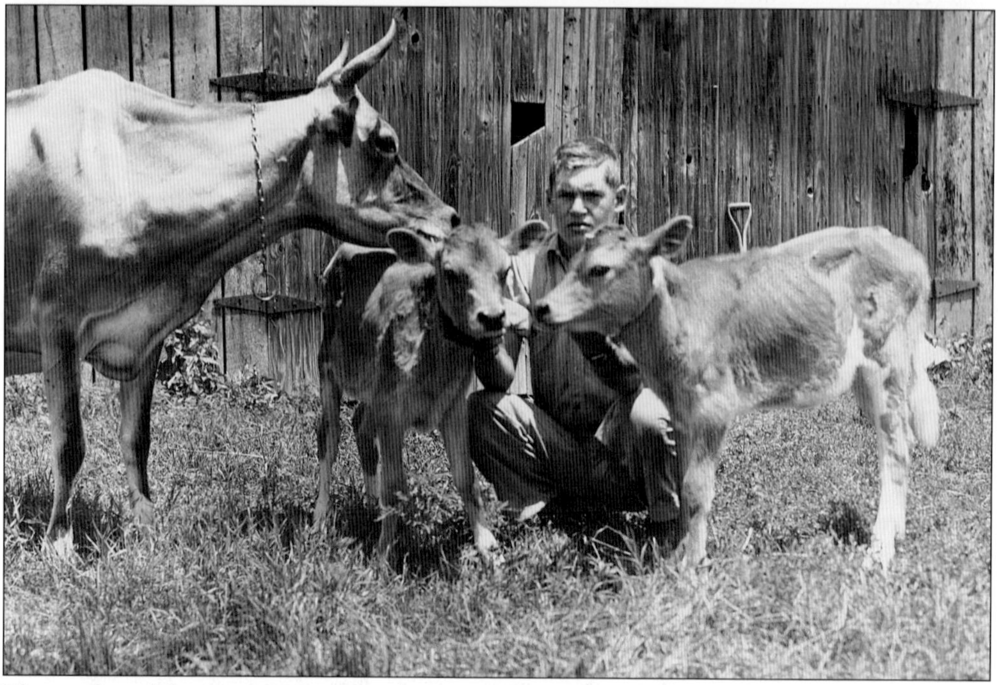

The cattle and dairy industries were also important to the county's economy. Here, "Chigger" Overton shows off a cow and two calves at his farm near Bethpage. (Photograph by W.C. Hackett, courtesy of Evelyn Hackett Tuttle.)

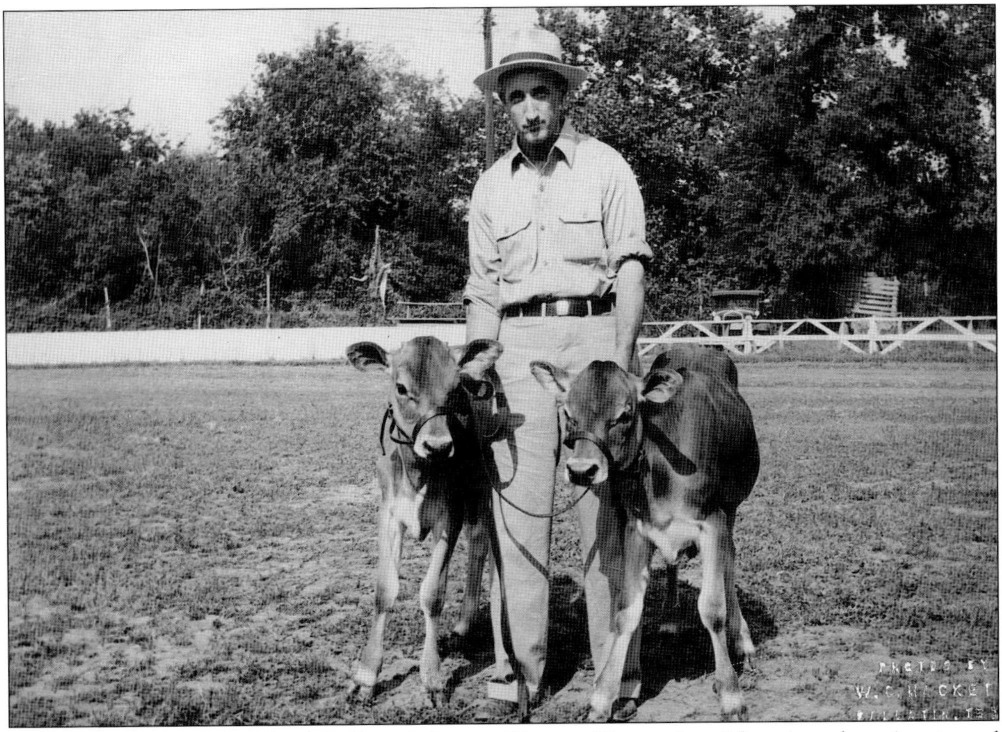

W.C. Hackett photographed Gallatin's Junius Gleaves Turner Jr. with twin calves Annie and Eva. (Courtesy of Kenneth C. Thomson Jr.)

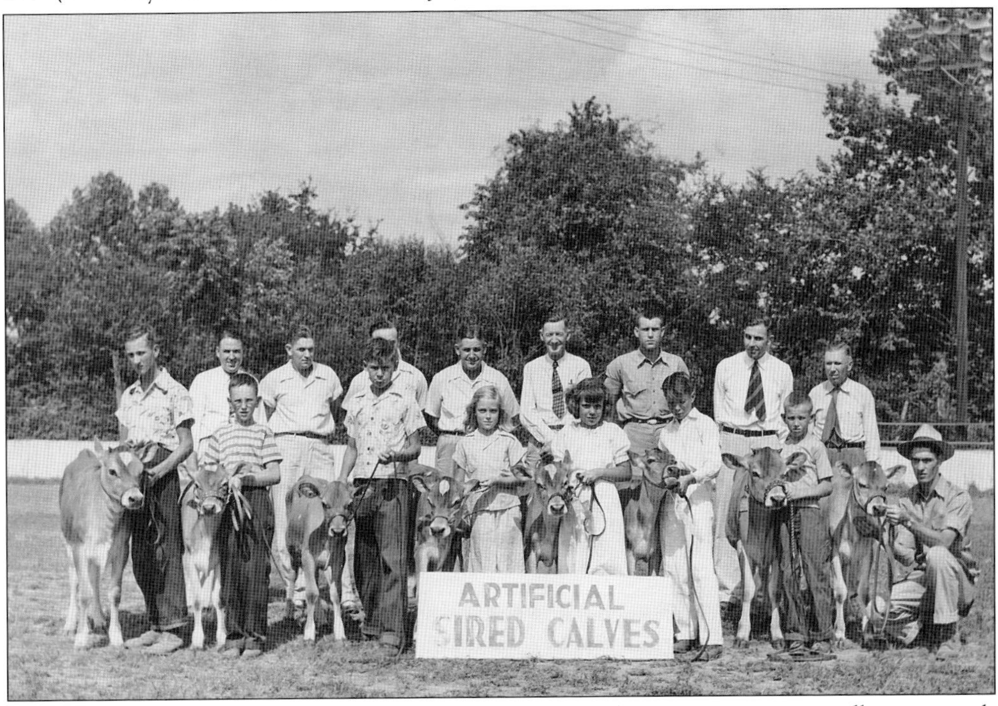

Decades before the cloning of "Dolly" the sheep, Gallatin youngsters proudly pose with artificially sired calves. (Photograph by W.C. Hackett, courtesy of Evelyn Hackett Tuttle.)

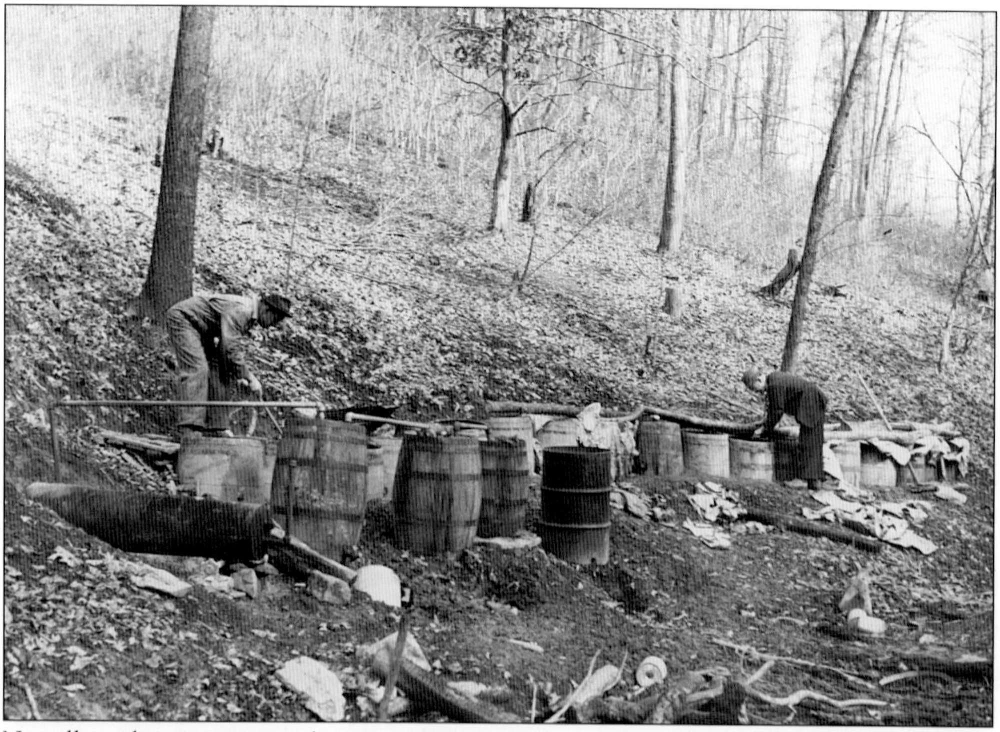

Not all rural activities were legitimate. W.C. Hackett photographed Sheriff Harris Reddick and Deputy Earnest Roberts as they examine fermented mash at an illegal still in rural Sumner County. The manufacturing of illegal "moonshine" reached its peak during the years of Prohibition but continued sporadically among the rural population throughout the remainder of the century. (Courtesy of Evelyn Hackett Tuttle.)

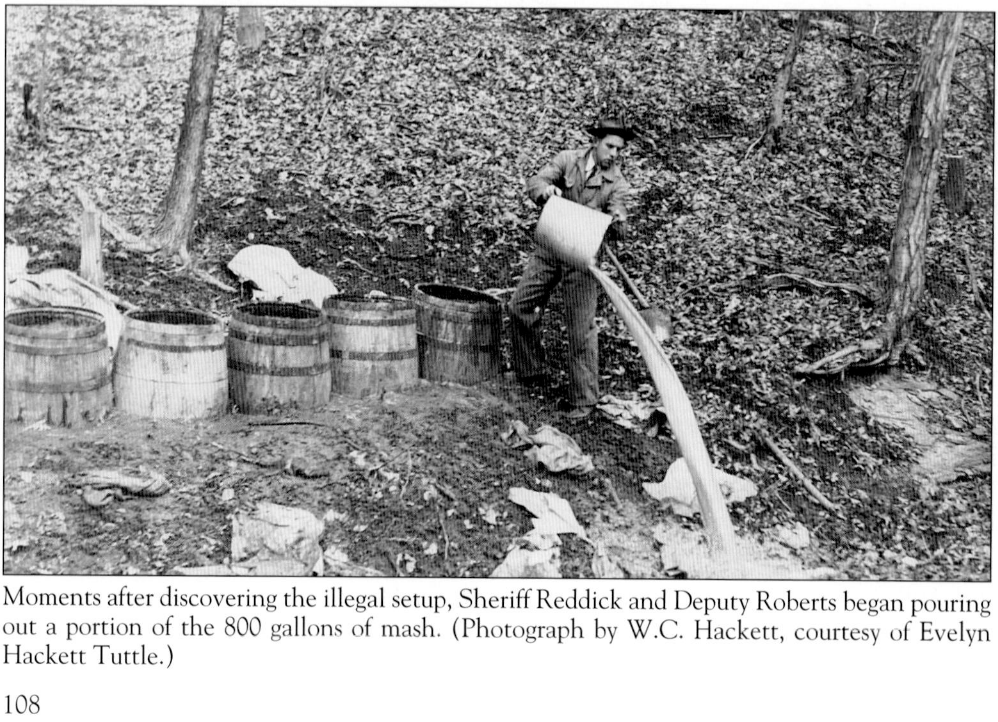

Moments after discovering the illegal setup, Sheriff Reddick and Deputy Roberts began pouring out a portion of the 800 gallons of mash. (Photograph by W.C. Hackett, courtesy of Evelyn Hackett Tuttle.)

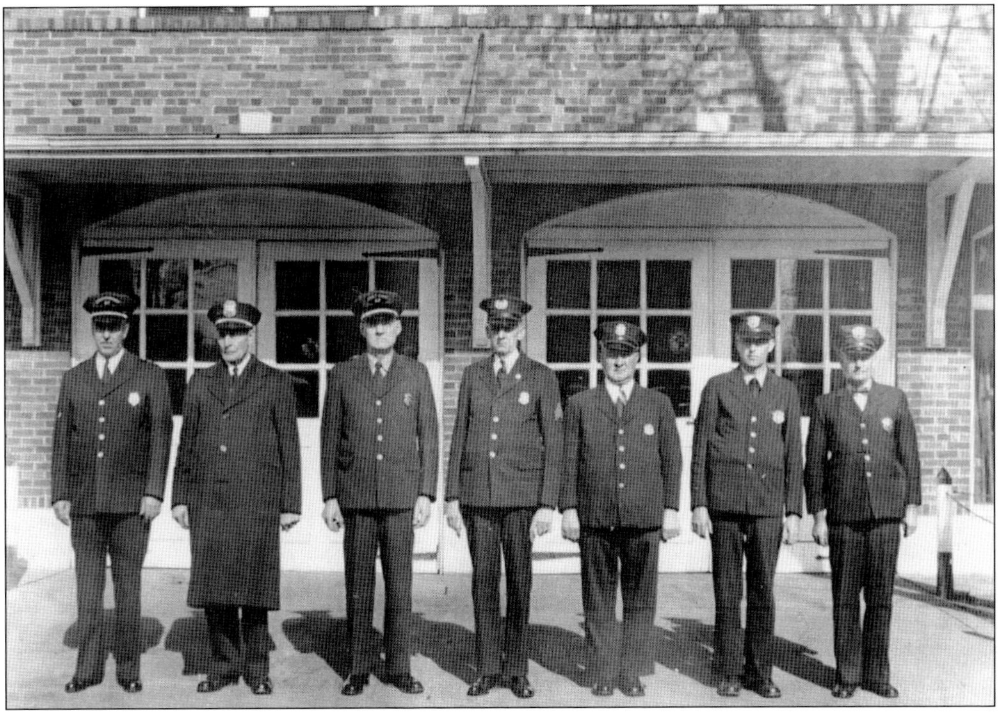

Communities looked to local police and fire departments for protection. Here, the police officers and firemen of Gallatin pose in front of the city hall. Pictured, from left to right, are as follows: Roy Weatherford, Bert Wallace, ? McCrory, Jim Trout, George Harrison, ? Jones, and A.P. Lee. (Courtesy of Allen Haynes.)

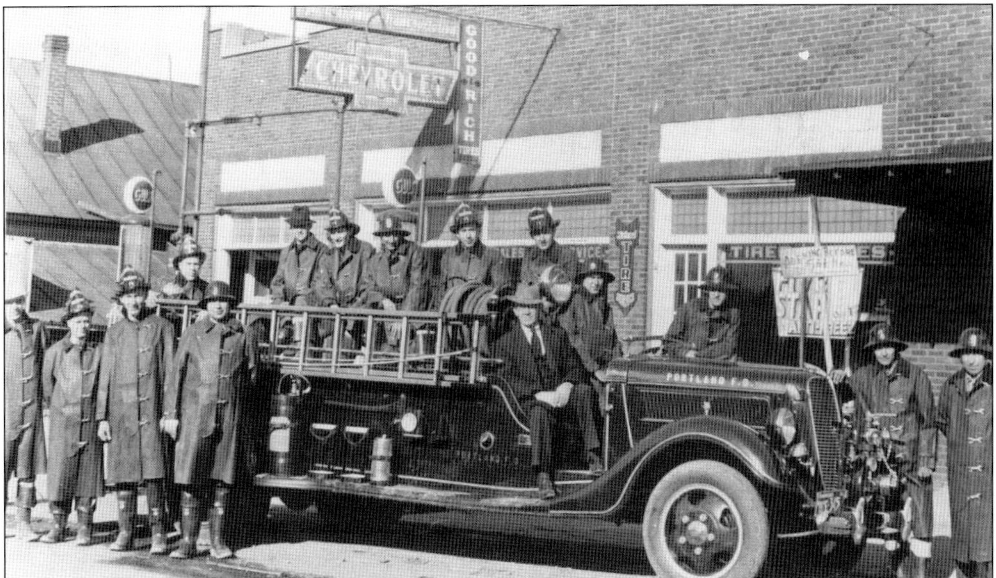

Dick Hill (in suit), who served as the mayor of Portland from 1933 to 1939, is pictured here with members of the Portland Fire Department. This Chevrolet dealership was housed in a former Ford dealership. (Courtesy of Allen Haynes.)

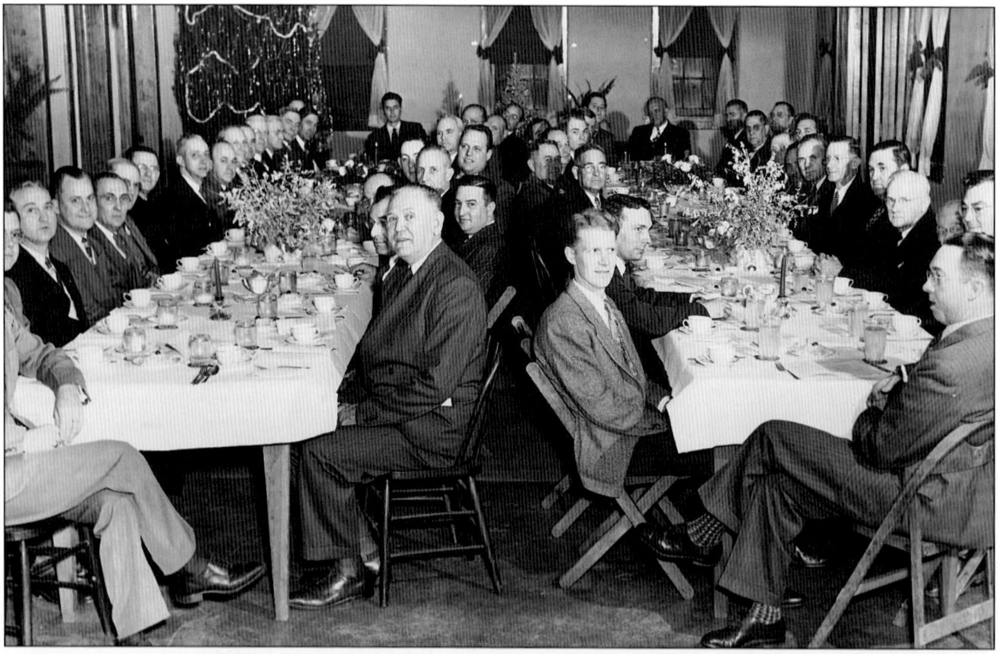

Another aspect of community life were the organizations which satisfied both service and social functions. Members of the Gallatin Rotary Club enjoy a Christmas dinner at the First Presbyterian Church. William P. Puryear Jr. sits at the head of the table to the left, while Church of Christ minister Brother Harold Leroy Olmstead sits at the head of the table on the right. (Photograph by W.C. Hackett, courtesy of Evelyn Hackett Tuttle.)

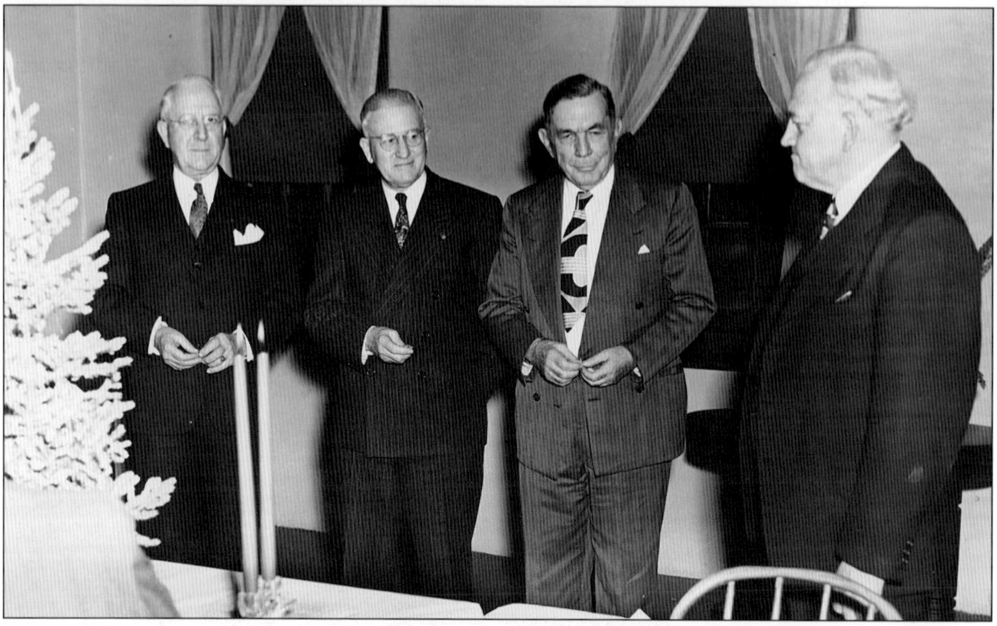

Pictured from left to right, Rotary members Leslie M. Ross (insurance), John T. Franklin (postmaster), Judge J. Woodall Murray Sr., and Brother Harold Leroy Olmstead (minister) meet at the same Rotary Christmas function in the late 1940s. (Photograph by W.C. Hackett, courtesy of Evelyn Hackett Tuttle.)

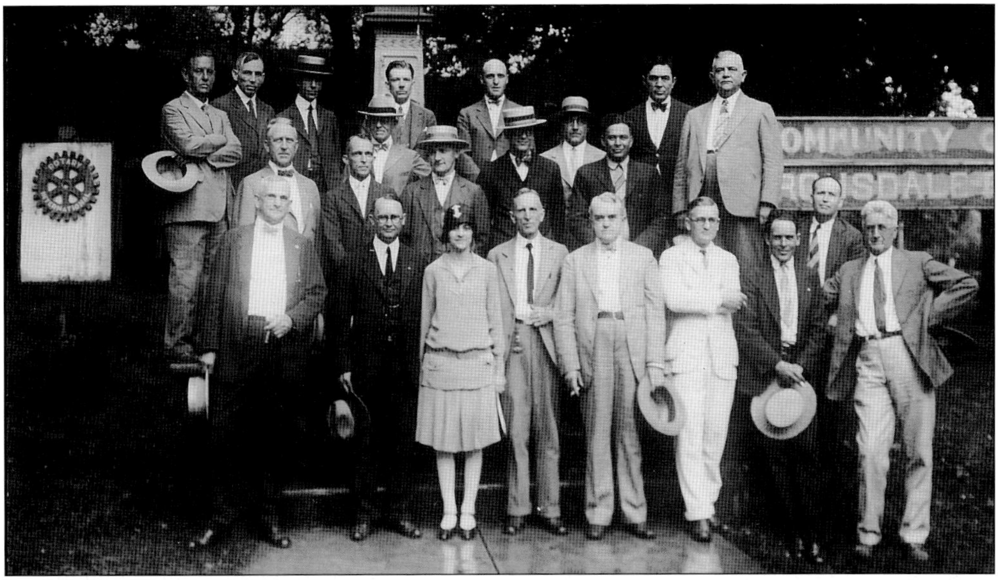

The Rotary Club of Gallatin is pictured in front of historic Trousdale Place. The woman is Virginia Mae (Brown) Patterson. Dr. Lewis Miller Woodson (front row, far left) and Dr. J.M. Ashburn (front row, far right) were mentioned in the Lackey cartoon on page 63. (Courtesy of Kenneth C. Thomson Jr.)

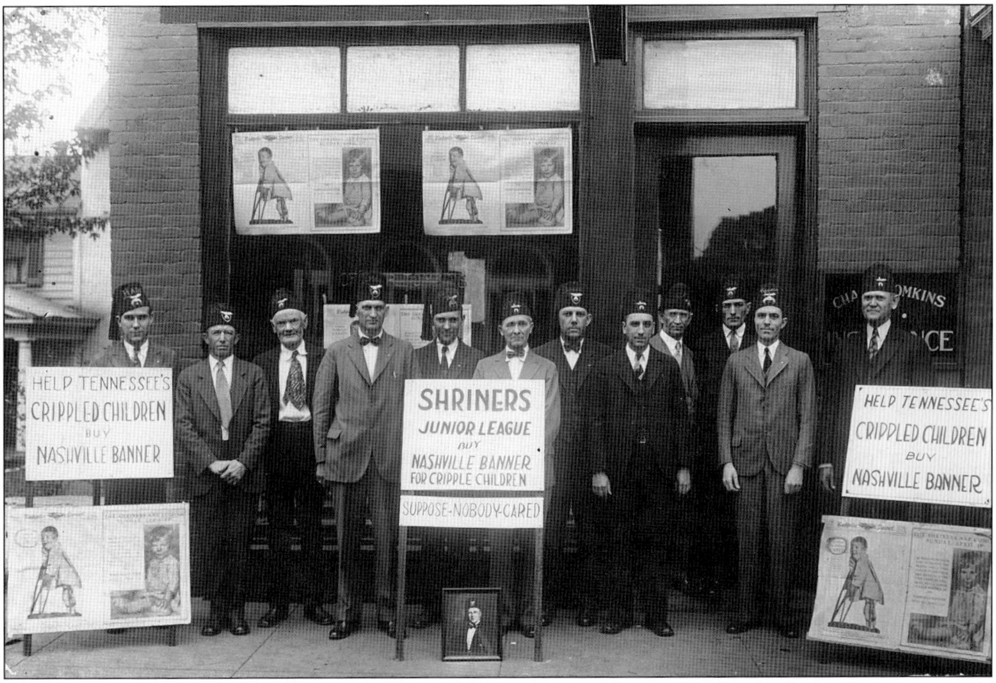

The Gallatin Shriners joined forces with the Junior League and the *Nashville Banner* for a fund-raiser to benefit crippled children. Harold Tillman Hix stands fifth from the left. (Courtesy of Kenneth C. Thomson Jr.)

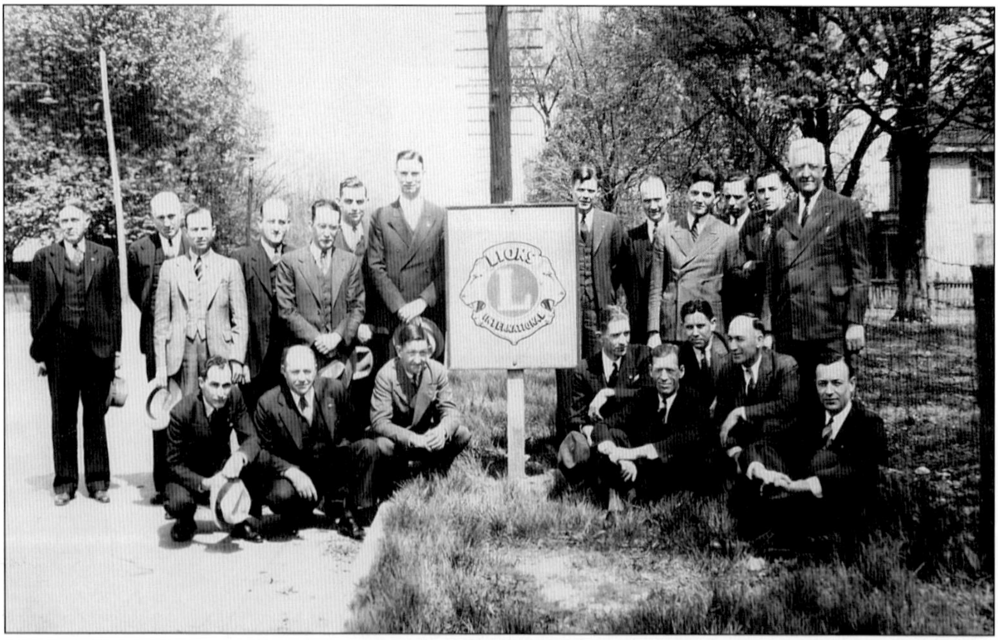

During the early part of the 20th century, the number of fraternal and service organizations grew. Here, members of Lions International pose beside the organizational sign on the outskirts of Gallatin. (Courtesy of the Bob Perry Collection, Sumner County Archives.)

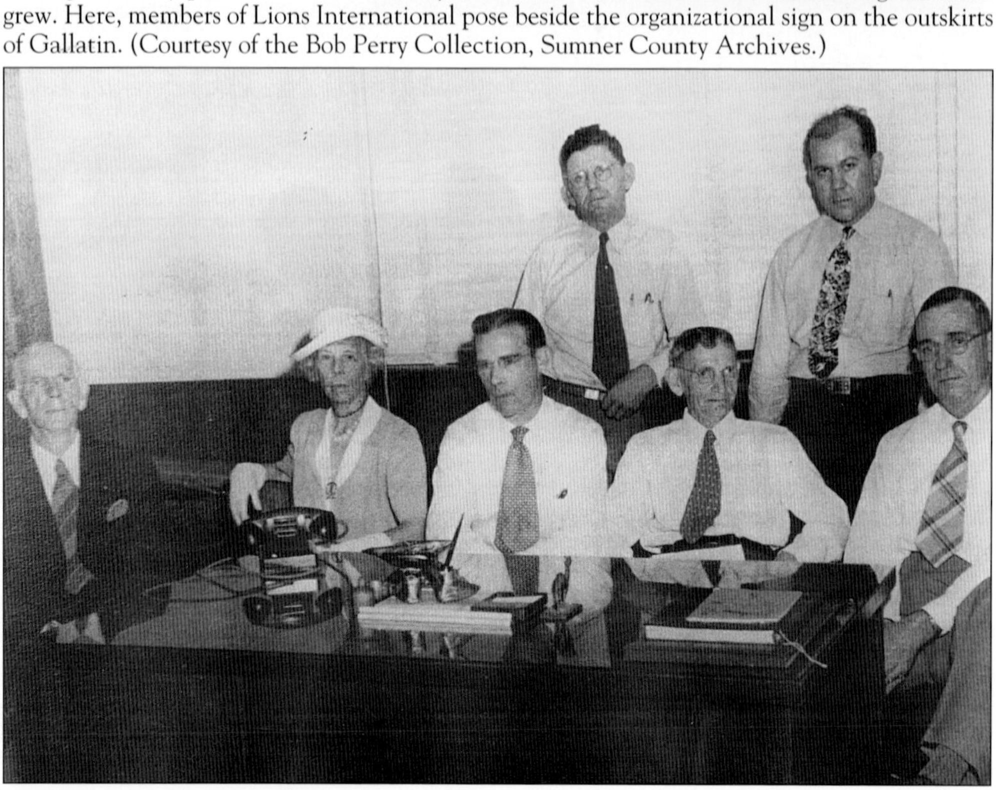

Members of the board at the Bank of Hendersonville meet, *c.* 1950. Members include, from left to right, Harvey Willis, Sarah Berry, Earl Hurt, Martin Curtis Sr., Horace Willis, Cornelius Breedlove, and Harold Roney. (Courtesy of Lee Curtis.)

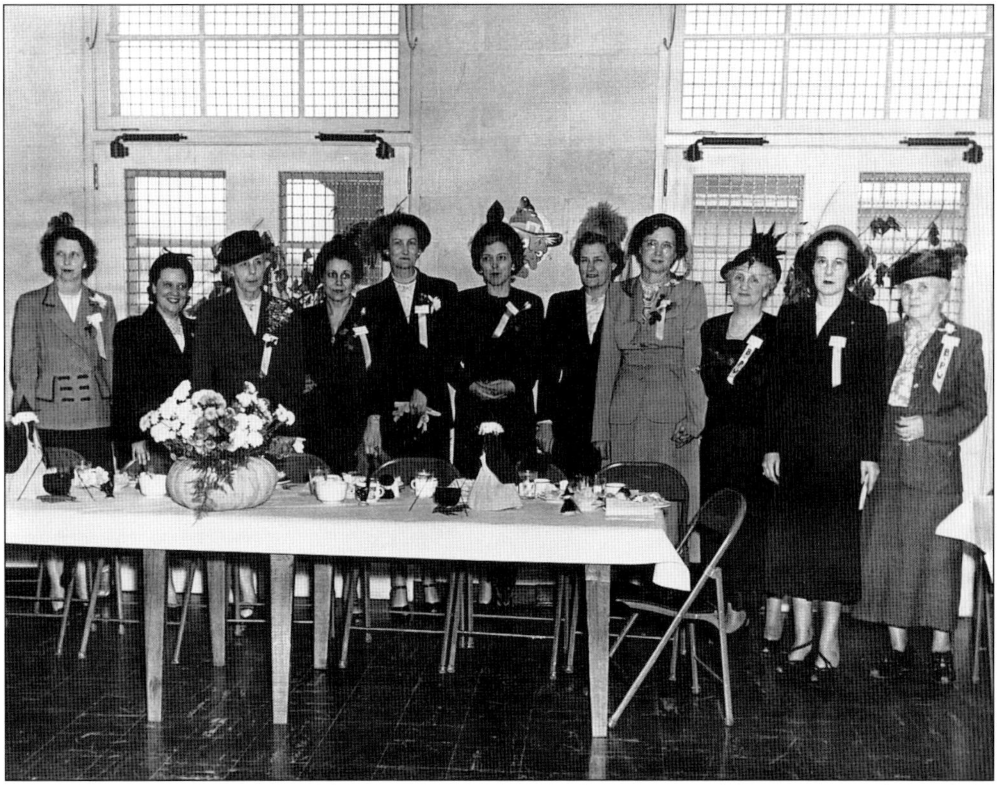

Women's organizations were likewise an active part of community life. Here, members of the Business and Professional Women meet for a luncheon. Pictured far right is Lizzie Payne, the Confederate widow of Edwin Sanders Payne. (Courtesy of Kenneth C. Thomson Jr.)

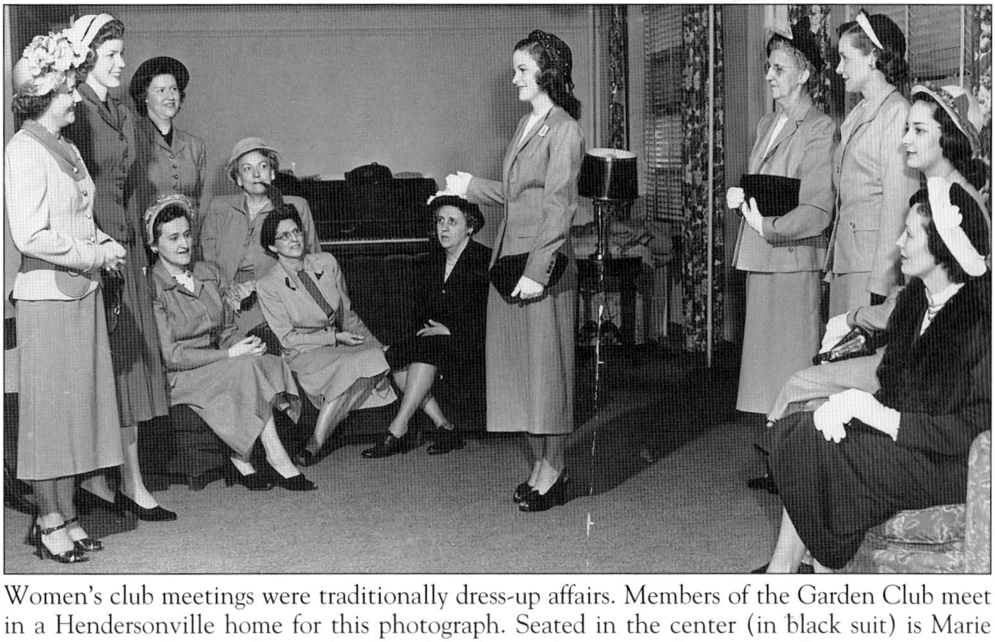

Women's club meetings were traditionally dress-up affairs. Members of the Garden Club meet in a Hendersonville home for this photograph. Seated in the center (in black suit) is Marie Comer of Monthaven, the mother of Jackie Comer. (Courtesy of Lee Curtis.)

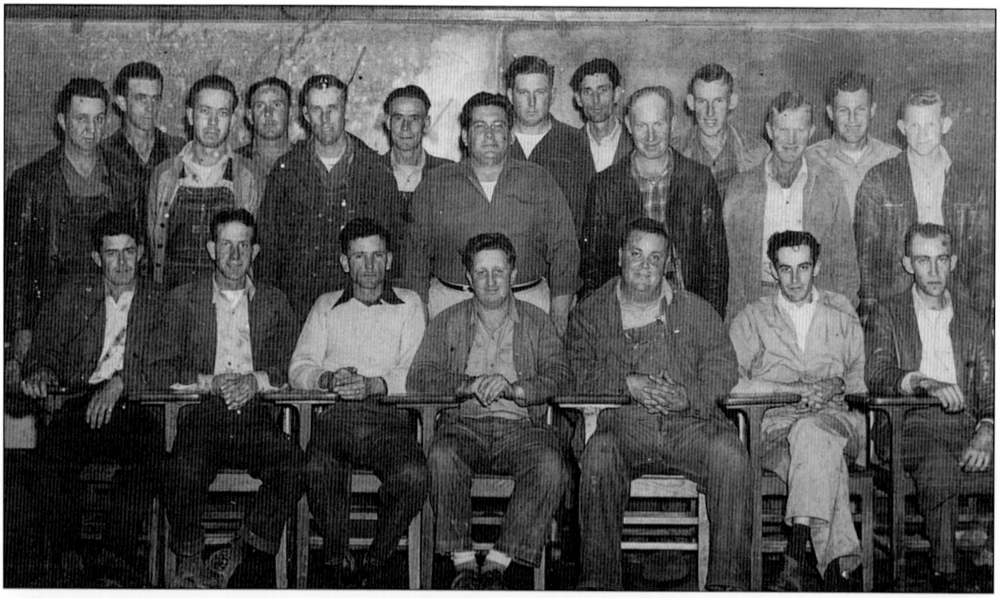

Following WW II, veterans took advantage of special classes in order to attain vocational training and improve their job prospects. (Courtesy of Allen Haynes).

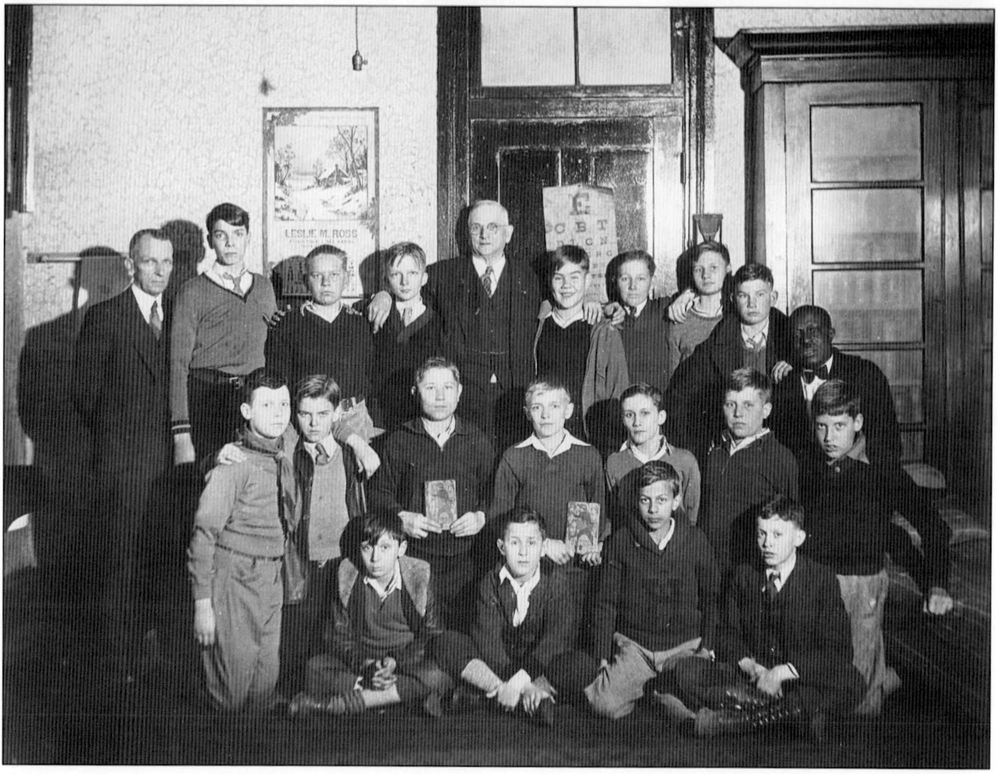

E.M. Stark photographed boy scouts in the office of Dr. Lewis Miller Woodson on the Gallatin Public Square. Dr. Woodson is pictured in the center of the back row and Presbyterian minister Rev. Charles Ramsey stands on the far left, back row. (Courtesy of Kenneth C. Thomson Jr.)

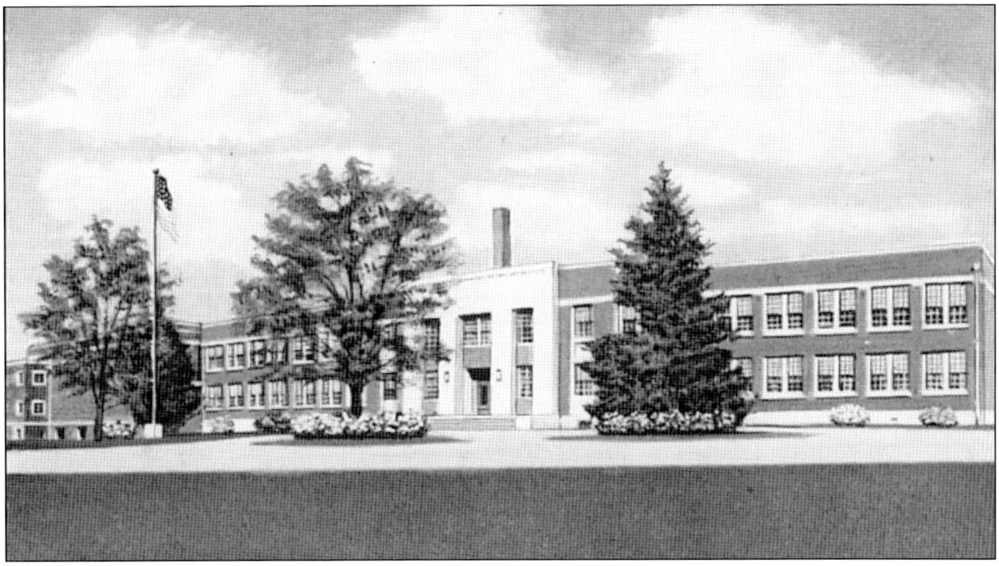

The new Gallatin High School, opened in the early 1930s, was featured on a postcard. (Courtesy of Kenneth C. Thomson Jr.)

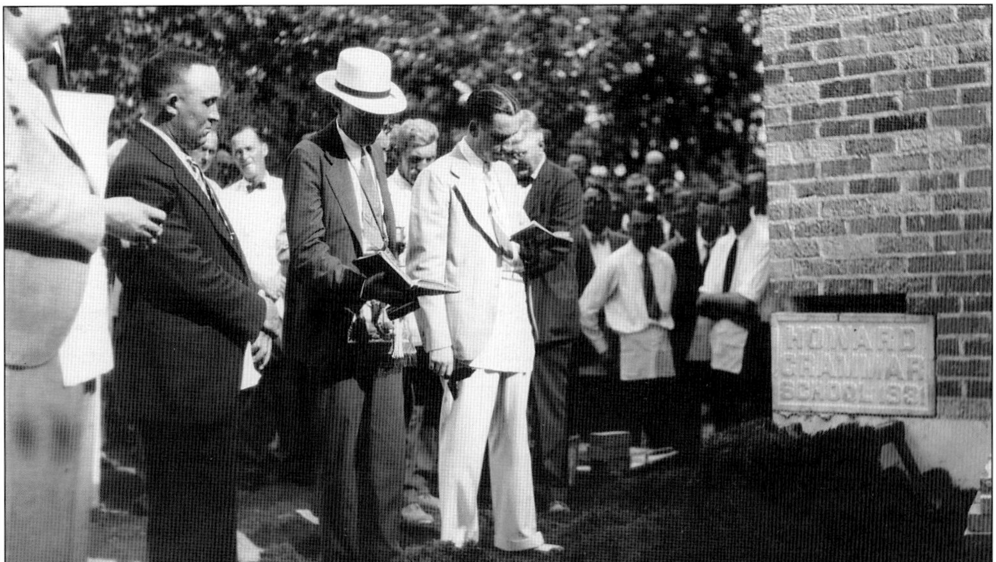

In 1931, the New Howard School opened on the site of the old Howard Female College in Gallatin. Designed by Nell Ferrell Harris (Mrs. W. Lee Harris), the school was built by contractors Robert and Madel Lassiter. This photograph shows the cornerstone of the building during dedication ceremonies. (Courtesy of Kenneth C. Thomson Jr.)

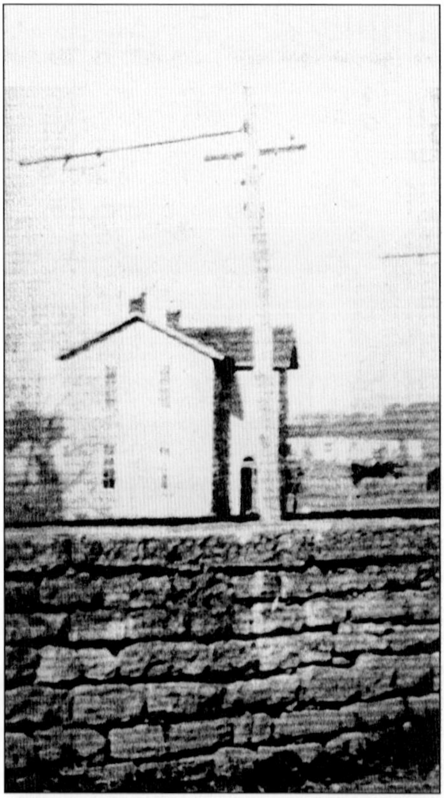

In the years before the creation of Old Hickory Lake, this Hendersonville school was located across Drakes Creek near the present-day Kroger store. (Courtesy of Quinton Coppage.)

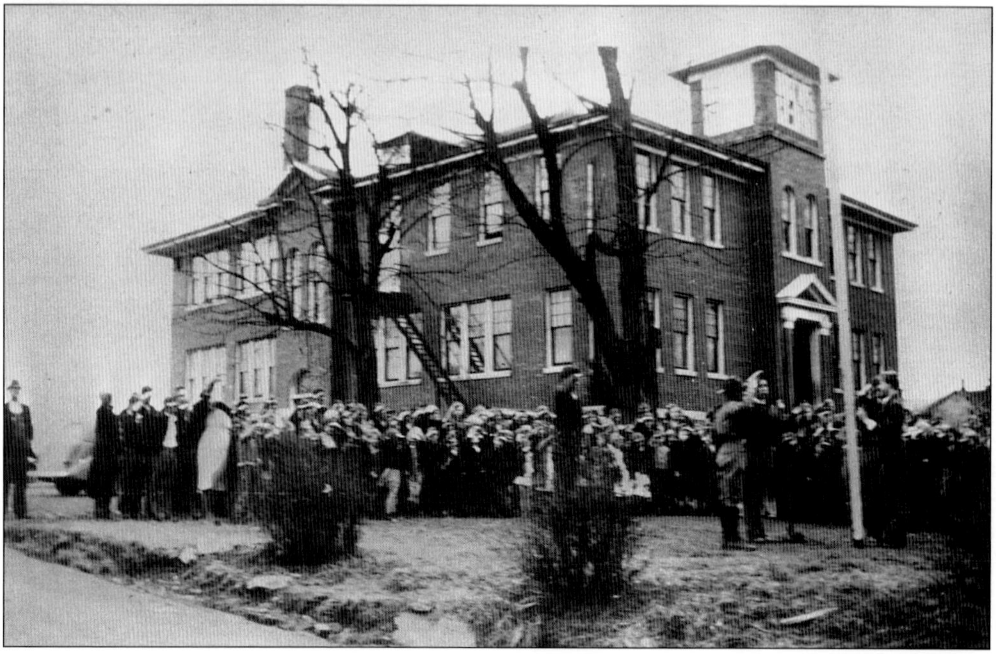

Hendersonville students gather in front of the high school for the raising of the flag and the pledge of allegiance. (Courtesy of the Bob Perry Collection, Sumner County Archives.)

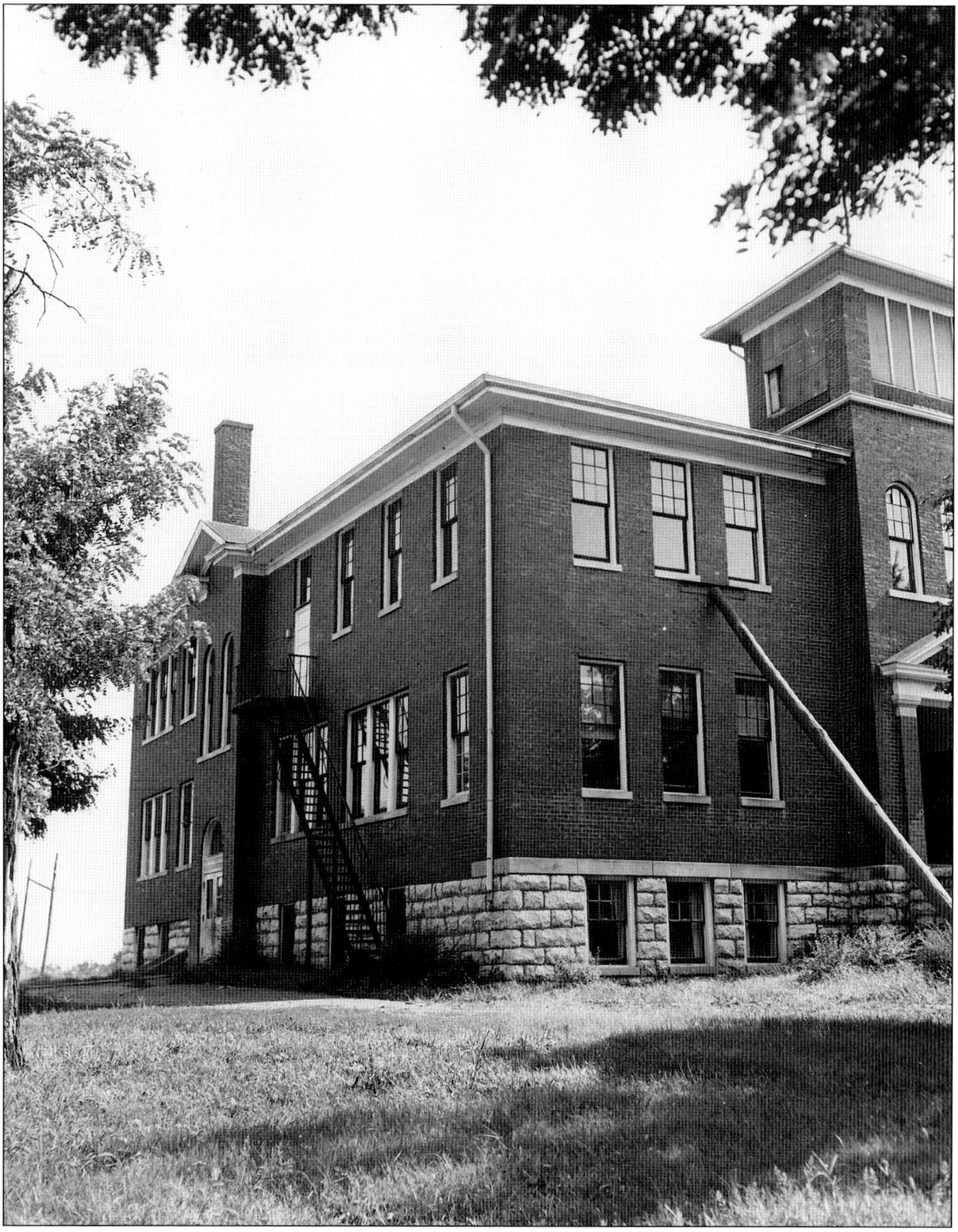

A later photograph of Hendersonville High School shows a remarkable view familiar to scores of students. When the brick wall buckled and threatened collapse, a telephone pole was used to prop up the structure. The pole remained in place for a number of years. (Courtesy of the Charles Roney Collection, Hendersonville's Martin Curtis Library.)

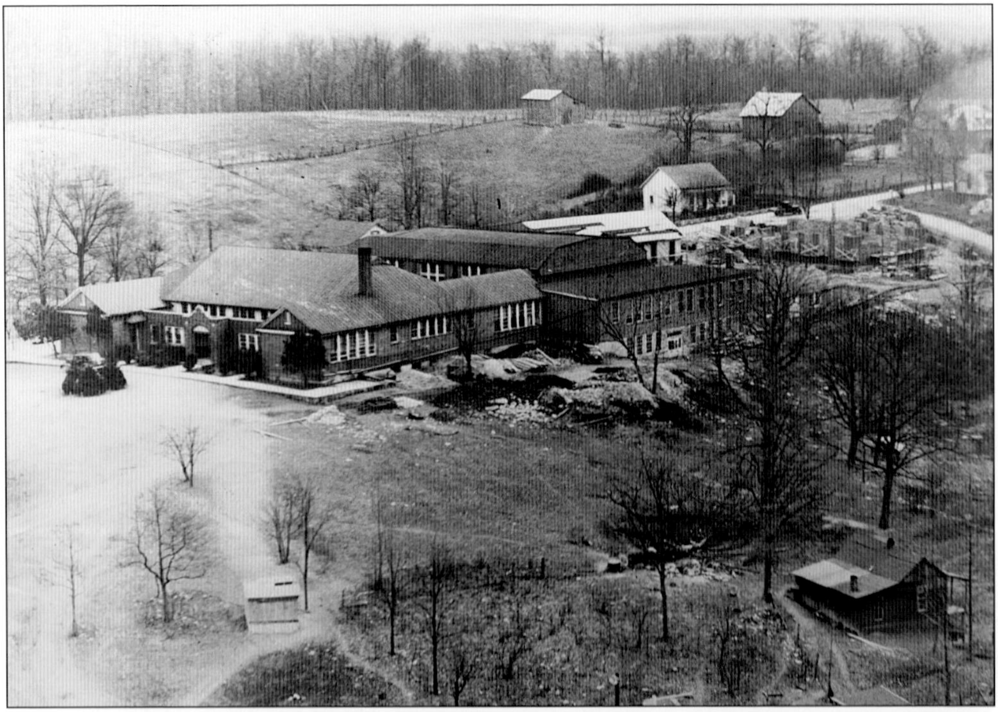

Built on the site of the town's old wooden school, this aerial shot shows Westmoreland School. The portion of the building under construction is the agricultural building. In December 1955, a fire of suspicious nature started in the basement cafeteria and spread quickly, destroying everything except the agriculture building, which was later used by the Westmoreland Manufacturing Company. (Photograph by H.G. Kirby, courtesy of John Creasy.)

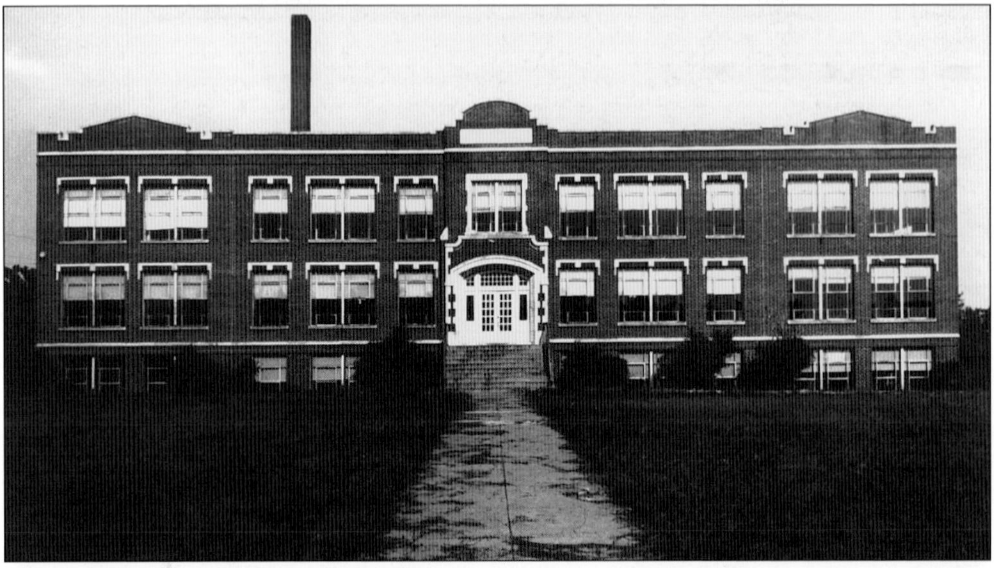

This handsome structure was the Sumner County High School of Portland. The community's rapid growth during the 1920s created overcrowded conditions that became the target of criticism. Construction of this three-story building provided relief for a number of years. (Courtesy of the Bob Perry Collection, Sumner County Archives.)

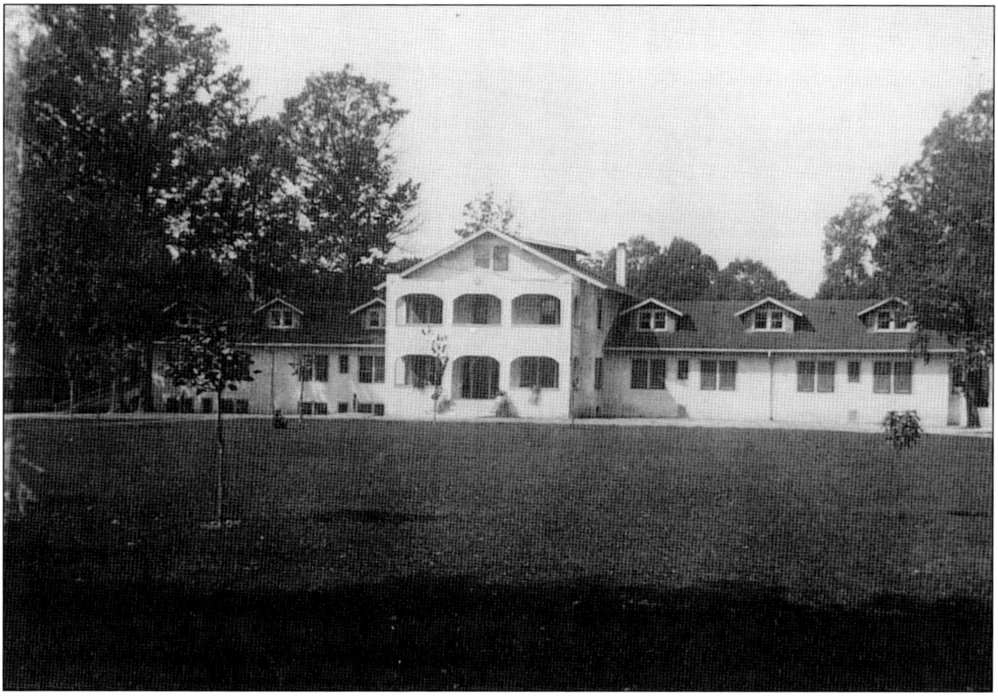

The Fountain Head Sanitarium, founded by the Seventh Day Adventists, continues to serve the county as the Highland Manor Nursing Home. (Courtesy of Allen Haynes.)

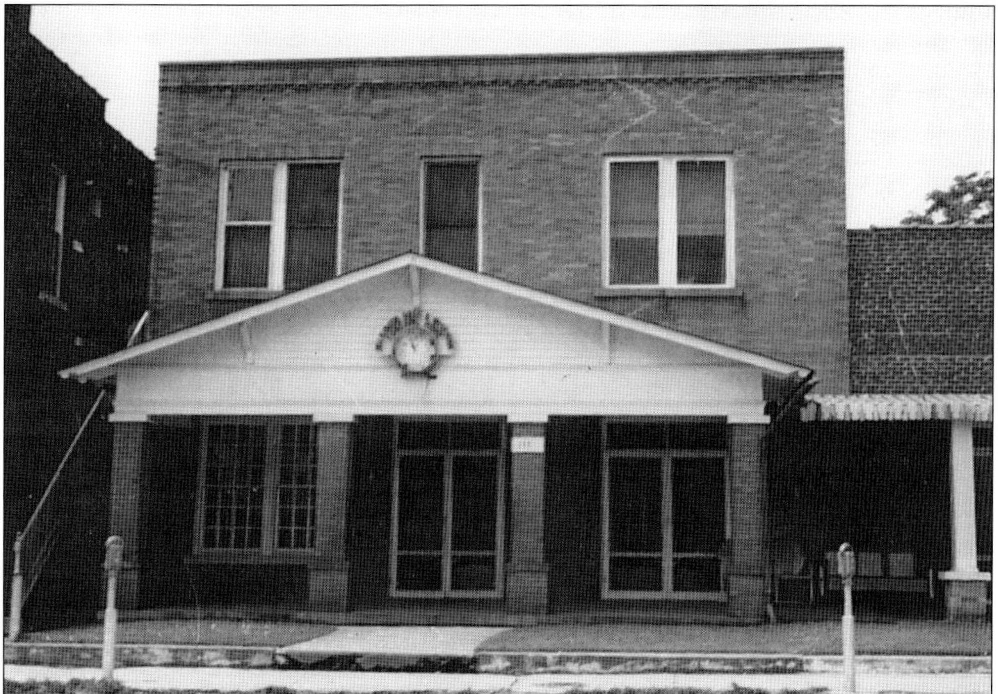

The Wilkerson Wiseman Funeral Home on Highway 109 in Portland, photographed here in 1951, was torn down in the late 1970s. (Courtesy of Allen Haynes.)

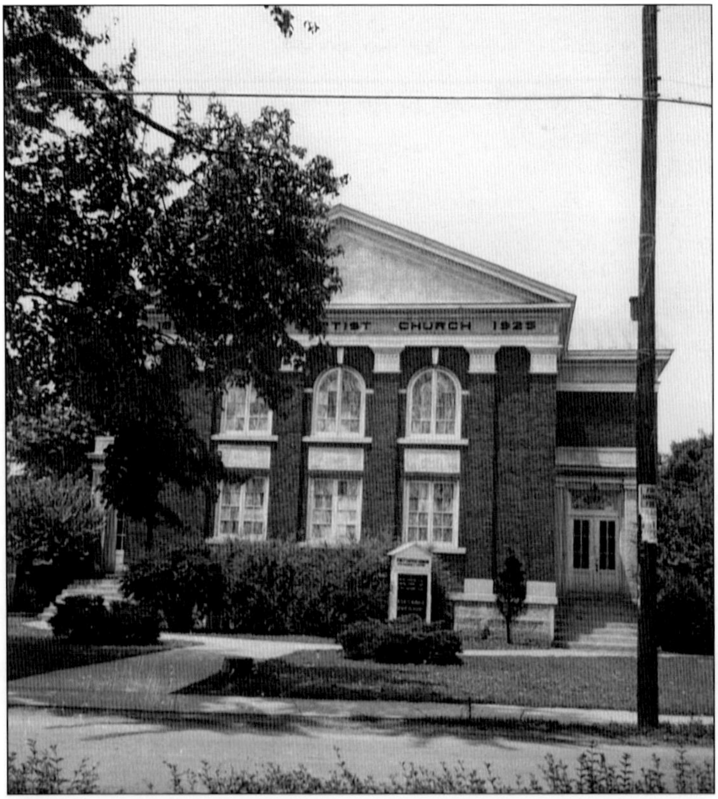

The First Baptist Church of Portland constructed this brick structure in 1925 to replace a smaller frame church. (Courtesy of Allen Haynes.)

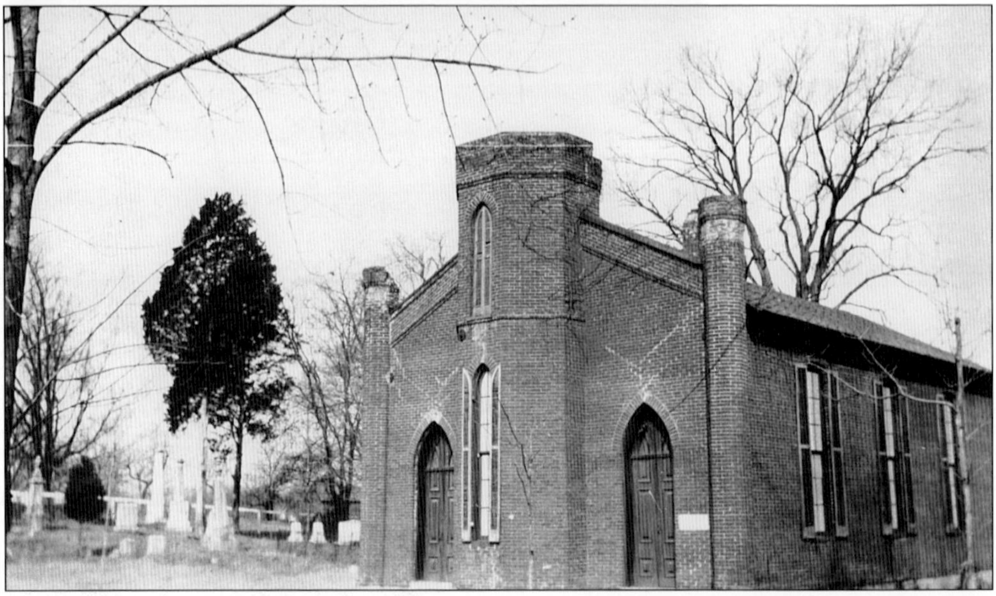

The First Presbyterian Church of Hendersonville was constructed in 1869, and its charming Gothic Revival styling and adjacent cemetery offer a visual respite in the center of town. In recent years, the church has undergone significant restoration, added an educational wing, and enclosed the grounds and cemetery. (Courtesy of the Bob Perry Collection, Sumner County Archives.)

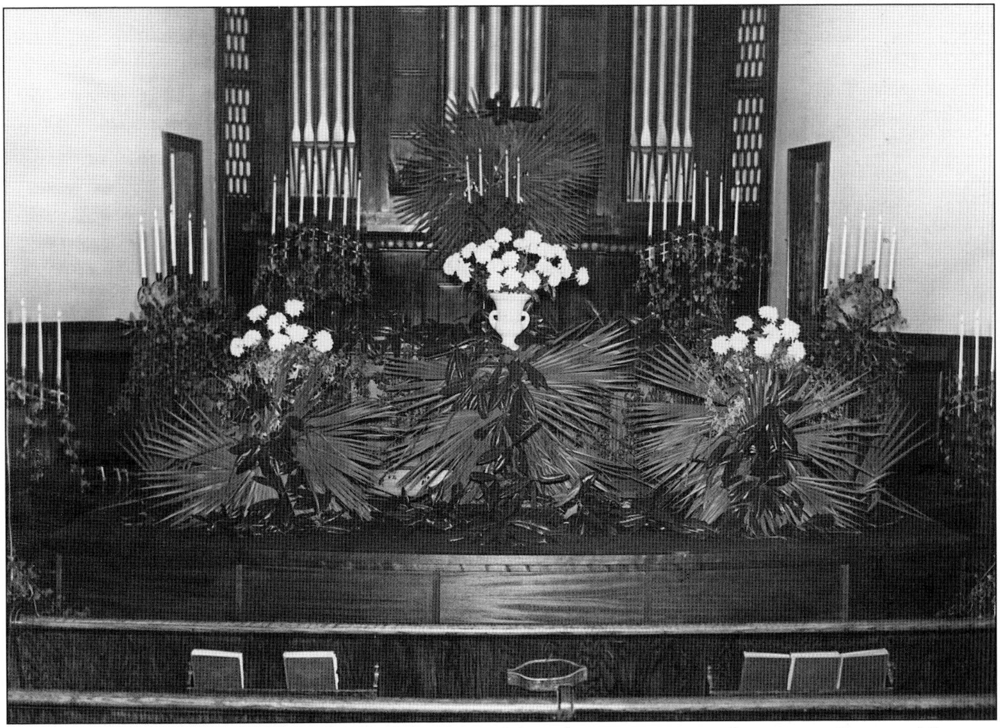

The interiors of local churches can be as beautiful as their exterior architecture. Pictured here is the interior of Gallatin's First Presbyterian Church with its magnificent pipe organ. (Courtesy of Kenneth C. Thomson Jr.)

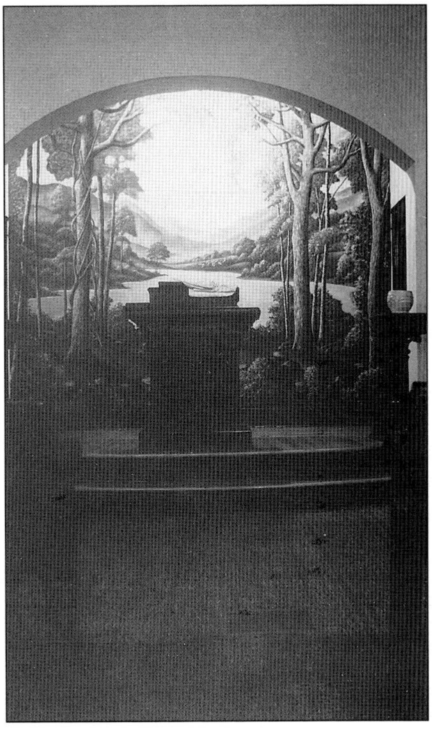

This beautiful mural hung over the baptistry at the old Hendersonville Church of Christ on West Main. That church was replaced in the 1980s by a new, modern structure on Rockland Road. (Courtesy of Quinton Coppage.)

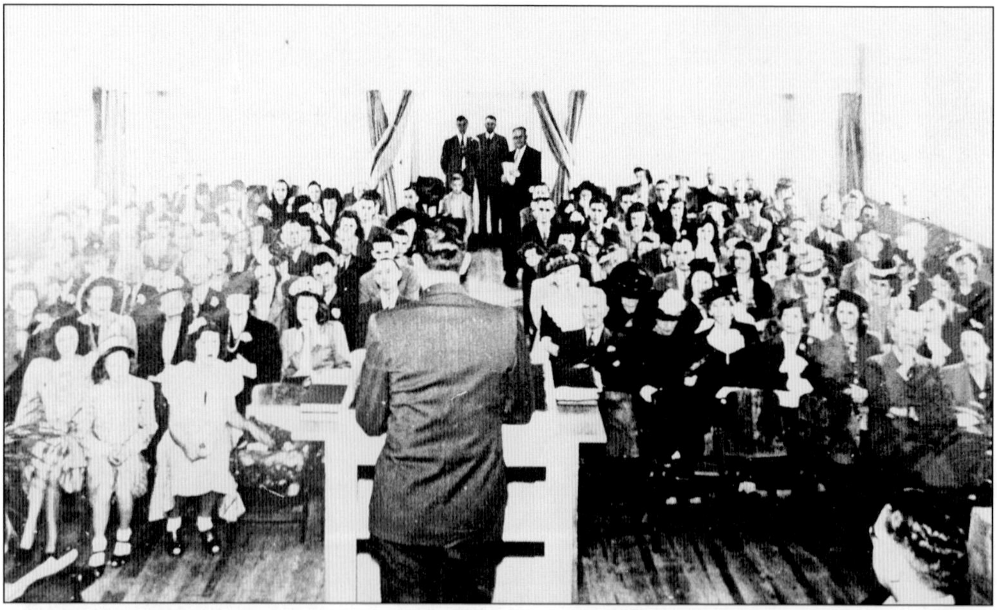

From its beginning in 1944 until the completion of its first building in 1947, the Hendersonville First Baptist Church conducted services every other Sunday afternoon at the First Presbyterian Church of Hendersonville. Throughout this period, Miss Sarah Berry, a staunch Presbyterian, attended all Baptist services in addition to those of her own church. She is pictured here (first full row on the right, fifth from right) at a Baptist service. (Courtesy of the First Baptist Church Archives.)

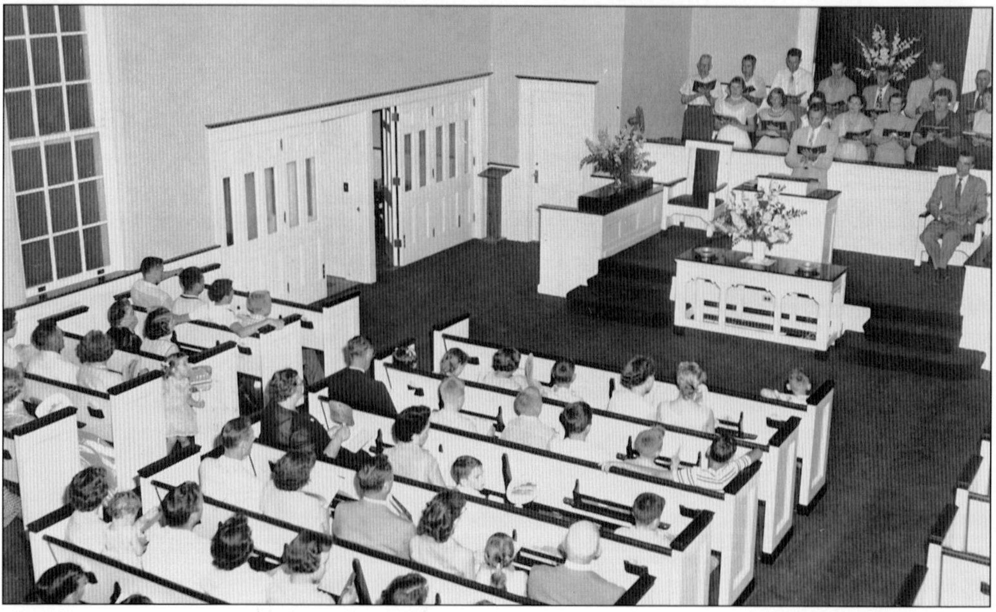

Church services were conducted in the chapel, the original sanctuary of the First Baptist Church of Hendersonville (1947–1966) before a larger sanctuary and Sunday school building were added. With the congregation's continued growth, a modern campus was built. On July 7, 1991 over 1,200 church members marched several miles to the new campus site. (Courtesy of the First Baptist Church Archives.)

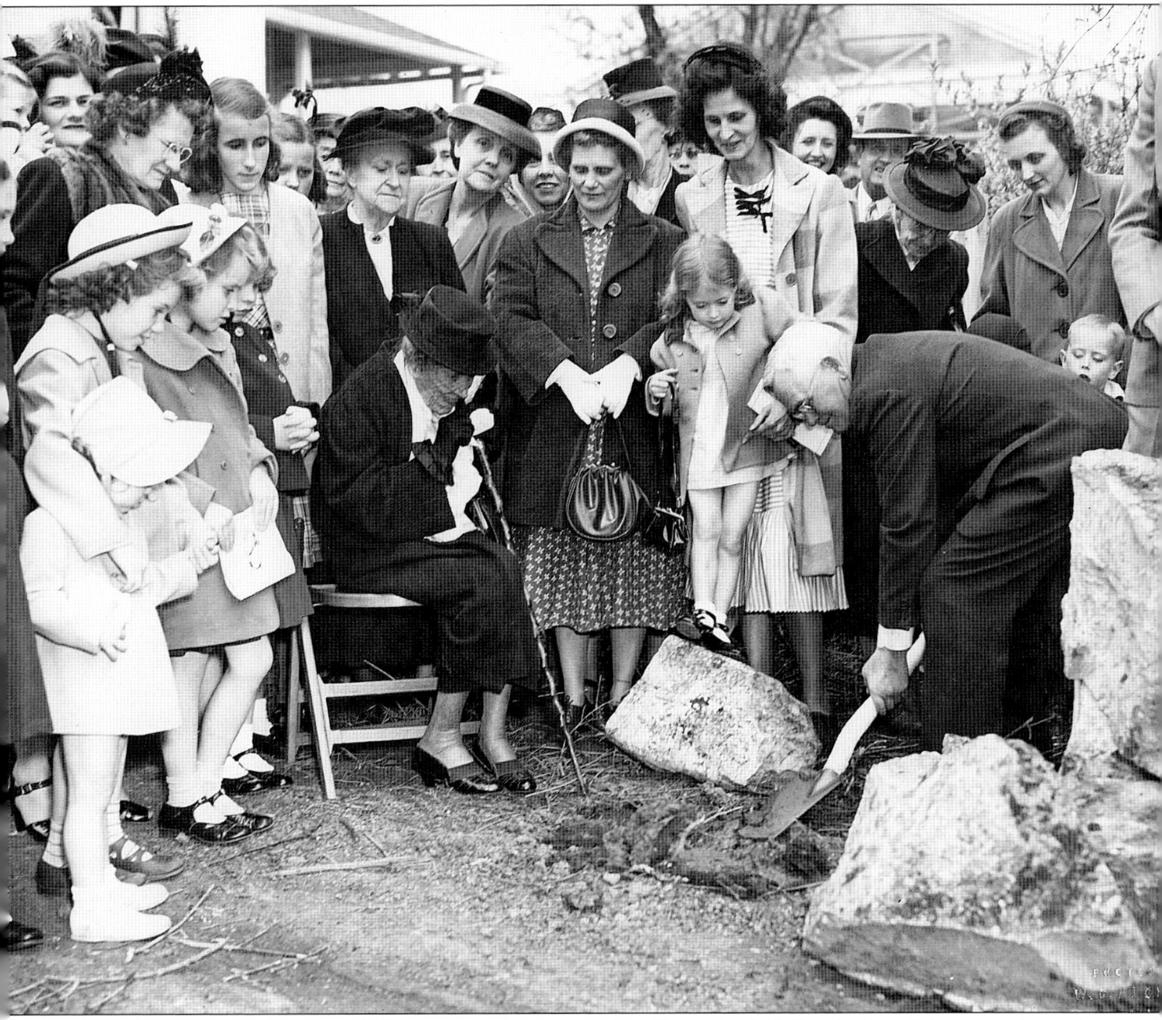

Surrounded by young and old, Mrs. Frances Paralee (Moseley) Dillard, the oldest member of the Gallatin Church of Christ (seated), looks on as Roy Cecil breaks ground for a new Sunday school building. Standing behind Mrs. Dillard is Susie Mentlo Anderson. (Photograph by W.C. Hackett, courtesy of Evelyn Hackett Tuttle.)

INDEX

T

U

V

W

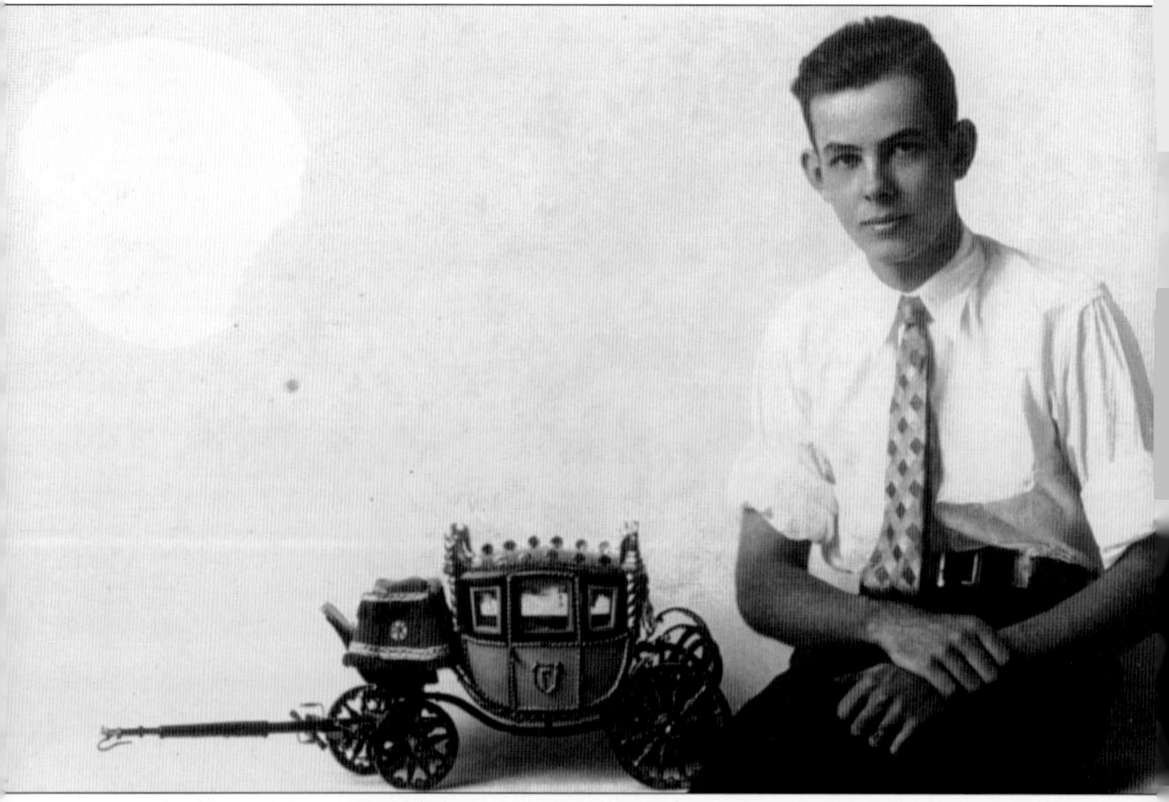

A youthful James Morgan Franklin is pictured here with the miniature carriage he constructed for entry in the Nashville Tennessean Chapter of the Fisher Body Craftsman's Guild competition. Construction took seven months, and Franklin made the tools used to stamp all brass pieces. He was the son of Horace Franklin whose company built fire engines and the Kraft Cheese container pictured on page 86. (Courtesy of Peggy Franklin Kobe.)

ACKNOWLEDGMENTS

In addition to the individual collectors who shared their wonderful photographs throughout this volume, the authors wish to thank the staff of the Sumner County Archives and Hendersonville's Martin Curtis Library.